Your future is just four parts away.

Welcome to the Becker CPA Exam Review! Congratulations on taking the first step to becoming a CPA. As the industry's leading partner in CPA Exam preparation, we know you're not just studying for an exam – you are preparing for your future. To help you get there, Becker CPA Exam Review is as close as you can get to the real thing. So let's get started.

Access Becker's CPA Exam Review course

Log in to your CPA Exam Review course anytime at **cpa.becker.com**. Watch our orientation video and download the mobile app to access your studies on the go. Your progress will automatically sync among all your devices, so you can pick up where you left off. For more on getting started, visit **becker.com/cpa-review/getting-started**.

Utilize the Becker resources

Make studying more organized with our study planner. With interactive tools to help you determine your ideal study schedule and to recommend your ideal exam-taking time, it's easy to plan your preparation so you can become Exam Day Ready℠. Here are the added benefits of Becker:

- Take advantage of unlimited practice tests, personalized by Adapt2U Technology
- Access 1-on-1 academic support from our experienced CPA instructors
- Test your knowledge with our simulated exams – the closest thing you can get to the actual CPA Exam itself

You're not in it alone!

For tips, stories and advice, visit our blog at **becker.com/blog**. You can also collaborate with other Becker students studying REG on our Facebook study group at **facebook.com/groups/BeckerREGStudyGroup/**.

C0-EKK-791

Submit your CPA Exam application

It takes time for your CPA Exam application to be approved – so don't wait until the last minute.

Once your CPA Exam application has been processed, your Notice to Schedule will give you a limited window of time to schedule your exam.

Your state board of accountancy sets the amount of time you have, so be sure to check your state's requirements.

Once you schedule your exam, add it to the study planner so we can share tips, strategies and more as your test date approaches.

Becker

Join the community!

Becker™

ACADEMIC HELP
Click on Contact Academic Support from within the course software at the top at cpa.becker.com

CUSTOMER SERVICE AND TECHNICAL SUPPORT
Call 1-877-CPA-EXAM (outside the U.S. +1-630-472-2213) or contact us at becker.com/contact-us

This textbook contains information that was current at the time of printing. Your course software will be updated on a regular basis as the content that is tested on the CPA Exam evolves and as we improve our materials. Note the version reference below and select your replacement textbook at **becker.com/cpa-replacements-upgrades** to learn if a newer version of this book is available to be ordered.

CPA Exam Review

Taxation and Regulation (REG)

For Exams Scheduled After January 9, 2024

V 1.0

COURSE DEVELOPMENT TEAM

Timothy F. Gearty, CPA, MBA, JD, CGMA	Editor in Chief, Financial/Regulation (Tax) National Editor
Angeline S. Brown, CPA, CGMA	Sr. Director, Product Development
Michael Potenza, CPA, JD	Sr. Director, Instruction and Client Partnerships, Curriculum
Lauren Chin, CPA	Director, Curriculum
Nancy Gauldie, CPA	Senior Manager, Curriculum
Wanda Kaminski, CPA	Senior Manager, Curriculum
Stephen Bergens, CPA	Manager, Accounting Curriculum
Bill Karalius, CPA	Sr. Specialist, Curriculum
Brittany Nance, CPA	Sr. Specialist, Curriculum
Angelle Cascio, CPA, CMA	Sr. Specialist, Curriculum
Savannah Hooper, CPA	Sr. Specialist, Curriculum
Anson Miyashiro	Manager, Course Development
Tim Munson	Project Manager, Course Development
Joe Antonio	Manager, Course Development
Shelly McCubbins, MBA	Project Manager, Course Development

CONTRIBUTING EDITORS

Heather Baiye, CPA, MBA	Christopher R. Issa, CPA
Michael Brown, CPA, CMA	Steven J. Levin, JD
Kelvin Chang, CFA, AWS-CSA, CPA (inactive)	Stephanie Morris, CPA, MAcc
Elliott G. Chester, CPA, CMA, CFE	Michelle Moshe, CPA, DipIFR
Courtney Chianello, CPA	Sandra Owen, JD, MBA, CPA
Zachariah M. Chism, CPA, CFE	Jennifer J. Rivers, CPA
Tom Cox, CPA, CMA	Josh Rosenberg, MBA, CPA, CFA, CFP
Michael Deldon, CPA	Jonathan R. Rubin, CPA, MBA
R. Thomas Godwin, CPA, CGMA	Susan M. Tillery, CPA/PFS
Liliana Hickman-Riggs, CPA, CMA, CIA, CFE, CITP, CFF, CGMA, FCPA, MS	Thomas N. Tillery, MA Ed, MSFS, CFP, ChFC, CLU, CRPC

This textbook is an essential part of Becker's CPA review course and is intended for use in conjunction with the Becker CPA review web and mobile applications ("Becker Apps"). Your use of and access to the Becker Apps is governed by the online end user license agreement (EULA). This textbook is to be used solely by the purchaser of the CPA review course and for personal use only. This textbook as a whole, and any parts therein, may not be shared, copied, reproduced, distributed, licensed, sold, or resold without the prior written consent of Becker Professional Development Corporation. Failure to comply with this notice may expose you to legal action for copyright infringement and/or disciplinary action pursuant to the Student Code of Conduct located at https://www.becker.com/cpa-review/student-code-of-conduct.

Permissions

Material from *Uniform CPA Examination Selected Questions and Unofficial Answers*, 1989–2023, copyright © by American Institute of Certified Public Accountants, Inc., is reprinted and/or adapted with permission.

Any knowing solicitation or disclosure of any questions or answers included on any CPA Examination is prohibited.

Copyright © 2023 by Becker Professional Education Corporation. All rights reserved.

ISBN: 978-1-950713-73-8

Printed in the United States of America.

No part of this work may be reproduced, translated, distributed, published or transmitted without the prior written permission of the copyright owner. Request for permission or further information should be addressed to the Permissions Department, Becker Professional Education Corporation.

Taxation and Regulation (REG)

Table of Contents

Introduction Intro-1

REG 1: *Federal Taxation of Individuals*
1. Filing Requirements and Filing Status R1-3
2. Gross Income: Part 1 .... R1-11
3. Gross Income: Part 2 .... R1-29
4. Adjustments R1-39
5. Itemized Deductions R1-49
6. Section 199A Qualified Business Income Deduction R1-63
7. Tax Computations and Credits R1-69

REG 2: *Property Taxation*
1. Basis and Holding Period of Assets R2-3
2. Gains and Losses R2-15
3. Cost Recovery R2-23

REG 3: *Entity Taxation*
1. C Corporation Overview R3-3
2. Differences Between Book and Tax R3-13
3. C Corporation Tax Computations and Credits R3-21
4. Calculating Loss Limitations for C Corporations R3-27
5. S Corporation Overview R3-29
6. Partnership Overview R3-41
7. Tax-Exempt Organization Overview R3-51
8. State and Local Tax Issues R3-55

REG 4: *Professional Responsibilities and Federal Tax Procedures*
1. Circular 230 .... R4-3
2. Professional Responsibilities and Tax Return Preparer Penalties R4-11
3. Federal Tax Procedures and Taxpayer Penalties R4-21
4. Legal Duties and Responsibilities R4-33

REG 5: *Business Law: Part 1*

1. Contracts: Part 1 .... R5-3
2. Contracts: Part 3 .... R5-13
3. Contracts: Part 3 .... R5-25
4. Agency R5-41
5. Suretyship R5-53
6. Secured Transactions R5-63

REG 6: *Business Law: Part 2*

1. Bankruptcy: Part 1 .... R6-3
2. Bankruptcy: Part 2 .... R6-11
3. Federal Laws and Regulations R6-17
4. Business Structures: Part 1 .... R6-27
5. Business Structures: Part 2 .... R6-41

Introduction
REG

1. Taxation and Regulation (REG) Overview 3
2. REG Exam: Summary Blueprint 3
3. Becker's CPA Exam Review: Course Introduction 3
4. The Uniform CPA Exam: Overview 4
5. Becker Customer and Academic Support 6

NOTES

Taxation and Regulation (REG) Overview

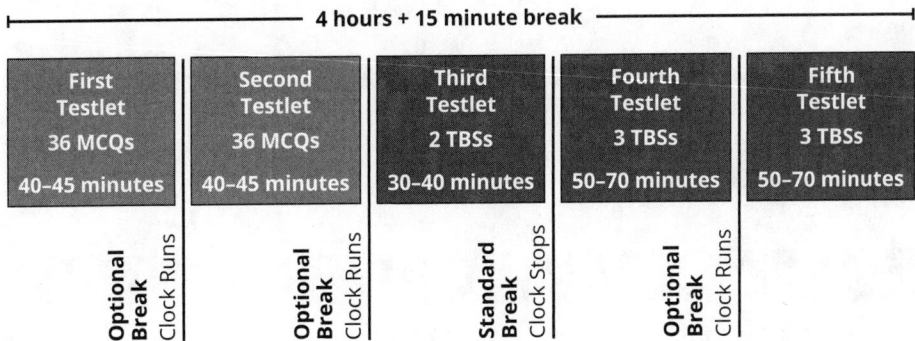

REG Exam: Summary Blueprint

Content Area Allocation	Weight
Ethics, Professional Responsibilities, and Federal Tax Procedures	10–20%
Business Law	15–25%
Federal Taxation of Property Transactions	5–15%
Federal Taxation of Individuals	22–32%
Federal Taxation of Entities (including tax preparation)	23–33%
Skill Allocation	**Weight**
Evaluation	—
Analysis	25–35%
Application	35–45%
Remembering and Understanding	25–35%

Becker's CPA Exam Review: Course Introduction

Becker Professional Education's CPA Exam Review products were developed with you, the candidate, in mind. To that end we have developed a series of tools designed to tap all of your learning and retention capabilities. The Becker lectures, comprehensive tests, and course software are designed to be fully integrated to give you the best chance of passing the CPA Exam.

Passing the CPA Exam is difficult, but the professional rewards a CPA enjoys make this a worthwhile challenge. We created our CPA Exam Review after evaluating the needs of CPA candidates and analyzing the CPA Exam over the years. Our course materials comprehensively present topics you must know to pass the examination, teaching you the most effective tactics for learning the material.

The Uniform CPA Exam: Overview

Exam Sections

The CPA Examination consists of three Core sections and three Discipline sections. You must pass all three Core sections and one of the Discipline sections to become a licensed CPA.

The three Core sections are:

Financial Accounting and Reporting (FAR)

The FAR section consists of a four-hour exam covering financial accounting and reporting for commercial entities under U.S. GAAP, not-for-profit accounting, and the basics of government accounting.

Auditing and Attestation (AUD)

The AUD section consists of a four-hour exam. This section covers all topics related to auditing, including audit reports and procedures, generally accepted auditing standards, attestation and other engagements, and government auditing.

Taxation and Regulation (REG)

The REG section consists of a four-hour exam, combining topics from business law and federal taxation, including the taxation of property transactions, individuals, and entities.

The three Discipline sections (you must pass one) are:

Business Analysis and Reporting (BAR)

The BAR section consists of a four-hour exam covering advanced financial accounting and reporting, government accounting, financial management, operations management, and managerial and cost accounting.

Information Systems and Controls (ISC)

The ISC section consists of a four-hour exam and includes topics related to information systems and data management, security, confidentiality and privacy, and system and organization controls (SOC) engagements.

Tax Compliance and Planning (TCP)

The TCP section consists of a four-hour exam and includes topics related to personal financial planning, entity tax compliance, entity tax planning, and property transactions.

Question Formats

The chart below illustrates the question format breakdown by exam section.

	Multiple-Choice Questions (MCQs)		Task-Based Simulations (TBSs)	
Section	Percentage	Number	Percentage	Number
FAR	50%	50	50%	7
AUD	50%	78	50%	7
REG	50%	72	50%	8
BAR	50%	50	50%	7
ISC	60%	82	40%	6
TCP	50%	68	50%	7

Each exam will contain testlets. A testlet is either a series of multiple-choice questions or a set of task-based simulations. For example, the Regulation examination will contain five testlets. The first two testlets will be multiple-choice questions and the third, fourth, and fifth testlets will contain task-based simulations. Each testlet must be finished and submitted before continuing to the next testlet. Candidates cannot go back to view a previously completed testlet or go forward to view a subsequent testlet before closing and submitting the earlier testlet. Our simulated exams contain these types of restrictions so that you can familiarize yourself with the functionality of the CPA Exam.

Exam Schedule

Candidates can schedule an exam date directly with Prometric (www.prometric.com/cpa) after receiving a notice to schedule.

Eligibility and Application Requirements

Each state sets its own rules of eligibility for the examination. Please visit www.becker.com/cpa-review/requirements as soon as possible to determine your eligibility to sit for the exam.

Application Deadlines

With the computer-based exam format, set application deadlines generally do not exist. You should apply as early as possible to ensure that you are able to schedule your desired exam dates. Each state has different application requirements and procedures, so be sure to gain a thorough understanding of the application process for your state.

Grading System

You must pass all three Core exams and one of the Discipline exams to become a CPA. You must score 75 or better on a part to receive a passing grade.

Becker Customer and Academic Support

You can access Becker's Customer and Academic Support from within the course software by clicking Contact Support at the top at:

cpa.becker.com

You can also access customer service and technical support by calling 1-877-CPA-EXAM (outside the U.S. +1-630-472-2213).

REG 1

Federal Taxation of Individuals

Module

1	Filing Requirements and Filing Status	3
2	Gross Income: Part 1	11
3	Gross Income: Part 2	29
4	Adjustments	39
5	Itemized Deductions	49
6	Section 199A Qualified Business Income Deduction	63
7	Tax Computations and Credits	69

NOTES

MODULE 1: Filing Requirements and Filing Status

REG 1

1 Individual Income Tax Formula

This module begins the discussion of individual income tax. The formula below provides a summary of the calculation of taxable income and federal income tax liability or refund for individuals. Ultimately, these items are reported on the individual income tax return, Form 1040.

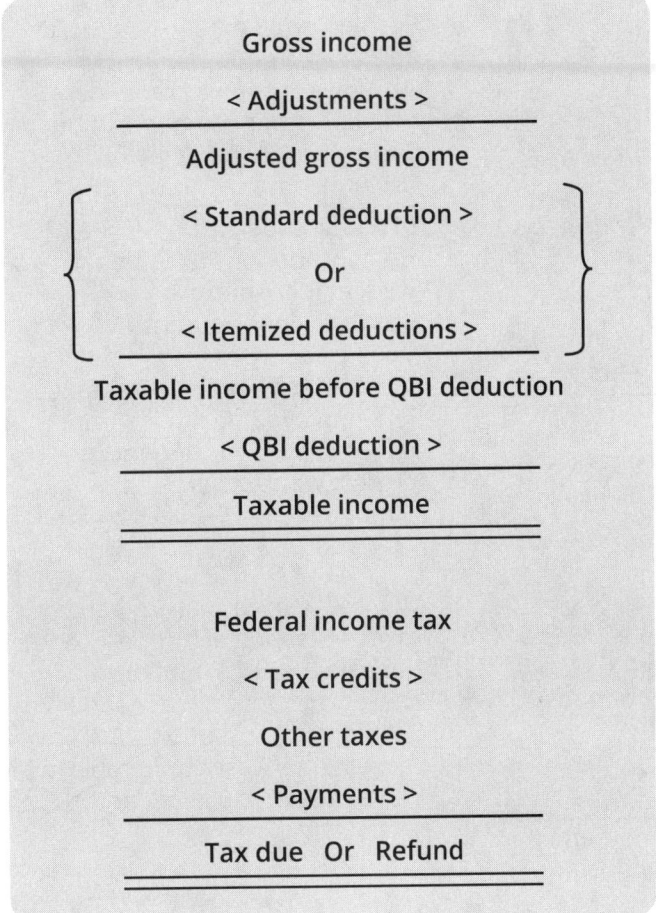

Gross income
< Adjustments >
Adjusted gross income
< Standard deduction >
Or
< Itemized deductions >
Taxable income before QBI deduction
< QBI deduction >
Taxable income

Federal income tax
< Tax credits >
Other taxes
< Payments >
Tax due Or Refund

Filing Requirements and Filing Status

2 Taxable Income Formula for Individuals

Taxable income is the base for the individual income tax. The formula below demonstrates the calculation of taxable income for individual taxpayers.

Gross income
- Wages
- Interest
- Dividends
- State tax refunds
- Alimony received*
- Business income
- Capital gain/loss
- IRA income
- Pension and annuity
- Rental income/loss
- K-1 flow-through income/loss
- Unemployment compensation
- Social Security benefits
- Other income

< Adjustments >
- Educator expenses
- IRA contributions (traditional)
- Student loan interest
- Health savings account
- Moving expenses**
- One-half self-employment taxes
- Self-employed health insurance
- Self-employed retirement
- Interest withdrawal penalty
- Alimony paid*

Adjusted gross income

< Itemized deductions >
- Medical (in excess of 7.5 percent of AGI)
- Taxes—state/local (property and either income or sales, up to $10,000)
- Interest expense (Home and Investment)
- Charitable contributions (AGI limit varies by type)
- Casualty/theft loss attributable to federal disaster (in excess of $100 floor and 10 percent of AGI)

Taxable income before QBI deduction

< QBI deduction >

Taxable income

*Only for alimony payments pursuant to divorce or separation agreements executed on or before December 31, 2018.

**Only for members of the armed forces moving pursuant to military order.

3 Filing Requirements for Individuals

3.1 Who Must File?

The first consideration when thinking about individual taxation is who must file a tax return. Generally, a taxpayer must file a return if his or her income is equal to or greater than the sum of:

1. the regular standard deduction amount (except for married filing separately), plus
2. the additional standard deduction amount for taxpayers age 65 or older or blind (except for married persons filing separately).

3.2 When to File

3.2.1 Due Date—April 15

Individual taxpayers must file on or before the 15th day of the fourth month following the close of the taxpayer's taxable year, which is April 15.

3.2.2 Extension

- **Automatic Six-Month Extension to October 15:** An automatic six-month extension (until October 15) is available for those taxpayers who are unable to file by the April 15 due date. The automatic six-month extension is not an extension for the payment of any taxes owed. Although granted automatically, the six-month extension must be requested by the taxpayer by filing Form 4868 by April 15.
- **Payment of Tax:** Even with an extension, the due date for payment of taxes remains April 15.

4 Filing Status

4.1 Single (Use the End-of-Year Test)

You are considered unmarried for the whole year if, on the last day of your tax year, you are either: unmarried or legally separated.

4.2 Joint Returns (Use the End-of-Year Test)

In order to file a joint return, the parties must be married at the end of the year, living together in a legally recognized common law marriage, or married and living apart (but not legally separated or divorced).

- If married during the year, a joint return may be filed, provided the parties are married at year-end.
- If divorced during the year, a joint return may not be filed.
- If one spouse dies during the year, a joint return may be filed.

4.3 Married Filing Separately

A married taxpayer may file a separate return even if only one spouse has income for the year. In a separate property state, spouses who elect to file using the married filing separately status must separately report their own income, credits, and deductions on their own individual income tax returns. In a community property state, most of the income, deductions, credits, etc., are split 50/50.

4.4 Qualifying Widow(er) With Dependent Child

- **Two Years After Spouse's Death:** A qualifying widow(er) is a taxpayer who may use the joint tax return standard deduction and rates for each of two taxable years following the year of death of his or her spouse, unless he or she remarries. In the event of a remarriage, the surviving spouse will file a tax return (joint or separate) with the new spouse.

- **Principal Residence for Dependent Child:** The surviving spouse must pay over half the cost of maintaining a household where a dependent child lives for the whole taxable year. The dependent child must be a child (including an adopted child but not a foster child) or stepchild of the surviving spouse.

4.5 Head of Household

Head of household status entitles certain taxpayers to pay lower taxes. The lower tax results from a larger standard deduction and "wider" tax brackets.

To qualify, the following conditions must be met:

1. The individual is unmarried, legally separated, or married and has lived apart from his or her spouse for the last six months of the year as of the close of the taxable year.

2. The individual is not a "qualifying widow(er)."

3. The individual is not a nonresident alien.

4. The individual maintains as his or her home a household that, for more than half the taxable year, is the principal residence of a qualifying person, including a dependent child, parent, or relative (as discussed below).

4.5.1 A Qualifying Child

Child, stepchild, legally adopted child, foster child, brother or sister, or a descendant of one of these who meets the definition of a dependent under the qualifying children rules.

4.5.2 Father or Mother (Not Required to Live With Taxpayer)

A dependent parent is not required to live with the taxpayer, provided the taxpayer maintains a home that was the principal residence of the parent for the entire year. Maintaining a home means contributing over half the cost of upkeep. This means rent, mortgage interest, property taxes, insurance, utility charges, repairs, and food consumed in the home.

4.5.3 Dependent Relatives (Must Live With Taxpayer)

Grandparents, brothers, sisters, aunts, uncles, nephews, and nieces (as well as stepparents, parents-in-law, sisters-in-law, or brothers-in-law) qualify as relatives. A dependent relative (other than a father or mother) must live with the taxpayer. Note that cousins, foster parents, and unrelated dependents do not qualify.

4.5.4 Summary of Who Meets Head-of-Household Qualifying Person Requirement

	Qualifying Dependent	Lives With Taxpayer
Child or descendant	Yes	Yes
Parents	Yes	No
Other relative	Yes	Yes

Pass Key

In order to avoid confusing the required time period for different filing statuses, just remember:

Widow/widower = Must be principal residence for dependent child for **whole** year.

Head of household = Must be principal residence for qualifying person for more than **half** a year.

5 Dependency Definitions

Certain tax benefits, such as an advantageous filing status or certain tax credits, require either a qualifying child or qualifying relative. Each category has requirements:

Qualifying Child
Close relative
Age limit
Residency and filing requirements
Eliminate gross income test
Support test

Or

Qualifying Relative
Support test
Under a specific amount of (taxable) gross income test
Precludes dependent filing a joint tax return test
Only citizens (residents of US/Canada or Mexico) test
Relative test
Or
Taxpayer lives with individual for whole year test

Taxpayers must obtain a Social Security number for any dependent who has attained the age of one as of the close of the tax year.

Filing Requirements and Filing Status REG 1

Pass Key

A taxpayer will be entitled to certain tax benefits for anyone whom a taxpayer "**CARES**" for, or whom they "**SUPORT**," even if the dependent:

- was born during the year; or
- died during the year.

5.1 Qualifying Child

If the parents of a child are entitled to claim the child but do not, no one else may claim the child unless that taxpayer's AGI is higher than the AGI of the highest parent.

In general, a child is a qualifying child of the taxpayer if the child satisfies the following:

1. Close Relative

Under the close relationship test, to be a qualifying child of a taxpayer, the child must be the taxpayer's son, daughter, stepson, stepdaughter, brother, sister, stepbrother, stepsister, or a descendant of any of these. An individual legally adopted by the taxpayer, or an individual who is lawfully placed with the taxpayer for legal adoption by the taxpayer, is treated as a child of the taxpayer. A foster child who is placed with the taxpayer by an authorized placement agency or by judgment, decree, or other order of any court of competent jurisdiction also is treated as the taxpayer's child.

2. Age Limit

The age limit test varies depending on the benefit. In general, a child must be younger than the taxpayer, and under age 19 (or age 24 in the case of a full-time student) to be a qualifying child (although no age limit applies with respect to individuals who are totally and permanently disabled at any time during the tax year). A "full-time" student is a student who attends an educational institution for at least part of each of five months during the taxable year. An "educational institution" is one that maintains full-time faculty and a daytime program.

3. Residency and Filing Requirements

Under the residency and filing requirement tests, a child must have the same principal place of abode as the taxpayer for more than one half of the tax year. The child also must be a citizen of the United States or a resident of the United States, Canada, or Mexico. Furthermore, the child cannot file a joint tax return for the year (unless it was filed only for a refund claim).

4. Eliminate Gross Income Test

The gross income test (see **SUPORT**) does not apply to a qualifying child.

5. Support Test

The qualifying child must not have contributed more than half of his or her own support. Support means the actual expenses incurred by or on behalf of the dependent. Social Security and state welfare payments are included in the dependent's total support, but only to the extent that such amounts are actually expended for support purposes. Scholarships received by a dependent are not included in determining the dependent's support if the dependent is a full-time student and the son, daughter, stepson, or stepdaughter of the taxpayer. This exclusion of scholarships from the support test does not extend to siblings or descendants.

5.2 Qualifying Relative

Taxpayers can apply the **SUPORT** rules to determine whether an individual meets the qualifying relative rules. In general, an individual is a qualifying relative of the taxpayer if the individual satisfies the following:

1. **Support Test**

   The taxpayer must have supplied more than one half (greater than 50 percent) of the support of a person in order to claim him or her as a qualifying relative. The same definition of support as related to a qualifying child applies.

2. **Under Gross Income Limitation**

   A person may not be claimed as a qualifying relative unless the qualifying relative's gross income is less than $4,700 (2023).

   - **Definition of Taxable Income:** Only income that is taxable is included for the purpose of the gross income limitation.

   - **Nontaxable Income**
     - Social Security (at low income levels)
     - Tax-exempt interest income (state and municipal interest income)
     - Tax-exempt scholarships

3. **Precludes Dependent Filing a Joint Return**

   A taxpayer does not meet the definition of qualifying relative if the taxpayer is a married dependent who files a joint return, unless there is no tax liability on the couple's joint return and there would not have been any tax liability on either spouse's tax return if they had filed separately.

4. **Only Citizens of the United States or Residents of the United States, Mexico, or Canada**

   The qualifying relative must be either a citizen of the United States or a resident of the United States, Mexico, or Canada.

5. **Relative**

   Children, grandchildren, parents, grandparents, brothers, sisters, aunts and uncles, nieces and nephews (as well as stepchildren, stepparents, stepbrothers or stepsisters, in-laws) can meet the definition of qualifying relative. Children include legally adopted children, foster children, and stepchildren. Foster parents and cousins are not considered to be relatives.

   Remember: A child born at any time during the year will qualify as a relative for qualifying-child or qualifying-relative purposes.

   Or:

6. **Taxpayer Lives With the Individual (if Non-relative) for the Whole Year**

   A non-relative member of a household (i.e., a person living in the taxpayer's home for the entire year) may be considered a qualifying relative provided the taxpayer's relationship with that person does not violate local law. Foster parents and cousins must live with the taxpayer the entire year because they are not considered to be relatives.

Filing Requirements and Filing Status

5.3 Multiple Support Agreements

Where two or more taxpayers together contribute more than 50 percent to the support of a person but none of them individually contributes more than 50 percent, the contributing taxpayers, all of whom must be qualifying relatives of (or lived the entire year with) the individual, may agree among themselves which contributor may claim the individual as a dependent for tax benefits.

- A contributor must have contributed more than 10 percent of the person's support in addition to meeting the other dependency tests in order to be able to claim him or her as a dependent.
- The joint contributors are required to file a multiple support declaration, Form 2120.

Example 1 Multiple Support Agreement

Facts: Peter, who is single and lives alone in Idaho, has no income of his own and is supported in full by the following people:

	Amount of Support	Percent of Total
Tim (an unrelated friend)	$2,400	48
Angie (Peter's sister)	2,150	43
Mike (Peter's son)	450	9
	$5,000	100%

Required: Under a multiple support agreement, Peter is considered a dependent of which of the following:

a. No one
b. Tim
c. Angie
d. Mike

Solution: Peter only meets dependency definition requirements for Angie.

	Tim	Angie	Mike
Support test	Yes	Yes	No
Under gross income	Yes	Yes	
Preclude joint filing	Yes	Yes	
Only U.S. citizens	Yes	Yes	
Relative, or	No	Yes	
Taxpayer lived with	No	N/A	

5.4 Children of Divorced Parents

- **General Rule (Custodial Parents):** Generally, the parent who has custody of the child for the greater part of the year qualifies to use the child as a dependent for tax benefit purposes (determined by a "time" test, not the divorce decree). It does not matter whether that parent actually provided more than one-half of the child's support. If the parents have equal custody during the year, the parent with the higher adjusted gross income will claim the tax benefits related to the dependent.

MODULE 2
Gross Income: Part 1

REG 1

1 Gross Income Overview

The first step in determining tax liability is to compute gross income.

1.1 Gross Income Definition

Generally, gross income means all income from whatever source derived, unless specifically excluded. (For example, if the taxpayer finds $4,000 under a floorboard in his house, cannot find the owner, and keeps the money, the $4,000 is income regardless of the fact that the taxpayer did not "earn" it.)

1.2 Determination of Amount of Income

Except in the cases of gain derived from dealings in property (discussed below), income is determined by the amount of cash, property (FMV), or services obtained. In cases of noncash income, the amount of the income is the *fair market value* of the property or services received.

> **Pass Key**
>
> | Event | | Income | Basis |
> |---|---|---|---|
> | Taxable | = | FMV | FMV |
> | Nontaxable | = | None | NBV |

> **Example 1   Noncash Income**
>
> **Facts:** A taxpayer performs services and receives a car with a fair market value of $3,000 as compensation.
>
> **Required:** Determine the amount of income for the taxpayer.
>
> **Solution:** The $3,000 FMV of the property received is income to the taxpayer.

1.3 Realization and Recognition

In order to be taxable, the gain must be both realized and recognized.

- **Realization:** Realization requires the accrual or receipt of cash, property, or services, or a change in the form or the nature of the investment (a sale or exchange).

- **Recognition:** Recognition means that the realized gain must be included on the tax return (i.e., there is no provision that permits exclusion or deferral under the Internal Revenue Code).

> **Illustration 1   Recognition Concept**
>
> A taxpayer owns stock for which he paid $100, and the stock goes up in value to $150. There is no realized gain even though there has been an increase in the taxpayer's wealth. Gain is realized when the shares are sold for $150 or exchanged for other property worth $150. If the gain is taxable, it would also be recognized on the tax return.

1.4 Timing of Revenue Recognition

- **Accrual Method:** Under the accrual method, recognition occurs according to the rules of GAAP (with some exceptions); that is, revenue is taxable when earned.
- **Cash Method:** Under the cash method, recognition occurs in the period the revenue is actually or constructively received in cash or fair market value (FMV) of property.

2 Specific Items of Income and Exclusions

2.1 Salaries and Wages

Gross income includes many forms of compensation for services.

- **Money:** All money received, credited, or available (constructive receipt).
- **Property:** The fair market value (FMV) of all property is included as gross income.
- **Bargain Purchases:** If an employer sells property to an employee for less than its fair market value, the difference is income to the employee.
- **Guaranteed Payments to a Partner:** Guaranteed payments are reasonable compensation paid to a partner for services rendered (or use of capital) without regard to the partner's income or loss sharing percentage. This earned compensation is also subject to self-employment tax.
- **Taxable Fringe Benefits (Non-statutory):** The fair market value of a fringe benefit not specifically excluded by law is includable in income. For example, an employee's personal use of a company car is included as wages in an employee's income. Furthermore, the amount included is subject to employment taxes and income and FICA tax withholdings.
- **Employer Contributions to Roth 401(k) Accounts:** If an employer-sponsored 401(k) plan allows, an employee can elect to designate certain employer contributions as Roth contributions. Roth contributions made by the employer to an employee's 401(k) account are included in the employee's income.
- **Portion of Life Insurance Premiums:** Premiums paid by an employer on a group term life insurance policy covering his employees are not income to the employees up to the cost on the first $50,000 of coverage per employee (nondiscriminatory plans only). Premiums above the first $50,000 of coverage are taxable income to the recipient and normally included in W-2 wages. (This amount is calculated from an IRS table, and it is not the entire amount of the premium in excess of the $50,000 coverage.)

2.2 Nontaxable Fringe Benefits

- **Life Insurance Coverage**

    Employees may exclude from income the value of life insurance premiums the employer pays on an employee's behalf for up to $50,000 of group-term life insurance.

- **Accident, Medical, and Health Insurance (Employer-Paid)**

    Premium payments are excludable from the employee's income when the employer paid the insurance premiums, but amounts paid to the employee under the policy are *includable in income unless such amounts are:*

    1. Reimbursement for medical expenses actually incurred by the employee; or

    2. Compensation for the permanent loss or loss of use of a member or function of the body.

- **De Minimis Fringe Benefits**

    De minimis fringe benefits are so minimal that they are impractical to account for and may be excluded from income. An example is an employee's personal use of a company computer.

- **Meals and Lodging**

    The gross income of an employee does not include the value of meals or lodging furnished to him or her in kind by the employer for the *convenience of the employer on the employer's premises*. Additionally, in order to be nontaxable, the lodging must be required as a condition of employment.

- **Employer Payment of Employee's Educational Expenses**

    Up to $5,250 may be excluded from gross income of payments made by the employer on behalf of an employee's educational expenses and/or student loans. The exclusion applies to both undergraduate and graduate-level education.

- **Employee Adoption Assistance Program**

    For 2023, a taxpayer can exclude from taxable income up to $15,950 of qualified adoption expenses paid by an employer. The exclusion is phased out for taxpayers with MAGI of $239,230–$279,230.

- **Dependent Care Assistance**

    Employees can exclude from gross income up to $5,000 of benefits paid or reimbursements by an employer for dependent care expenses. Qualifying dependents include dependent children under age 13 and a spouse or other dependent physically or mentally incapable of self-care.

- **Qualified Tuition Reduction**

    Employees of educational institutions studying at the undergraduate level who receive tuition reductions may exclude the tuition reduction from income. Graduate students may exclude tuition reduction only if they are engaged in teaching or research activities and only if the tuition reduction is in addition to the pay for the teaching or research. To be excludable, tuition reductions must be offered on a nondiscriminatory basis.

- **Qualified Employee Discounts**

  Employee discounts on employer-provided merchandise and service are excludable as follows:

  - **Merchandise Discounts**

    The excludable discount is limited to the employer's gross profit percentage. Any excess must be reported as income.

  - **Service Discounts**

    The excludable discount on services is limited to 20 percent of the fair market value of the services. Any excess discount must be reported as income.

- **Employer-Provided Parking**

  The value of employer-provided parking up to $300 per month (2023) may be excluded. The exclusion is available even if the parking benefit is taken by the employee in place of taxable cash compensation.

- **Transit Passes**

  The value of employer-provided transit passes up to $300 per month (2023) may be excluded.

- **Qualified Non-Roth Retirement Plans**

  - **Contributions Made by Employer (Nontaxable)**

    Generally, payments made by an employer to a qualified non-Roth retirement plan are not income to the employee at the time of contribution.

  - **Contributions Made by Employee (Nontaxable)**

    Employees can elect to contribute part of their salary into certain qualified non-Roth retirement plans pretax, so the employee is not taxed on that income.

  - **Benefits Received (Taxable)**

    The amount that is exempt from tax (plus any income earned on such amount) is taxable to the employee in the year in which the amount is distributed or made available to the employee.

- **Flexible Spending Arrangements (FSAs)**

  A *flexible spending arrangement* stems from a Section 125 employee flexible benefit plan. The plan allows employees to receive a pretax reimbursement of certain (specified) incurred expenses.

  - **Pretax Deposits Into Employee's Account**

    Employees have the ability to elect to have part of their salary (generally up to $3,050 for 2023) deposited pretax into a flexible spending account designated for them. These deposits must be done via salary reduction directly by the employer, and the employee is not taxed on that income. The employee has the option to use the deposited funds to pay for qualified health care and/or qualified dependent care costs, and submits claims to the plan administrator for reimbursement.

  - **Forfeit Funds Not Used Within 2½ Months After Year-End**

    An employee generally must use the money in an FSA within the plan year. Funds not used within 2½ months after the year-end are forfeited. However, this grace period only applies if the employer amended the plan accordingly. Alternatively, the employer may amend the plan to allow an employee to carry over up to $610 per year (2023) to use in the following year.

2.3 Interest Income

2.3.1 Taxable Interest Income

The items below represent taxable interest income:

- Interest from federal bonds.
- Interest from industrial development bonds.
- Interest from corporate bonds.
- Part of the proceeds from an installment sale is taxable as interest.
- Interest paid by the federal or state government for late payment of a tax refund is taxable.
- For certain taxpayers and certain bonds, the amortization of a bond premium is an offset (reduction) to the interest received and a reduction to the bond's basis, and the amortization of a bond discount is an addition to the interest received and an addition to the bond's basis.

2.3.2 Tax-Exempt Interest Income (Reportable but Not Taxable)

The following items must be reported on the tax return but are not taxable:

- **State and Local Government Bonds/Obligations:** Interest on state and local bonds/obligations is tax-exempt. Furthermore, mutual fund dividends for funds invested in tax-free bonds are also tax-exempt.
- **Bonds of a U.S. Possession:** Interest on the obligation of a possession of the United States, such as Guam or Puerto Rico, is tax-exempt.
- **U.S. Series EE Savings Bonds:** Interest on U.S. Series EE savings bonds issued after 1989 is tax-exempt when:
    - it is used to pay for higher education (reduced by tax-free scholarships) of the taxpayer, spouse, or dependents;
    - the taxpayer is over age 24 when bond is issued;
    - a married taxpayer files a joint return; and
    - the taxpayer meets certain income requirements.

The exclusion of interest from U.S. Series EE savings bonds is phased out when the taxpayer's modified AGI reaches a certain level (2023).

Filing Status	Modified AGI
Single/head of household	$91,850–$106,850
Married filing jointly	$137,800–$167,800

When a taxpayer uses bonds to pay for a child's education, the bonds must be registered in the taxpayer's and/or spouse's name. The child can be listed as a beneficiary on the bond, but not as a co-owner.

2.3.3 Forfeited Interest (Adjustment) (Penalty on Withdrawal From Savings)

Forfeited interest is a penalty for early withdrawal of savings (generally on a time deposit, such as a certificate of deposit, at a bank). The bank credits the interest to the taxpayer's account and then, in a separate transaction, removes certain interest as a penalty for withdrawing the funds before maturity. The interest received is taxable on the taxpayer's income tax return, but the amount forfeited is also deductible as an adjustment in the year the penalty is incurred. Thus, the taxpayer only pays tax on the amount of interest actually received. Note, however, that the amount of forfeited interest is deducted separately and not netted with interest income on the tax return.

2.4 Dividend Income

2.4.1 Source Determines Taxability

A dividend is defined by the Internal Revenue Code as a distribution of property by a C corporation out of the company's earnings and profits. The taxability of the dividend is determined by the amount of the company's earnings and profits:

- Corporate earnings and profits → taxable dividend
- No earnings and profits and taxpayer has basis in stock → nontaxable and reduces basis of stock
- No earnings and profits and no stock basis → taxable capital gain income

2.4.2 Taxable Dividends

All dividends that represent distributions of a corporation's earnings and profits (similar to retained earnings) are includable in gross income.

- **Taxable Amount (to Recipient Shareholder)**
  - Cash = Amount received
  - Property = Fair market value

2.4.3 Preferential Tax Rate for Qualified Dividends

Qualified dividends are those paid by domestic or certain qualified foreign corporations.

- **Qualified Dividends Holding Period**: To be qualified dividends, the stock must be held for more than 60 days during the 120-day period that begins 60 days before the ex-dividend date (the date on which a purchased share no longer is entitled to any recently declared dividends).

- **Nonqualified Dividends:**
  - Employer stock held by an employee stock ownership plan (ESOP)
  - Amounts taken into account as investment income (for purposes of the limitation on investment expenses)
  - Short sale positions
  - Certain foreign corporations
  - Dividends paid by credit unions, mutual savings banks, building and loan associations, mutual insurance companies, and farmer's cooperatives.

Qualified dividends are taxed at the same preferential tax rates as long-term capital gains (LTCGs):

	2023 Taxable Income			
Tax Rate	Single	Head of Household	Married Filing Jointly	Married Filing Separately
0%	$0–$44,625	$0–$59,750	$0–$89,250	$0–$44,625
15%	$44,626–$492,300	$59,751–$523,050	$89,251–$553,850	$44,626–$276,900
20%	Over $492,300	Over $523,050	Over $553,850	Over $276,900

2.4.4 Tax-Free Distributions

The following items are excluded from gross income:

- **Return of Capital**

    Return of capital exists when a C corporation distributes funds but has no earnings and profits. The taxpayer will simply reduce (but not below zero) his or her basis in common stock held.

- **Stock Split**

    When a stock split occurs, the shareholder will allocate the original basis over the total number of shares held after the split.

- **Stock Dividend (Unless Cash or Other Property Option/Taxable FMV)**

    Unless the shareholder has the option to receive cash or other property (which would then be taxable at the FMV of the dividend), the basis of the shares after distribution depends on the type of stock received.

    - Same stock—original basis is divided by total shares
    - Different stock—original basis is allocated based on the relative FMV of the different stock

- **Life Insurance Dividend**

    Dividends caused by ownership of insurance with a mutual company (premium return).

2.4.5 Capital Gain Distribution

Distributions by a corporation that has no earnings and profits, and for which the shareholder has recovered his or her entire basis, are treated as taxable gross income.

2.5 State and Local Tax Refunds

The receipt of a state or local income tax refund in a subsequent year is not taxable if the taxes paid did not result in a tax benefit in the prior year.

- Itemized in prior year = State or local refund is taxable.
- Standard deduction used in prior year = State or local refund is nontaxable.

Gross Income: Part 1

> **Illustration 2 — Nontaxable and Taxable State and Local Tax Refunds**
>
> Carlos, a single individual, used the standard deduction on his Year 10 federal individual income tax return. In Year 11, he received a $150 state income tax refund. The $150 tax refund is not includable in his Year 11 income because he did not itemize in Year 10 and, therefore, did not receive a tax benefit from the state income taxes paid. If he had received a tax benefit from deducting the state taxes when paid in Year 10, a Year 11 (or later) refund of those taxes would be taxable income for federal income tax purposes when received, regardless of whether or not the taxpayer itemized deductions in the year the refund was received.

2.6 Payments Pursuant to a Divorce

2.6.1 Alimony/Spousal Support Payments

Alimony or spousal support payments made pursuant to a divorce or separation agreement executed on or before December 31, 2018, are included in gross income by the recipient and deductible by the payor spouse. For divorce or separation agreements executed after December 31, 2018, alimony received is not included in gross income, and alimony paid cannot be deducted. To be deemed alimony under the tax law:

- payments must be legally required pursuant to a written divorce (or separation) agreement;
- payments must be in cash (or its equivalent);
- payments cannot extend beyond the death of the payee-spouse;
- payments cannot be made to members of the same household;
- payments must not be designated as anything other than alimony; and
- the spouses may not file a joint tax return.

> **Pass Key**
>
> On the CPA Exam, if a real date is provided (e.g., 2017 or 2018) instead of a generic date (e.g., Year 1 or Year 2), candidates should use that as a tip-off that there is a date-specific tax treatment that needs to be considered. The CPA Exam will only use real dates when it is necessary for the candidate. A clear example of this is a question about alimony in which the year is indicated so the candidate can correctly decide whether that amount is includable in income.
>
> Candidates should also apply any assumptions given in a question and assume that the information provided in the question is material.

2.6.2 Child Support

- **Nontaxable:** If any portion of the payments is fixed by the decree or agreement as being for the support of minor children (or is contingent on the child's status, such as reaching a certain age), such portion is not deductible by the spouse making payment and is not includable by the spouse receiving payment.

- **Payment Applies First to Child Support:** If the decree or agreement specifies that payments are to be made both for alimony and for support, but the payments subsequently made fall short of fulfilling these obligations, the payments will be allocated first to child support (until the entire child support obligation is met) and then to alimony.

2.6.3 Property Settlements (Nontaxable)

If a divorce settlement provides for a lump-sum payment or property settlement by a spouse, that spouse gets no deduction for payments made, and the payments are not includable in the gross income of the spouse receiving the payment.

2.7 Business Income or Loss (Schedule C)

Net business income or loss from a sole proprietorship is calculated on Schedule C and reported on Form 1040 as a single item (the specific line item is business income or loss).

2.8 Gains and Losses on Disposition of Property

Gain or loss on the disposition of property is measured by the difference between the amount realized and the adjusted basis. Gains and losses are given tax effect (recognized) only when the asset is sold or disposed by other means. Whether on a cash or accrual method of accounting, taxpayers who sell stock or securities on an established securities market must recognize gains and losses as of the trade date, not the settlement date. The basic formula in determining the gain or loss is as follows:

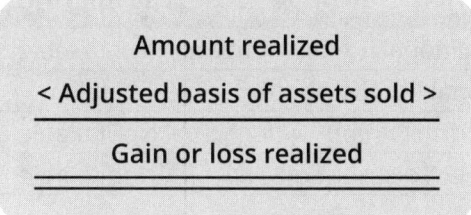

2.9 IRA Distributions

Distributions for IRAs consist of principal (contributions) and earnings. The tax treatment of a distribution depends on whether the distribution is from a traditional IRA or a Roth IRA.

Any taxable distributions from IRAs are taxed as ordinary income regardless of the type of income, such as capital gain, that was earned while the funds were invested.

2.9.1 Distributions From Traditional IRAs

- Distributions of principal (contributions) are taxable if the taxpayer took a deduction for the contribution when made.
- Distributions of earnings are always taxable, whether or not the taxpayer deducted the contribution when made.
- A distribution from a nondeductible, traditional IRA is allocated between principal (contributions) and earnings pro rata based on relative amounts in the IRA account at the time of the distribution.
- Taxpayers are required to start taking required minimum distributions (RMDs) by April 1 of the year following the year in which the taxpayer reaches age 73.

Gross Income: Part 1

2.9.2 Distributions From Roth IRAs

- Distributions of principal (contributions) from a Roth IRA are never taxable because taxpayers are not allowed to deduct contributions to a Roth IRA.
- Distributions of earnings from a Roth IRA are only taxable if the distribution is a nonqualified Roth distribution.
- A *qualified distribution* is a distribution from a Roth IRA that:
    1. Is made at least five years after the first day of the year in which the taxpayer made his or her first contribution to the Roth IRA, and
    2. Meets one of the following requirements:
        —taxpayer is age 59½ or older;

        —taxpayer is disabled;

        —taxpayer is a *first-time* homebuyer (has not owned a home for two years) and uses the distribution to purchase a home (maximum $10,000); or

        —distribution is made to a beneficiary after the taxpayer's death.
- Distributions from Roth IRAs are considered to first come from principal (contributions), then earnings.

Type of Distribution	Principal (Contributions)	Earnings
Nondeductible traditional IRA distribution	Nontaxable	Taxable
Deductible traditional IRA distribution	Taxable	Taxable
Qualified Roth IRA distribution	Nontaxable	Nontaxable
Nonqualified Roth IRA distribution	Nontaxable	Taxable

Illustration 3 — Automated Diagnostic and Validation Check: Gross Income

Mary, a CPA, is preparing the Year 1 federal income tax return for her client, Isabelle Irwin, who is 62 years old and single. Isabelle received a $20,000 distribution for her individual retirement account (IRA) during the current year. Her only other source of income for the year was interest and dividend income from a mutual fund.

Mary received the following messages in a software diagnostic report when she was preparing Isabelle's Year 1 federal income tax return:

Form 1040: Dividend Income	Box 49	Qualified dividends

The amount of the total ordinary dividends in Box 48 that are qualified dividends was not entered in Box 49. An amount must be entered in Box 49. If the amount of qualified dividends is zero, enter a zero (0).

Form 1040: IRA Distribution	Box 73	Type of IRA

No entry was made to identify the type of IRA in Box 73. The type of IRA needs to be selected from the options provided:

- Roth
- Traditional Deductible IRA
- Traditional Nondeductible IRA

Form 1040: IRA Distribution	Box 74	Date IRA was opened

The date the IRA was opened was incorrectly entered with only the month and day, but not the year. The year that the account was opened needs to be added.

Form 1040: IRA Distribution	Box 75	Date of distribution

The date the distribution was made was not entered in Box 75.

Action Needed:

Mary should enter the amount of the dividends that qualify for the preferential capital gains rates in Box 49 Qualified Dividends. This amount is provided in Box 1b of the Form 1099-DIV.

The tax treatment of the IRA distribution depends on the type of IRA, so Mary needs to select the appropriate type from the list provided in Box 73. If the distribution is from a Roth IRA, the tax preparation software needs the date the account was opened and the date of the distribution. This information is used to determine whether the distribution was made at least five years after the first day of the year in which the taxpayer made the first contribution to the account.

Because Isabelle is over age 59½, the distribution is a qualified Roth distribution that is 100 percent nontaxable as long as the five-year test is met. If it is not met, the contributions (principal) distributed are nontaxable, but the earnings distributed are taxable.

Gross Income: Part 1

Example 2 IRA Distribution

Facts: Sally opened an IRA when she was 55 years old and contributed $5,000. Several years later, when the account had grown to $8,000, she withdrew $6,000 to pay for a three-week European vacation.

Required: Determine the amount of Sally's taxable ordinary income from the IRA distribution under four different assumptions:

1. Traditional IRA, deduction was taken for the contribution
2. Traditional IRA, deduction was not taken for the contribution
3. Roth IRA, amount was withdrawn four years after the contribution
4. Roth IRA, amount was withdrawn six years after the contribution

Solution:

1. $6,000 taxable ordinary income

   Traditional IRA and Sally deducted the contribution, so both distribution of principal (contribution) and earnings are taxable. A distribution of any amount is 100 percent taxable.

2. $2,250 taxable ordinary income

   Traditional IRA and Sally did not deduct the contribution, so the distribution of principal (contribution) is not taxable. Distribution of earnings for a traditional IRA are always taxable. The $8,000 account balance consists of 62.5 percent principal (5,000 contribution / 8,000 total) and 37.5 percent earnings (3,000 earnings / 8,000 total), so 37.5 percent of the distribution is taxable. $6,000 distribution × 37.5% taxable portion = $2,250.

3. $1,000 taxable ordinary income

   The Roth IRA distribution was made before the account had been open for five years, so it is a nonqualified distribution. Distribution of principal (contribution) is not taxable but the earnings are taxable. A distribution from a Roth IRA is considered to come first from principal (contribution), then earnings, so the $6,000 distribution consists of $5,000 nontaxable principal and $1,000 taxable earnings.

4. $0 taxable ordinary income

   The Roth IRA has been open for at least five years and Sally is at least age 59½ (55 years old at contribution + Withdrawal six years later = 61 years old at time of distribution). The distribution is a qualified Roth distribution and neither the principal (contribution) nor the earnings are taxed.

2.9.3 Penalty Tax (10 Percent)

Generally, a premature distribution before age 59½ is subject to a 10 percent penalty tax (in addition to regular income tax) if the individual has not met an exception.

2.9.4 Exception to Penalty Tax (Still Subject to Ordinary Income Tax)

There is no penalty if the premature distribution was used to pay:

- **Homebuyer** (first time): Distribution used toward the purchase of a first home within 120 days of distribution ($10,000 maximum exclusion)
- **Insurance** (medical): If unemployed with 12 consecutive weeks of unemployment compensation
- **Medical** expenses in excess of percentage of AGI floor
- **Disability** (permanent or indefinite disability, but not temporary disability)
- **Education:** College tuition, books, fees, etc.
- **Adoption or birth** of child made within one year from the date of birth or adoption ($5,000 maximum exclusion)
- **Disaster:** Qualified natural disaster ($22,000 maximum per disaster)
- **Death** or terminal illness

2.9.5 Rollover From Traditional to Roth IRA

Taxpayers can transfer funds from a traditional IRA to a Roth IRA. The amount transferred is taxed as if it is a distribution: Contributions that were not deducted are nontaxable, and both contributions that were deducted and earnings are taxable ordinary income. However, the withdrawal from the traditional IRA is not subject to the 10 percent early withdrawal penalty if the taxpayer contributes the entire amount to a Roth IRA account within 60 days of the withdrawal.

2.10 Annuities

An annuity is a contract between a taxpayer and an insurance company in which the taxpayer contributes a lump-sum payment (or series of payments) and in return receives regular annuity payments over time. There are two basic types of annuities: 1) fixed period annuities, in which payments are received over a fixed period of time; and 2) life annuities, in which payments are received over the taxpayer's lifetime.

Each annuity payment received by the taxpayer consists of return of investment (contributions), which are nontaxable, and earnings, which are taxed as ordinary income. How much of each annuity payment is nontaxable return of investment and how much is taxable earnings depends on whether the annuity is a fixed period annuity or a life annuity.

2.10.1 Fixed Period Annuity Payments

The annuity exclusion ratio, which is the portion of each annuity payment that is a nontaxable return of investment, is the original investment divided by the expected value of the annuity. For a fixed period annuity, the expected value of the annuity is the amount of each payment times the number of payments.

> ### Example 3 — Fixed Period Annuity
>
> **Facts:** Zoe purchased an annuity for $60,000 that would pay her $750 per month for 120 months (10 years).
>
> **Required:** Calculate the amount of the taxable portion of each annuity payment received.
>
> **Solution:**
>
> Expected value of the annuity = $750 monthly annuity payment × 120 months = $90,000
>
> Annuity exclusion ratio = $60,000 original investment / $90,000 expected value = 66.7% return of capital
>
> Taxable portion of each annuity payment = 100% − 66.7% = 33.3% × $750 monthly payment = **$249.75**

2.10.2 Life Annuity Payments

For a life annuity, the number of annuity payments to be received is unknown, so taxpayers must use IRS life expectancy tables to determine the portion of each annuity payment that is a nontaxable return of investment. The original investment is divided by the appropriate factor from the IRS tables. The IRS factor represents the taxpayer's life expectancy at the time he or she starts receiving the annuity payments. The factor ranges from 360 months for taxpayers age 55 or under to 160 months for taxpayers age 71 or older. The portion of each annuity payment that is a nontaxable return of investment is the original investment divided by the IRS life expectancy factor.

If a taxpayer lives longer than the IRS estimated life expectancy, the entire amount of any additional payments received are taxable. If the taxpayer dies before receiving the expected number of payments, the remaining unrecovered investment is deducted on the taxpayer's final income tax return.

> ### Example 4 — Life Annuity
>
> **Facts:** John purchased an annuity for $60,000 that would pay him $600 per month for the rest of his life. John is 64 years old at the annuity start date, so the IRS life expectancy factor is 260 months.
>
> **Required:** Calculate the amount of the taxable portion of each annuity payment received.
>
> **Solution:**
>
> Nontaxable return of capital = $60,000 original investment / 260 months = $230.77
>
> Taxable portion of each monthly annuity payment = $600.00 − $230.77 = **$369.23**
>
> What if John lived for 270 months? The last ten $600 monthly payments would be fully taxable because he has recovered all of his original investment over the first 260 months.
>
> What if John died after 250 months? The remaining unrecovered investment of $2,307.70 ($230.77 × 10 months) is deducted on John's final income tax return.

2.11 Rental Income—Passive Activity

Net rental income or loss is calculated on Schedule E and reported as a single line item on Form 1040 (the specific line item is rental real estate, royalties, ...).

2.12 Unemployment Compensation

A taxpayer must include in gross income the full amount received for unemployment compensation.

2.13 Social Security Income

Social Security benefits received might be included in income. Taxpayers are classified into five categories depending on the level of modified adjusted gross income, which is defined as AGI plus tax-exempt interest plus 50 percent of Social Security benefits. Taxpayers must include in income the lesser of 50 percent (or 85 percent, depending on income) of Social Security received or 50 percent (or 85 percent, depending on income) of the excess modified AGI over the threshold.

- Low Income = No Social Security benefits are taxable (income equal to or less than $25,000 for single filers or equal to or less than $32,000 for MFJ).
- Lower Middle Income = Less than 50 percent of Social Security benefits are taxable.
- Middle Income = 50 percent of Social Security benefits are taxable (income over: single $25,000/MFJ $32,000).
- Upper Middle Income = Between 50 percent and 85 percent of Social Security benefits are taxable.
- Upper Income = 85 percent of Social Security benefits are taxable (income over: single $34,000/MFJ $44,000).

2.13.1 Modified Adjusted Gross Income

Modified adjusted gross income (modified AGI), or provisional income, includes the following items:

- Any income excluded because of the foreign-earned income exclusion.
- Any exclusion or deduction claimed for foreign housing.
- Any interest income from series EE bonds that was able to be excluded because of qualified higher education expenses.
- Any deduction claimed for student loan interest or qualified tuition and related expenses.
- Any employer-paid adoption expense that was excluded.
- Any deduction claimed for an annual (non-rollover) contribution to a traditional IRA.

2.14 Year of Death Income

A final income tax return is filed in the year of death. A personal representative will file the tax return for a single taxpayer, while a surviving spouse may file a joint return. The final income tax return is due at the same time the decedent's return would have been due, generally April 15 following the year of death.

The decedent's income includible on the final income tax return is generally determined as if the person were still alive, with the taxable period ending on the date of death. The method of accounting used by the decedent before death also determines the income includible on the final return. Income earned or received after death is reported on the federal estate tax return.

2.15 Taxable Miscellaneous Income

2.15.1 Prizes and Awards

The fair market value of prizes and awards is taxable income. An exclusion from income for certain prizes and awards applies when the winner is selected for the award without entering into a contest (i.e., without any action on the winner's part) and assigns the award directly to a governmental unit or charitable organization.

2.15.2 Gambling Winnings and Losses

- **Winnings:** Gambling winnings are included in gross income.
- **Losses:** Unless the taxpayer is in the trade or business of gambling (which follows specific reporting rules), gambling losses may only be deducted to the extent of gambling winnings. Gambling losses include the expenses the taxpayer incurred in connection with the gambling activity. Gambling losses are deductible on Schedule A as an itemized deduction.

2.15.3 Damages Awards

To decide whether a damages award is excludable, one must determine what the damages were paid "in lieu of." Thus, if a damage award is compensation for lost profit, the award is *income*.

2.15.4 Punitive Damages

Punitive damages are fully taxable as ordinary income if received in a business context or for loss of personal reputation. Punitive damages received by an individual in a personal injury case are also taxable except in wrongful death cases where state law has limited wrongful death awards to punitive damages only.

2.15.5 Cancellation of Debt (COD) Income

If a taxpayer borrows money from a commercial lender and the lender later cancels or forgives part or all of the debt, the canceled debt is generally included in the taxpayer's income. COD income is not taxable in the following situations:

- Debt is discharged through insolvency.
- Taxpayer is insolvent when the debt is canceled.
- Cancellation of nonrecourse secured loan, including foreclosure on personal residence (treated as a sale of the forfeited secured property).
- Student loans forgiven by lender are not included in borrower's taxable income (2021–2025).

> **Example 5**   **COD Income**
>
> **Facts:** Mary owes the bank $80,000 on an unsecured recourse note. She satisfies the note in full with a payment of $30,000. The bank accepts this payment and forgives the remaining $50,000 of debt.
>
> **Required:** Determine Mary's taxable income as a result of the cancellation of debt.
>
> **Solution:** The debt is unsecured recourse debt and none of the exceptions apply, so Mary has taxable cancellation of debt income of $50,000.

2.16 Partially Taxable Miscellaneous Items (Scholarships and Fellowships)

- **Degree-Seeking Student:** Scholarships and fellowship grants are excludable only up to amounts actually spent on tuition, fees, books, and supplies (not room and board) provided:
    - The grant is made to a degree-seeking student;
    - No services are to be performed as a condition to receiving the grant; and
    - The grant is not made in consideration for past, present, or future services of the grantee.
- **Non-degree-Seeking Student:** Scholarships and fellowships awarded to non-degree-seeking students are fully taxable at FMV.
- **Tuition Reductions:** Graduate teaching assistants and research assistants who receive tuition reductions are taxed on the reduction if it is their only compensation, but not if the reduction is in addition to other taxable compensation.

2.17 Nontaxable Miscellaneous Items

- **Life Insurance Proceeds (Nontaxable):** The proceeds of a life insurance policy paid because of the death of the insured are excluded from the gross income of the beneficiary.
    - The interest income element on deferred payout arrangements is fully taxable.
    - If the proceeds are used to pay for long-term care, accelerated death benefits received by an insured who is terminally ill (provided there is certification that the insured is expected to die within 24 months), is chronically ill, or requires assisted living are not taxable.
    - For policies issued after August 17, 2006, if the policy is company-owned (COLI), the employer beneficiary may exclude from gross income benefits received (no more than the total amount of premiums and other amounts paid by the policyholder). Any excess received beyond the amount of premiums and other amounts paid by the policyholder would be taxable. The gross income inclusion requirement for the COLI is not applicable, however, if proper notice and consent requirements are met and any of the following situations apply:
        —The insured was a qualified highly compensated officer, director, or employee and a U.S. citizen or resident.
        —Proceeds were paid to a member of the insured's family.
        —The beneficiary is a family member or another individual (not the policyholder).
        —The beneficiary is a trust for the benefit of the insured's family (or the estate of the insured).
- **Gifts and Inheritances (Nontaxable):** Gross income does not include property received from a gift or inheritance; however, any income received from such property (e.g., interest income, rental income, etc.) after the property is in the hands of the recipient is taxable.
- **Medicare Benefits (Nontaxable):** Exclude from gross income basic Medicare benefits received under the Social Security Act.
- **Workers' Compensation (Nontaxable):** Exclude from gross income compensation received under a workers' compensation act for personal injury or sickness.

Gross Income: Part 1 — REG 1

- **Personal (Physical) Injury or Illness Award (Nontaxable):** Exclude from gross income damages received as compensation for personal (physical) injury or illness.
- **Accident Insurance: Premiums Paid by Taxpayer (Nontaxable):** Exclude from gross income all payments received (even with multiple recoveries) if the individual paid all premiums for the insurance.
- **Foreign-Earned Income Exclusion:** Taxpayers working abroad may exclude from gross income up to $120,000 (2023) of their foreign-earned income. In order to qualify for the exclusion, the taxpayer must satisfy one of the following two tests:
    1. **Bona Fide Residence Test:** The taxpayer must have been a bona fide resident of a foreign country for an entire taxable year.
    2. **Physical Presence Test:** The physical presence test requires that the taxpayer must have been present in the foreign country for 330 full days out of any 12-consecutive-month period (which may begin on any day).

Note: The exclusion cannot exceed the taxpayer's foreign-earned income reduced by the taxpayer's foreign housing exclusion ($120,000 foreign-earned income exclusion × 16% = $19,200 maximum). Furthermore, the amount of excluded income and housing is used to determine the income tax rate for the taxpayer for the year (i.e., although it is not taxed, the excluded income could cause other income to be taxed at higher rates, as if the excluded income were taxable).

MODULE 3
Gross Income: Part 2

REG 1

1 Business Income or Loss, Schedule C

Net income from self-employment is computed on Schedule C. The net income from the sole proprietorship is then transferred to Form 1040 as one amount.

> Gross business income
> < Business expenses >
> Profit or loss

1.1 Gross Income

Items that normally would be revenue in a trade or business or other self-employed activity (such as director or consulting fees) are included as part of gross income on Schedule C.

- Cash = Amount received (cash basis)
- Property = Fair market value
- Cancellation of debt

1.2 Expenses

Expenses include items that one would expect to find in business, such as:

- Cost of goods (inventory is expensed when sold).
- Salaries and commissions paid to others.
- State and local business taxes paid.
- Office expenses (e.g., supplies, equipment, and rent).
- Actual automobile expenses (depreciation expense is limited to only that portion used for business) or a standard mileage rate (65.5 cents per mile for 2023).
- Business meal expenses at 50 percent.
- Depreciation of business assets.
- Employee benefits.
- Legal and professional services.
- Bad debts actually written off for an accrual basis taxpayer only (the direct write-off method, not the allowance method, is used for tax purposes).

- Interest expense on business loans (interest expense paid in advance by a cash basis taxpayer cannot be deducted until the tax year/period to which the interest relates). The business interest expense deduction is limited to the sum of:
  - business interest income;
  - 30 percent of adjusted taxable income (ATI); and
  - floor plan financing interest expense.

  ATI is taxable business income for the year excluding all interest income and interest expense. Floor plan financing is debt that is typically used to acquire motor vehicles held for sale or lease where the debt is secured by the acquired inventory.

  Disallowed business interest expense can be carried forward indefinitely. The limitation does not apply if the taxpayer's average annual gross receipts are $29 million or less (2023) for the prior three taxable years.

1.3 Nondeductible Expenses (on Schedule C)

- Salaries paid to the sole proprietor (considered a withdrawal).
- Federal income tax.
- Personal portion of:
  - Automobile, travel, and meal expenses.
  - *Interest expense:* This may be reported as an itemized deduction if mortgage interest or investment interest is paid.
  - *State and local tax expense:* Report as an itemized deduction on Schedule A.
  - *Health insurance of a sole proprietor:* Although this is not reported on Schedule C as an expense, it is reported as an adjustment to arrive at AGI.
- Bad debt expense of a cash basis taxpayer (who never reported the income).
- *Charitable contributions:* Report as an itemized deduction on Schedule A.
- Entertainment expenses

1.4 Net Business Income or Loss

1.4.1 Net Business Income Is Taxable

There are two federal taxes on net business income:

1. Income tax
2. Self-employment (SE) tax
   - An adjustment to income is allowed for one-half of SE tax (Medicare plus Social Security) paid. This allows the sole proprietor the ability to "deduct" the employer portion of the SE tax as an adjustment to gross taxable income (of which the net Schedule C amount is a part).
   - All self-employment income is subject to the 2.9 percent Medicare tax.
   - Up to $160,200 (2023) is subject to the 12.4 percent Social Security tax (so a total of 15.3 percent on self-employment earnings up to $160,200 in 2023).
   - The SE tax is calculated on 92.35 percent of self-employment income.

> **Example 1** — **Calculation of Self-Employment Tax**
>
> **Facts:** Tyler earns $20,000 from his consulting business, which he runs as a sole proprietorship. This was the only income he had in the current year.
>
> **Required:** Determine Tyler's self-employment tax.
>
> **Solution:** Tyler's self-employment tax is $2,826 calculated as follows:
>
> $20,000 × 92.35% = $18,470
>
> $18,470 × 15.3% = $2,826

1.4.2 Net Business Loss

A business with a loss may deduct the loss against other sources of income subject to overall excess business loss and net operating loss (NOL) limitations.

1.5 Hobby Losses

If an activity is not "engaged in for profit" by a taxpayer, the activity is a hobby for tax purposes, rather than a business, and deduction of the expenses related to the activity are limited.

1.5.1 Determining Whether Activity Is Engaged in for Profit

In determining whether an activity is engaged in for profit by the taxpayer, all the facts and circumstances are taken into account. To determine whether a profit motive exists for an activity, the following nine factors provided in the tax law are taken into consideration:

- Does the taxpayer carry on the activity in a businesslike manner and maintain complete and accurate books and records?
- Is the taxpayer an expert in the accepted practices of the activity, or does he or she seek expert advice?
- Does the taxpayer devote much of his or her personal time and effort to carrying on the activity?
- Is there an expectation that assets used in the activity may appreciate in value?
- Has the taxpayer engaged in other activities in the past and converted them from unprofitable to profitable?
- Does the activity have a history of sustained losses beyond reasonable start-up losses or unforeseen circumstances beyond the control of the taxpayer?
- Does the activity have occasional large profits, even though there are losses in other years?
- Does the taxpayer have substantial income or capital from sources other than the activity?
- Does the activity have elements of personal pleasure or recreation?

1.5.2 Three-of-Five Year Presumption

If an activity is profitable for three out of five consecutive years, the activity is presumed to be an activity engaged in for profit (a business). Rather than the taxpayer having the burden of proving that the activity is engaged in for profit, the IRS has the burden of proving that it is *not* engaged in for profit.

Gross Income: Part 2 REG 1

1.5.3 Tax Treatment of Activity Not Engaged in for Profit (Hobby)

If an activity is not engaged in for profit, the taxpayer cannot deduct the ordinary and necessary expenses that would be deductible if the activity were a business. No expenses related to the activity can be deducted, but the taxpayer is still required to include the revenue from the activity in taxable gross income (as other income).

2 Rental Income or Loss

2.1 General

Rental activity is reported on Schedule E. The basic formula for the determination of net rental income or loss is as follows:

> Gross rental income
> Prepaid rental income
> Rent cancellation payment
> Improvement-in-lieu of rent
> < Rental expenses >
> ─────────────────────────
> Net rental income   Or   Net rental loss

2.2 Rental of Residence

- **Rented Fewer Than 15 Days**

    If the residence is rented for fewer than 15 days per year, it is treated as a personal residence. The rental income is excluded from income, and mortgage interest (first or second home) and real estate taxes are allowed as itemized deductions. Depreciation, utilities, and repairs are *not* deductible.

- **Rented 15 or More Days**

    If the residence is rented for 15 or more days, and is used for personal purposes for the greater of (i) more than 14 days or (ii) more than 10 percent of the rental days, it is treated as a personal/rental residence. Expenses must be prorated between personal and rental use. However, a different proration method is used for mortgage interest and property taxes than is used for other property-related expenses (e.g., utilities, insurance, depreciation, etc.). Rental use expenses are deductible only to the extent of rental income.

2.3 Nonresidence (Rental Property)

For rental property, the taxpayer includes income received from the property in gross income and deducts all expenses allocated to the rental property on Schedule E of Form 1040. Rental losses are considered passive and will be deductible only to the extent of passive income. An exception to this rule allows an active participant in rental activity to deduct up to $25,000 of rental losses against nonpassive income.

> **Illustration 1 Vacation Home Rental**
>
> Julie rents her vacation home for two months and lives there for one month (during the other 11 months, Julie lives in the city). Thus, of the three-month period the vacation home is used, one-third is personal and two-thirds is rental. Assume that Julie's gross rental income is $6,000, her real estate taxes are $2,400, interest is $3,600, utilities are $4,800, and related depreciation is $7,200.
>
> These amounts are deductible in the following order:
>
> | | | Rental (Schedule E) | Personal (Schedule A) |
> |---|---|---|---|
> | Gross rental income | | $ 6,000 | – |
> | Deduct: Taxes | $2,400 | | |
> | Interest | 3,600 | | |
> | | $6,000 × 2/12* | (1,000) | $5,000—Schedule A |
> | Balance | | $ 5,000 | |
> | Deduct: Utilities | $4,800 × 2/3** | (3,200) | $1,600—Not Deductible |
> | | | $1,800 | |
> | Deduct: Depreciation | $7,200 × 2/3** | | |
> | | $4,800 but limited to*** | (1,800) | $2,400—Not Deductible |
> | Net income | | $ 0 | |
>
> *Allocated based on rental period/total annual period.
>
> **Allocated based on rental period/total annual usage.
>
> ***The additional $3,000 ($4,800 − 1,800) is not deductible, but is carried over to next year and applied against future income from this property.

3 Income or Loss From Flow-Through Business Entities

A flow-through entity's income, gains, losses, and deductions "flow through" to the owners and are taxed at the individual owner's level, rather than the entity level.

3.1 Types of Flow-Through Entities

- Partnerships
- S corporations
- LLCs that are taxed as partnerships or S corporations
  - If there are two or more owners, the default entity type is a partnership.
  - The partnership can elect to be taxed as a C corporation and if qualified, can then elect S status.

3.2 Ordinary Business Income and Separately Stated Items

Flow-through entities file annual information returns with the IRS, reporting the amount of the entity's ordinary business income or loss and separately stated items. The flow-through entity also provides each partner/shareholder a Schedule K-1 with the partner/shareholder's share of the flow-through entity's ordinary business income or loss and separately stated items.

3.2.1 Separately Stated Items

Certain items of income, gain, loss, and deduction that receive special treatment at the individual level (e.g., preferential tax rate, netting process, limitations) are carved out and flowed through separately to the owner. Common separately stated items include:

- Rental real estate income (loss)
- Interest income
- Dividend income
- Royalties
- Net short-term capital gain (loss)
- Net long-term capital gain (loss)
- Net Section 1231 gain (loss)
- Charitable contributions
- Section 179 expense deduction
- Guaranteed payments to partners *(partnerships only)*

3.2.2 Guaranteed Payments to Partners

Guaranteed payments are compensation paid by a partnership to a partner, either for services rendered or for the use of capital, that are determined without regard to the partnership's income.

- The payments are a business expense that reduces partnership ordinary income (loss).
- They flow through as a separately stated item of income on the recipient partner's Schedule K-1 and are included in the partner's taxable gross income.

3.2.3 Distributions to Partners and Shareholders

Distributions to partners and S corporation shareholders are not taxable income. The partnership/S corporation's income is taxed to the owners when it is earned, regardless of whether or when it is distributed to the owners.

3.3 Self-Employment Income

3.3.1 Guaranteed Payments for Services

Guaranteed payments to partners for services provided to the partnership are self-employment income to the recipient. Guaranteed payments are therefore subject to self-employment (Social Security and Medicare) tax in addition to income tax.

A shareholder in an S corporation receives a salary, rather than a guaranteed payment, for services provided to the corporation. The shareholder is employed by the corporation, not self-employed, so half of the Social Security and Medicare taxes are paid by the corporation and half are withheld from the shareholder's salary.

3.3.2 Owner's Share of Ordinary Business Income

A partner's allocable share of partnership ordinary business income is self-employment income subject to self-employment tax if the partner is actively involved in the operations of the business. If the partner is not actively involved, such as a limited partner who is not allowed to participate in managing the partnership, then the partner's allocable share of ordinary business income is not self-employment income.

A shareholder's allocable share of S corporation ordinary business income is not self-employment income, regardless of whether or not the shareholder is actively involved in the operations of the business. This avoidance of self-employment tax is one reason that a business may choose to organize as an S corporation rather than a partnership.

3.4 Business Loss Limitations

3.4.1 Tax Basis Loss Limitation

A taxpayer's tax basis in his or her ownership interest in a flow-through entity is basically the investment in the ownership interest, adjusted for items such as income, deductions, distributions, and, in some cases, debt.

A loss can only be flowed through to the owner's individual income tax return and deducted to the extent of the owner's tax basis. A loss in excess of the owner's tax basis is suspended until tax basis is reinstated in future years, and is carried forward indefinitely.

Any suspended losses due to insufficient tax basis remaining when the owner disposes of his or her interest in the flow-through entity are lost.

Example 2 — Tax Basis Loss Limitation

Facts: Don Carson is a 25 percent partner in Able, Brown, and Carson (ABC) Partners. Don's basis in his partnership interest at the beginning of Year 1 is $50,000. Don received $30,000 in distributions in Year 1. ABC Partners had a Year 1 ordinary business loss of $100,000.

Required: Calculate Don Carson's deductible ABC Partners ordinary business loss and ending tax basis in his partnership interest.

Solution:

ABC Partners' Year 1 ordinary business loss	$100,000
	× 25%
Don's share of Year 1 ordinary business loss	$ 25,000
Year 1 beginning tax basis in partnership interest	$ 50,000
Less: Year 1 distributions	(30,000)
Basis before Year 1 ordinary business loss	20,000
Deductible loss passed through to Don	(20,000)
Ending basis in partnership interest	$ 0
Suspended loss carryforward ($25,000 − $20,000)	$ 5,000

Illustration 2 — Automated Diagnostic and Validation Check: Loss Limitations

Mary, a CPA, is preparing the Year 1 federal income tax return for her client, Virginia Voss. Virginia is a 25-percent partner in a bicycle repair shop, Ace Bike Repairs, and is actively involved in the operations of the business. Virginia started a new activity—organizing and guiding week-long self-contained bike tours in the local area. Virginia had been doing this on a volunteer basis for the local bike club for several years but has decided to branch out on her own and try to start a cycling tour business.

Mary received the following messages in a software diagnostic report when she was preparing Virginia's Year 1 federal income tax return:

Form 1040:	Box 65	Tax basis in partnership interest

An ordinary business loss for Ace Bike Repairs partnership is included in Box 64, but no amount is entered in Box 65 for the partner's year-end tax basis in the partnership interest. The amount of the tax basis in the partnership interest is required for determining the amount of deduction for the ordinary business loss.

Form 1040:	Box 71	Activity code

The activity code for the Virginia's Cycling Tours activity has not been entered. Please review the information and enter the correct activity code.

Form 1040:	Box 72	Activity engaged in for profit

The box indicating whether an activity is engaged in for profit has not been checked. Review the factors provided in the tax law for determining whether an activity is engaged in for profit and check the box to indicate whether the activity is engaged in for profit.

Action Needed:

Mary needs to determine the tax basis of Virginia's partnership interest before the current year ordinary business loss and enter the amount in Box 65 of the tax preparation software. Virginia's deduction of her share of the Ace Bike Repairs partnership ordinary business loss is limited to her tax basis in her partnership interest.

Mary should also review the factors provided in the tax law for determining whether an activity is engaged in for profit. She should select the correct activity code in the tax software to indicate the type of activity and check the box to indicate whether the activity is engaged in for profit. If an activity is engaged in for profit, revenue from the activity is included in gross income and all ordinary and necessary business expenses can be deducted, even if there is a net loss. If an activity is *not* considered to be engaged in for profit, revenue from the activity is included in gross income but no expenses related to the activity can be deducted.

3.4.2 Excess Business Loss Limitation

Taxpayers are not allowed to deduct an overall "excess business loss" for the year. This limitation is applied to the taxpayer's combined active sources of business income and loss for the year, including Schedule C, rental activities, and income/losses from flow-through entities. The excess business loss limitation is applied after any other applicable loss limitations.

An excess business loss for the year is the excess of aggregate business deductions for the year over the sum of aggregate business income for the year plus a threshold amount. For 2023, the threshold amount is $578,000 (married filing jointly) and $289,000 (all other taxpayers). The combined business loss for the year in excess of the threshold amount is carried forward as a net operating loss (NOL).

NOLs generated before 2018 can offset 100 percent of a future year's taxable income, but can only be carried forward 20 years. NOLs generated after 2017 can be carried forward indefinitely.

NOL carryforwards from post-2017 tax years can offset 100 percent of taxable income in 2019 and 2020. Starting in 2021, any NOL carryforwards from post-2017 tax years can only offset 80 percent of taxable income after deducting any pre-2018 NOL carryforwards.

Example 3   **Excess Business Loss Limitation**

Facts: Betsy Chapel, a single taxpayer, has portfolio income of $600,000 in the current year. She is also an active participant in two businesses: a sole proprietorship and a partnership.

Sole proprietorship current year business income	$ 500,000
Share of partnership current year ordinary business loss	(900,000)

Required: Calculate the amount of Betsy's current year taxable gross income.

Solution: Betsy's combined business income (loss) for the current year is a $400,000 loss ($500,000 sole proprietorship income − $900,000 share of partnership ordinary business loss). She is allowed to deduct $289,000 (2023) against her other sources of income in the current year. The remaining $111,000 ($400,000 combined business loss − $289,000 loss deducted) is carried forward as a net operating loss (NOL).

NOTES

MODULE 4 Adjustments

REG 1

1 Overview

Adjustments for AGI (often referred to as "above-the-line" deductions, or "deductions to arrive at AGI") include the following:

- Educator expenses
- Traditional IRA contribution deduction
- Student loan interest deduction
- Health savings account deduction
- Moving expenses (only for members of the U.S. Armed Forces moving pursuant to military order)
- Deductible part of self-employment tax
- Self-employed health insurance deduction
- Deduction for contributions to certain self-employed retirement plans
- Penalty on early withdrawal of savings
- Alimony paid (only for divorce or separation agreements executed on or before December 31, 2018)
- Attorney fees paid in certain discrimination and whistle-blower cases

Pass Key

The CPA Examination will often refer to "adjustments" as "deductions to arrive at adjusted gross income."

2 Educator Expenses

- Eligible educators can deduct up to $300 of qualified expenses paid. If spouses are filing jointly and both are eligible educators, the maximum deduction is $600.
- Neither spouse can deduct more than $300 of his or her qualified expenses.
- An eligible educator is a kindergarten through grade 12 teacher, instructor, counselor, principal, or aide working in a school for at least 900 hours during a school year.

Adjustments REG 1

- Qualified expenses include ordinary and necessary expenses paid in connection with books, supplies, equipment (including personal protective equipment and supplies, computer equipment, software, and services), and other materials used in the classroom.
  - Deductible expenses also include costs of professional development.
  - An ordinary expense is one that is common and accepted in one's educational field.
  - A necessary expense is one that is helpful and appropriate for one's profession as an educator (does not have to be required).
- Qualified expenses do not include expenses for homeschooling or for nonathletic supplies for courses in health or physical education. Qualified expenses must be reduced by the following amounts:
  - Excludable U.S. series EE and I Savings Bond interest from Form 8815.
  - Nontaxable qualified state tuition program earnings.
  - Nontaxable earnings from Coverdell education savings accounts.
  - Any reimbursements received for these expenses that were not reported on Form W-2.

3 Individual Retirement Account Contributions

The three types of individual retirement accounts (IRAs) are:
- Deductible traditional IRA
- Roth IRA
- Nondeductible traditional IRA

3.1 Contributions

3.1.1 General Rule

The annual maximum contribution to IRAs is limited to the lesser of:

2023	Under Age 50	Age 50 and Over
Unmarried	$6,500 Or Earned income	$7,500 Or Earned income
Married	$13,000 ($6,500 each) Or Earned income of married couple	$15,000 ($7,500 each) Or Earned income of married couple

The annual limits apply to the sum of a taxpayer's contributions to deductible IRAs, nondeductible IRAs, and Roth IRAs.

- **Earned Income Includes:**
  - Salary and wages
  - Commissions
  - Bonuses
  - Alimony (for divorce or separation agreements executed before December 31, 2018)
  - Net earnings from self-employment
  - Non-tuition fellowship and stipend payments treated as taxable compensation
- **Earned Income Does Not Include:**
  - Interest and dividends
  - Annuity income
  - Pensions
  - Alimony (for divorce agreements executed after December 31, 2018)

3.1.2 Retirement Savings Contribution Credit

Eligible taxpayers may also be entitled to a tax credit for contributions to either a traditional IRA or a Roth IRA, subject to certain limitations.

3.2 Deductible Traditional IRA Contributions

Contributions to traditional IRAs may or may not be deductible. The traditional IRA is deductible from gross income to arrive at adjusted gross income. The adjustment is allowed for a year only if the contribution is made by the due date of the tax return for individuals, which is April 15 (filing extensions are not considered).

- Earnings on deductible traditional IRA contributions accumulate tax free until withdrawn.
- Distributions of both principal (contributions) and earnings from deductible traditional IRAs are taxable as ordinary income and may be subject to applicable early withdrawal penalties.
- Minimum distributions are required to be taken by April 1 of the year following the year in which the taxpayer reaches age 73.

3.2.1 Limitations on Deduction of Traditional IRA Contributions

A taxpayer's deduction for a traditional IRA contribution is limited if the taxpayer or spouse participates in an employer-sponsored plan.

- **Participation in Employer-Sponsored Retirement Plans:** If a taxpayer participates in an employer-sponsored retirement plan, AGI limitations apply to the deduction allowed for the contribution made to the traditional IRA. The allowed deductible contribution phases out proportionately within the following ranges:

Filing Status	2023 AGI Phase-out
Unmarried	$73,000–$83,000
Married filing jointly	$116,000–$136,000

Adjustments

REG 1

- **Special Rule:** If a married taxpayer is not an active participant in an employer's retirement plan, but the spouse is, the deduction for the spouse who is not an active participant is phased out based on the following AGI limitations:

Filing Status	2023 AGI Phase-out
Married filing jointly	$218,000–$228,000 (couple's AGI)
Married filing separately	$0–$10,000 (each spouse is subject to this limitation—both the participant and the nonparticipant)

3.2.2 Summary Chart for Married Individuals

Traditional IRA Income Phase-Out Ranges for Married Individuals

2023 Modified AGI Phase-out	Spouse 1 has earned income		If Spouse 2 has no earned income
	In ESRP?	Can IRA be deducted?	Can IRA be deducted?
N/A	No	Yes	Yes
<$116,000	Yes	Yes	Yes
$116,000–$136,000	Yes	Yes*	Yes
$136,001–$217,999	Yes	No	Yes
$218,000–$228,000	Yes	No	Yes**
>$228,000***	Yes	No	No

Note: If Spouse 2 has earned income, follow the same rules as Spouse 1.

ESRP = Employer Sponsored Retirement Plan

*The IRA deduction for the *working* spouse is phased out.

**The IRA deduction for the *nonworking* spouse is phased out.

***At modified AGI of more than $228,000, neither the working spouse nor the nonworking spouse can deduct their traditional IRA.

> **Example 1** **Phase-out of Traditional IRA Deduction**
>
> **Facts:** Kristi, a 40-year-old single taxpayer, is an active participant in her employer's retirement plan. Kristi's 2023 AGI is $75,000.
>
> **Required:** Calculate Kristi's maximum IRA deduction.
>
> **Solution:** Kristi's maximum 2023 IRA deduction is $5,200, calculated as follows:
>
> | | |
> |---|---:|
> | 2023 AGI | $ 75,000 |
> | Less phase-out threshold | (73,000) |
> | Excess over phase-out threshold | 2,000 |
> | Divided by $10,000 phase-out range | ÷ 10,000 |
> | Phase-out percentage | 20% |
> | × maximum IRA deduction allowed | 6,500 |
> | Phase-out amount | 1,300 |
> | 2023 allowable IRA deduction | $ 5,200 |
>
> *Question:* What is Kristi's maximum IRA deduction if she does not participate in an employer-sponsored retirement plan?
>
> *Answer:* $6,500. She would not be subject to the AGI limitations if she did not participate in an employer-sponsored retirement plan.

3.3 Roth IRA Contributions

- Contributions to a Roth IRA are not deductible when made.
- Earnings accumulate tax free while in a Roth IRA account.
- No deduction is allowed for Roth IRA contributions, so distribution of principal (contributions) is tax free. Distribution of earnings may be taxable, depending on whether the distribution is "qualified" or "nonqualified."

3.3.1 Allowable Roth Contributions

The ability to contribute to a Roth IRA is limited by modified AGI.

Filing Status	2023 MAGI Phase-out
Unmarried	$138,000–$153,000
Married filing jointly	$218,000–$228,000
Married filing separately	$0–$10,000

Adjustments

3.4 Nondeductible Traditional IRA

If a taxpayer's deduction for a contribution to a traditional IRA is limited, a nondeductible traditional IRA contribution can be made instead. The overall limitation still applies to the combined deductible and nondeductible contributions ($6,500 or earned income).

- Earnings on nondeductible traditional IRA contributions accumulate tax free until withdrawn.
- Distributions from a nondeductible traditional IRA will be taxed as follows:
  - Taxable: Earnings (taxed as ordinary income)
  - Nontaxable: Principal contributions (because not deducted when contributed)

IRA Summary			
	Deductible Traditional IRA	*Nondeductible Traditional IRA*	*Roth IRA*
Maximum contribution (2023):	$6,500 combined annual maximum contribution with $1,000 additional "catch up" contribution for age 50 and older		
Above-the-line deduction for contribution:	Yes	No	No
Withdrawals of contributions:	Taxable	Nontaxable	Nontaxable
Withdrawals of earnings:	Taxable	Taxable	Nontaxable (if qualified distribution) Taxable (if nonqualified distribution)

4 Student Loan Interest Expense

The adjustment for education loan interest is limited to $2,500.

- All interest payments qualify for the adjustment.
- It is phased out for AGI between:

2023	
Unmarried	$75,000–$90,000
MFJ	$155,000–$185,000

- Deduction is completely phased out at AGI equal to or more than $90,000 (2023) for unmarried taxpayers (single or head of household) and $185,000 (2023) for married taxpayers filing jointly. Married taxpayers must file jointly to claim the adjustment.
- A dependent may not claim the adjustment.
- The taxpayer must be legally obligated to pay the loan (e.g., interest paid by a parent on a child's student loan will not qualify for the adjustment).
- Interest is only deductible on loans incurred by a taxpayer solely to pay for qualified education expenses (e.g., general loans such as a home equity line of credit would not qualify).

5 Health Savings Accounts

5.1 Pretax Contribution

Health savings accounts (HSAs) enable workers with high-deductible health insurance plans to make pretax contributions of up to $3,850 in 2023 ($7,750 for families) to cover health care costs. These amounts are increased by $1,000 for taxpayers age 55 or older. No contributions are allowed once a taxpayer becomes covered by Medicare Parts A or B.

5.2 Excludable Distributions

Any amount paid or distributed out of an HSA that is used exclusively to pay the qualified medical expenses of any account beneficiary is not includable in gross income. Note that distributions for qualified drugs include only those prescribed by a physician.

- Distributions made prior to age 65 that are not used to pay qualified medical expenses are includable in gross income and subject to an additional 20 percent tax.

5.3 High-Deductible Plan Defined

A high-deductible health insurance plan is a plan that has at least a $1,500 annual deductible for self-only coverage and a $3,000 annual deductible for family coverage plans (2023).

- **Out-of-Pocket Limitation:** Annual out-of-pocket expenses paid under the plan must be limited to $7,500 for self-only coverage plans and $15,000 for family coverage plans (2023). Out-of-pocket expenses include deductibles, co-payments and other amounts (other than premiums) that must be paid for plan benefits.

5.4 Archer Medical Savings Account (MSA) Contributions

No new Archer MSAs could be established after the year 2007; however, any accounts established prior to 2008 are allowed to continue.

- Archer MSAs are similar to IRAs, but they are used for health care. Typically, they are used only if an HSA is unavailable, as HSAs are generally more flexible.
- Qualified participants are self-employed individuals or employees of small businesses (fewer than 50 employees).
- These accounts were designed to be and must be used in conjunction with a high-deductible (2023: $2,650–$3,950 self-only coverage/$5,300–$7,900 family coverage) health insurance plan.
- The maximum out-of-pocket expenses limit is $5,300 for self-only coverage plans and $9,650 for family coverage plans (2023).

6 Moving Expenses

Moving expense deductions are only allowed for members of the Armed Forces (or spouses and dependents) on active duty who move pursuant to a military order and incident to a permanent change of station.

7 Self-Employment Tax (50 Percent)

Self-employed taxpayers with net business income are subject to two taxes: income tax and self-employment (Social Security and Medicare) tax. Fifty percent of the self-employment tax is deducted to arrive at adjusted gross income.

8 Self-Employed Health Insurance

Self-employed individuals may deduct all of the health insurance premiums paid for the taxpayer, spouse, and dependents, provided that the plan is set up in the name of the self-employed individual or the individual's business. The deduction is limited to the amount of the taxpayer's self-employment income. The health insurance premiums are deducted above the line (adjustment), rather than as an itemized deduction subject to a percentage of AGI floor.

9 Self-Employed Retirement Plan Contributions

Self-employed taxpayers are allowed to deduct contributions made to qualified self-employed non-Roth retirement plans as an above-the-line deduction (adjustment) for AGI. As with employer-sponsored non-Roth plans, the earnings are not taxed until they are distributed. Distributions from the plan are fully taxable as ordinary income and are subject to the same early and late distribution penalties as other retirement plans. For self-employed retirement plans that are designated as Roth plans, contributions are nondeductible and qualified distributions are nontaxable.

The maximum amount that a self-employed taxpayer can contribute to a self-employed retirement plan each year depends on the type of plan. The most common self-employed retirement plans are simplified employee pension (SEP) IRAs, savings incentive match plan for employees (SIMPLE) IRAs, and Solo 401(k)s.

9.1 SEP IRA

The 2023 maximum contribution to a SEP IRA is the lesser of:

- 20 percent of self-employment net income reduced by one-half of self-employment tax deduction; or
- $66,000 ($73,500 for taxpayers age 50 or older).

9.2 SIMPLE IRA

The 2023 maximum contribution to a SIMPLE IRA is the lesser of:

- 100 percent of self-employment net income reduced by one-half of self-employment tax deduction; or
- $15,500 ($19,000 for taxpayers age 50 and older).

9.3 Solo 401(k)

The 2023 maximum contribution to an individual 401(k) is the lesser of:

- 20 percent of self-employment net income reduced by one-half of self-employment tax deduction; or
- $66,000 ($73,500 for taxpayers age 50 or older).

Example 2 — Calculating Maximum Allowable Deductible Contribution to SEP IRA

Facts: Peter has self-employment net income (after the deduction for one-half of the self-employment tax, but before any SEP IRA contribution) of $100,000.

Required: Calculate Peter's maximum allowable deductible contribution to his SEP IRA self-employed retirement plan for 2023.

Solution:

Self-employment net income (after deduction for one-half of self-employment tax)	$100,000
Times	× 20%
Maximum allowable deductible contribution	$ 20,000

---

10 Penalty on Early Withdrawal of Savings

A penalty assessed on the early withdrawal of savings from a certificate of deposit or other time savings account is deductible at arriving at adjusted gross income.

This penalty is also considered interest forfeited because of the early withdrawal of savings before maturity.

11 Alimony

Alimony payments to a former spouse are adjustments deductible to arrive at AGI only for divorce or separation agreements executed on or before December 31, 2018.

11.1 Alimony/Spousal Support (Income to Payee/Adjustment to Payor)

Payments for the support of a former spouse are income to the spouse receiving the payments and are deductible to arrive at adjusted gross income (adjustment) by the contributing spouse. The following conditions must exist for alimony to be deductible:

- Payments must be legally required under a written divorce (or separation) decree or agreement;
- Payments must be in cash (or its equivalent);
- Payments cannot extend beyond the death of the payee-spouse;
- Payments cannot be made to members of the same household; and
- Payments must not be designated as anything other than alimony.

11.2 Child Support (Nontaxable to Payee/Nondeductible to Payor)

- **Nontaxable**

    If any portion of the payment is fixed by the decree or agreement as being for the support of minor children (or is contingent on the child's status, such as reaching a certain age), such portion is not deductible by the spouse making payment and is not includable in income by the spouse receiving payment.

- **Payment Applies First to Child Support**

    If the decree or agreement specifies that payments are to be made both for alimony and for support, but the payments subsequently made fall short of fulfilling these obligations, the payments will be allocated first to child support (until the entire child-support obligation for the year is met), and then to alimony.

11.3 Property Settlements (Nontaxable/Nondeductible)

If the divorce settlement provides for a lump-sum payment or property settlement by a spouse, that spouse gets no deduction for payments made, and the payments are not includable in the gross income of the spouse receiving the payment.

12 Attorney Fees Paid in Discrimination Cases

In certain cases, an adjustment is allowed for attorney fees paid in connection with age, sex, racial discrimination, and whistle-blower cases. The adjustment amount is limited to the amount claimed as income from the judgment.

MODULE 5: Itemized Deductions

REG 1

1 Standard Deduction

Those who do not itemize receive a standard deduction, with the amount determined based on filing status:

2023	
Single	$13,850
Head of household	20,800
Married filing jointly or surviving spouse	27,700
Married filing separately*	13,850
*Available only if both taxpayer and spouse do not itemize.	

1.1 Additional Standard Deduction for Age 65 or Older and/or Blindness

The standard deduction for a taxpayer who is age 65 or over or blind is increased by an additional amount.

2023	Unmarried	Married
One Qualified Taxpayer		
65 or blind	$1,850	$1,500
Both 65 and blind	3,700	3,000
Two Qualified Taxpayers		
Each 65 *or* blind		$3,000
Both 65 *and* blind		6,000

> **Illustration 1 — Additional Standard Deduction**
>
> - Bob and Suzanne DeFilippis are both age 66 and file a married filing joint income tax return. For tax year 2023, the standard deduction would be $30,700 ($27,700 plus $3,000) because each spouse is age 65 or over.
> - For tax year 2023, Ed Joback, a blind, single taxpayer, may claim a standard deduction of $15,700 if he is under age 65 ($13,850 plus $1,850), or $17,550 ($13,850 plus $3,700) if he is age 65 or over.

1.2 Standard Deduction: Dependent of Another

For 2023, the standard deduction amount for a taxpayer who is a dependent of another taxpayer is the greater of $1,250 or earned income plus $400. Thus, a dependent taxpayer with $1,300 earned income could claim a standard deduction of $1,700 ($1,300 plus $400). The dependent's standard deduction remains limited by the regular standard deduction for the tax year. Dependent taxpayers may claim the same additional standard deduction as other taxpayers for blindness and/or age 65-or-over status.

2 Itemized Deductions

Itemized deductions are referred to as "from AGI" deductions and are reported on Schedule A of an individual taxpayer's Form 1040. A taxpayer itemizes deductions when "from AGI" deductions are greater than the standard deduction. Taxpayers who are married filing separately must both take the standard deduction or both itemize. One spouse cannot take the standard deduction and the other spouse itemize.

2.1 Medical Expenses

2.1.1 Payments

Payments on behalf of the following individuals qualify:

- Filing taxpayer
- Spouse
- Dependent who received more than half of his or her support from the filing taxpayer

Note: The definition of "dependent" for this purpose does not consider the dependent's gross income or the joint return requirement. Thus, there is no limitation to the dependent's gross income when it relates to medical or dental expenses (however, all other dependency tests will continue to apply).

Support over 50 percent	Yes
Under taxable gross income limit	No
Precludes joint return	No
Only citizens	Yes
Relative *or*	Yes
Taxpayer lives with	Yes

2.1.2 Timing of Deduction

Include as potentially deductible expenses:

- Paid (cash or check) amounts during the year.
- Amounts charged to a credit card during the year (regardless of when paid).
- Payments made for a deceased spouse (deductible in the year paid, even if it is different from the year the spouse died).
- Amounts reimbursed to the taxpayer (or anyone else for the taxpayer) by hospital, health, or accident insurance must reduce otherwise allowable expense (before the percentage of AGI floor is applied).

> **Pass Key**
>
> Individuals are typically "cash basis." Therefore, generally in order to be tax deductible, the item must have been:
> - incurred as an expense
> - paid or charged to credit card before year-end

2.1.3 Calculation of Deductible Medical Expenses

Qualified medical expenses to the extent that they exceed medical insurance reimbursement and the 7.5 percent of AGI floor are deductible.

```
        Qualified medical expenses
        < Insurance reimbursement >
        Qualified medical expenses "paid"
        < 7.5% of AGI >
        Deductible medical expenses
```

2.1.4 Types of Deductible Medical Expenses

- Medicine and prescription drugs, including Medicare part D premiums
- Doctors
- Medical and accident insurance premiums (including qualified long-term care premiums, although the deduction is limited based on the age of the taxpayer)
- Medically necessary surgery
- Transportation to medical facility
  - Actual costs, or
  - Allowance (22 cents per mile for 2023)
- Physically disabled costs

    Expenses incurred by the physically disabled for the removal of structural barriers in their residences to accommodate a disability are treated as medical expenses.

2.1.5 Types of Nondeductible Medical Expenses

- Elective surgery, elective cosmetic operations, drugs that are illegal, travel, vitamins, the part of Social Security tax paid for basic Medicare, funerals, cemetery lots, and insurance against loss of earnings due to sickness or accident (note that cosmetic surgery required due to an accident or deformity can qualify).
- Life insurance.
- Capital expenditures (up to the increase in the fair market value (FMV) of the property because of the expenditure).

- Health club memberships recommended by a doctor for general health care (it would have to be more specific to make it deductible).
- Personal hygiene and other ordinary personal expenses (e.g., toothpaste, toiletries, over-the-counter medicines, bottled water, diaper service, maternity clothes, etc.).

2.1.6 Insurance Reimbursement

Amounts repaid to the taxpayer (or anyone else for the taxpayer) by hospital, health, or accident insurance must reduce otherwise allowable expense (before the percentage of AGI floor is applied).

- Reimbursement of expenses by an employer (or by policies provided by an employer) that exceed the total of medical or dental expenses paid by a taxpayer will be included as part of gross income.
- Reimbursement of any expense deducted in a prior year will be included as part of gross income in the year received.

2.1.7 Percentage of AGI Floor

Only medical expenses in excess of 7.5 percent of AGI floor are deductible.

2.2 State, Local, and Foreign Taxes

For cash-method taxpayers, deductible taxes are generally deductible in the year paid. For accrual-method taxpayers, taxes are generally deductible in the year in which they accrue. Itemized deductions for state and local income taxes, state and local property taxes, and sales tax are limited to $10,000 in the aggregate. In addition, foreign real property taxes, other than those incurred in a trade or business and those incurred with respect to property held as an investment, are not deductible.

2.2.1 Real Estate Taxes (State and Local Taxes)

- The taxpayer must be legally obligated to pay in order to deduct the taxes.
- Prorate taxes in year of sale/purchase.
- Taxes paid under protest are deductible. Subsequent recovery is included in gross income.
- Real estate taxes do not include street, sewer, and sidewalk assessment taxes.
- Taxes paid through an escrow account are deductible when paid to the taxing authority.
- Foreign real estate taxes paid are only deductible if paid in carrying on a trade or business
- Real estate taxes on land held for appreciation may be capitalized or deducted at the option of the taxpayer.
- Real estate taxes allocated to part of the home that is used exclusively for business may be deductible on Schedule C.

2.2.2 Personal Property Taxes (State and Local Taxes)

Personal property taxes are those assessed by state and local governments on personal property owned by the taxpayer, such as vehicles and boats. To be deductible, the tax must be based on the value of the personal property and paid during the tax year.

2.2.3 Income Taxes (State, Local, and Foreign Taxes)

- Estimated taxes paid during the year are deductible.
- Taxes withheld from paychecks during the year are deductible.
- Assessments for a prior year's tax that are paid in the current year are deductible.
- Refunds are included in gross income (if the tax was deducted in a prior year) and should not be netted against the current year itemized tax deduction.

2.2.4 Sales Tax

A taxpayer may elect to deduct either state and local income taxes or state and local general sales taxes. If the taxpayer chooses to deduct the sales tax, the amount is determined by either:

- the total amount of actual general sales taxes paid; or
- the relevant IRS table, plus any amount of sales tax paid for a motor vehicle, boat, or other IRS-approved items.

Note: A "tax benefit rule" applies to the impact of sales tax. If a taxpayer itemizes deductions in a year and takes a deduction for state income taxes instead of a deduction for sales taxes in that year, the tax benefit rule will calculate the taxability of the state tax refund on the extra benefit received from claiming the higher state income tax deduction instead of what would have been allowed if the state sales tax had been deducted.

2.2.5 Nondeductible Taxes

The following taxes are not deductible as itemized deductions on Schedule A:

Federal taxes (including Social Security)

Inheritance taxes for states

Business (on Schedule C) and rental property taxes (on Schedule E)

Pass Key

Once again, "cash basis" taxpayers are entitled to a deduction in the year an item is paid or charged. Note that there is no "matching" to the year the tax is applicable.

2.3 Interest Expense

2.3.1 Home Mortgage Interest

Deductions are allowed for "qualified residence interest" on a first or a second home (a taxpayer's principal residence and one other residence). A home that is used for personal purposes for at least 14 days in a tax year qualifies as a "second home." Mortgage interest allocated to part of the home that is used exclusively for business may be deductible on Schedule C and mortgage interest allocated to rental of the home may be deductible on Schedule E.

Interest on up to $750,000 ($375,000 MFS) of home-related indebtedness is deductible as home mortgage interest. Interest on excess principal (over $750,000, or $375,000 MFS) is treated as personal interest and, as such, is not deductible. Qualified indebtedness may be in the form of original acquisition debt or a home equity loan, but must meet the following:

- Incurred in buying, constructing, or substantially improving the taxpayer's principal and second home; and
- Secured by the home.

Points related to the debt on the home are deductible immediately. Points related to refinancing must be amortized over the period of the loan.

2.3.2 Investment Interest Expense

The investment interest deduction for individuals is limited to net taxable investment income.

- **Include as Net Taxable Investment Income**
    - Interest
    - Dividends (other than qualified dividends)
    - Short-term capital gains
    - Royalties (in excess of expenses)
    - Net long-term capital gains and qualified dividends (only if the taxpayer elects not to claim the reduced capital gains tax rate)

- **Dividend Income From Stock Purchased With Borrowed Funds**

    Any dividend income from stock purchased with borrowed funds that the taxpayer treats as investment income for purposes of the limitation on investment interest expense is not a qualified dividend available for preferential 15 percent tax rate.

- **Exclude From Net Taxable Investment Income**

    Interest expense used to purchase tax-free bonds is not deductible (because the interest earned on the bonds is not taxable).

- **Disallowed Expense: Carry Forward**

    The excess of investment interest paid over the "allowed" investment interest deducted can be carried forward indefinitely.

Pass Key

An easy way to understand and remember this rule is to think of it like the limitations on gambling losses. Investments (a risk/gamble) have the limitation of not being permitted to deduct a "net investment expense."

2.3.3 Personal (Consumer) Interest Is Not Deductible

Personal interest includes interest on:

- A personal note to a bank or person for borrowed funds
- Life insurance loans
- Bank credit cards or other revolving charge accounts
- A purchase of personal property such as autos, television sets, clothes, etc.
- Federal, state, or local tax underpayments
- A home equity loan not used to improve the home

2.3.4 Prepaid Interest (Allocate to Proper Period)

Prepaid interest must be allocated over the period of the loan, even for a cash basis taxpayer. (Remember that prepaid interest received is taxable as income in the year received and is not allocated.)

2.3.5 Educational Loan Interest (Adjustment/Not Itemized Deduction)

Educational loan interest is a deduction to arrive at adjusted gross income and not an itemized deduction.

2.4 Charitable Contributions

2.4.1 Types of Contributions

- **Charity:** Items given to qualifying charitable organizations (tax deductible).
- **Gifts:** Items given to individuals (e.g., needy family) (nondeductible).
- **Political Contributions:** Items given to candidates (nondeductible).

2.4.2 Amount of Deduction

A charitable contribution may be in the form of cash or property. The amount of the deduction for contributions of property depends on whether the property is ordinary income property or long-term capital gain (LTCG) property.

The amount of the deduction for ordinary income property is the lesser of the property's adjusted basis or its fair market value (FMV) at the time it is contributed. Ordinary income property includes:

- Inventory
- Short-term assets (held for one year or less)
- Investment or personal-use assets that have depreciated in value
- Depreciation recapture on long-term, business-use assets

The amount of the deduction for LTCG property is its FMV at the time of the contribution. LTCG property is appreciated capital gain property that has been held for more than one year and includes:

- Investment assets
- Personal-use assets
- Gain in excess of ordinary income depreciation recapture for long-term, business-use assets

2.4.3 AGI Limitations on Amount of Deduction

The maximum allowable deduction for charitable contributions depends on the type of property contributed and the type of charity to which the contribution was made.

	Public Charities	Private Operating Foundations	Private Nonoperating Foundations
Cash	60% of AGI	60% of AGI	30% of AGI
Ordinary income property	50% of AGI	50% of AGI	30% of AGI
Long-term capital gain property	30% of AGI	30% of AGI	20% of AGI

A private operating foundation actively conducts charitable activities and distributes funds to its own charitable programs. A private nonoperating foundation distributes funds to other charitable organizations.

When a taxpayer has charitable contributions that are subject to different AGI limitations, the AGI limitations are applied first to cash (60% AGI limit), then ordinary income property (50% AGI limit), then LTCG property (30% AGI limit).

2.4.4 Carryover of Excess Charitable Contributions (Five Years)

All charitable contribution carryovers are applied on a first-in, first-out basis, after current year contributions are deducted, subject to the percentage of income limitations.

Example 1 — Charitable Contribution Deduction

Facts: Joe Kelly itemizes deductions and made the following charitable contributions during the year:

- **United Way:** Cash $15,000
- **Goodwill:** Personal furniture (cost $25,000 three years ago, FMV at date of contribution $10,000)
- **Art Museum:** Sculpture (cost $20,000 five years ago, FMV at date of contribution $30,000)

Kelly's adjusted gross income (AGI) for the year is $100,000.

Required: Calculate the taxpayer's charitable contributions deduction for the year.

Solution:

Cash: The $15,000 cash contribution to United Way, a public charity, is subject to the 60 percent of AGI limitation.

1.	Limitation for contributions subject to 60% limit (AGI $100,000 × 60%)	$60,000
2.	Cash contribution to United Way	15,000
3.	Allowable deduction for cash contribution *(lesser of 1 or 2)*	**15,000**

(continued)

(continued)

Ordinary Income Property: The personal furniture contributed to Goodwill, a public charity, has depreciated in value, so it is ordinary income property and is subject to the 50 percent of AGI limitation. The amount of the contribution is the lesser of the cost basis or the FMV at the date of contribution, which is $10,000.

4. Limitation for contributions subject to 50% limit:
   AGI $100,000 × 50% $50,000
   Less: cash contribution allowed *(line 3)*   (15,000) $35,000
5. Contribution of ordinary income property to Goodwill (FMV)   10,000
6. Allowable deduction for ordinary income property contribution
   (lesser of 4 or 5)   **10,000**

LTCG Property: The sculpture contributed to the Art Museum, a public charity, is a long-term investment or personal-use asset that has appreciated in value, so it is long-term capital gain (LTCG) property and is subject to the 30 percent of AGI limitation. The amount of the contribution is the FMV at the date of contribution, which is $30,000.

7. Limitation for contributions subject to 30% limit:
   Lesser of:
   - AGI $100,000 × 30% $30,000 (a)
   - AGI $100,000 × 50% $50,000
     Less: cash contribution allowed *(line 3)*   (15,000)
     Less: ordinary income property contribution
     allowed *(line 6)*   (10,000)   25,000 (b)
8. Limitation of deduction *(lesser of a or b)* $25,000
9. Contribution of LTCG property to Art Museum (FMV)   30,000
10. Allowable deduction for LTCG property contribution
    (lesser of 8 or 9)   **$25,000**

11. Total charitable contributions deduction:
    Cash $15,000
    Ordinary income property   10,000
    LTCG property   25,000
       Total charitable contribution deduction   **$50,000**
12. Charitable contribution carryforward:
    LTCG property contribution (FMV) $30,000
    Less: amount deducted in current year   (25,000)
    LTCG property contribution carryforward $ 5,000

Itemized Deductions

2.4.5 Consideration Received for Contribution

The taxpayer may only deduct the excess contribution over the consideration received. Charitable organizations that receive contributions of more than $75 in exchange for services or property must provide the donor with a written statement that estimates the value of the deductible portion of the payment.

> **Illustration 2   Deductible Contribution**
>
> - Raffle tickets bought at a charity bazaar that have a chance of winning a prize do not give rise to a charitable deduction.
> - JoAnn Veiga buys a ticket to a charity ball for $200. The actual value of attending the ball was $50. Veiga may take a charitable deduction of $150.

2.4.6 Timing of Deduction

A deduction is allowed only for the tax year in which the contribution is made:

- **Cash or Check:** Actually paid.
- **Credit Card:** When charged, a contribution made by a bank credit card is deductible in the year the charge is made, even if payment to the bank for the charge occurs the following year.

2.4.7 Contribution for Services

A taxpayer may deduct out-of-pocket expenses incurred as a result of providing services to a charity. This includes the cost of driving to and from the volunteer work. The taxpayer may take 14 cents per mile (2023) or the actual cost of gas and oil. With either method, the taxpayer may also include parking and tolls.

2.4.8 Student Living in Taxpayer's Home

A charitable deduction may be taken for the expense incurred when the taxpayer takes into the home a full-time student (e.g., an exchange student). The student may not be beyond the 12th grade. The total deduction is up to $50 per month for each full month (15 or more days) the student is in the home and attending school.

2.4.9 Substantiation Requirements

Regardless of the amount of the cash contribution, taxpayers must keep records that substantiate their deductions. Either a bank record (e.g., canceled check or itemization on a bank statement with the charity's name) or a written acknowledgement from the charity is required. The acknowledgment must be obtained by the earlier of the filing date or the due date of the return.

For contributions of more than $500 of noncash property, the taxpayer must file Form 8283, giving certain information. In addition, taxpayers claiming more than $5,000 for any one item or group of similar items, such as a stamp collection, need a written appraisal for each such item or group donated, except that no appraisal is needed for publicly traded securities.

2.5 Casualty Losses (10 Percent of AGI Floor)

Casualty losses of nonbusiness property are deductible to the extent that each individual loss exceeds $100 and that the aggregate of these excess losses (excess over $100) exceeds 10 percent of AGI. The $100 floor applies to each separate casualty event. The losses are only deductible if sustained in a presidentially declared disaster area.

2.5.1 Amount of Loss

The amount regarded as a casualty loss is the difference between the market value of the property immediately before the casualty and its fair market value (FMV) immediately afterward. However, the loss may not exceed the adjusted basis of the property. Whichever amount is used must be reduced by the amount of any insurance recovery.

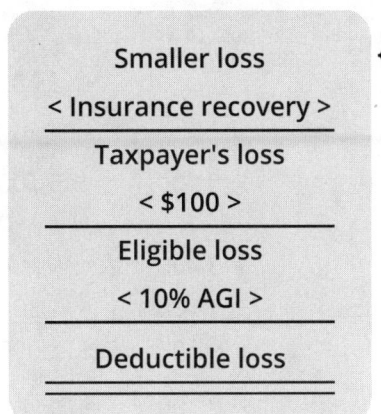

1. Lost cost/adjusted basis
2. Decreased FMV

Smaller loss
< Insurance recovery >
Taxpayer's loss
< $100 >
Eligible loss
< 10% AGI >
Deductible loss

2.5.2 Failure to Notify Insurer

A casualty loss for nonbusiness property cannot be deducted unless:

- an insurance claim was filed; or
- the losses are not covered by insurance.

2.5.3 Lost, Misplaced, or Broken Property

No casualty loss deduction is allowed for lost, misplaced, or broken property.

2.6 Miscellaneous Itemized Deductions (2 Percent of AGI Floor)

The Tax Cuts and Jobs Act of 2017 suspended all miscellaneous itemized deductions subject to the 2 percent of AGI floor for tax years 2018–2025.

Itemized Deductions

2.7 Gambling Losses

Gambling losses remain fully deductible, but only to the extent of gambling winnings.

Example 2 — Automated Diagnostic and Validation Check: Itemized Deductions

Facts: Mary, a CPA, is preparing the Year 2 federal income tax return for her client, Alice Adams. Alice is single and itemizes deductions on her individual income tax return every year. Alice's adjusted gross income (AGI) was $85,000 for Year 1 and $100,000 for Year 2. The following comparison of Alice's itemized deductions for Years 1 and 2 has been provided by Mary's tax preparation software:

Two-Year Comparison of Itemized Deductions	Year 1	Year 2	Difference
Medical/dental expenses (after 7.5% AGI floor)	$ 0	$ 5,000	$ 5,000
State and local taxes:			
Income taxes	$ 5,000	$ 5,000	$ 0
Sales taxes	0	0	0
Real estate taxes	3,000	5,500	2,500
Personal property taxes	1,500	1,500	0
Total state and local taxes	$ 9,500	$12,000	$ 2,500
Lesser of total taxes or $10,000	$ 9,500	$10,000	$ 500
Home mortgage interest	5,500	8,500	3,000
Charitable contributions	1,000	10,000	9,000
Casualty/theft losses (after per casualty and AGI floor)	0	0	0
Total itemized deductions	$16,000	$33,500	$17,500

Required: The comparison report shows that Alice's Year 2 total itemized deductions are significantly higher than her itemized deductions in the previous year. Please review this report to determine what might be causing the changes. Identify up to four items that you believe should be further analyzed, then state the issue and how Mary should follow up with the client.

(continued)

(continued)

Solution:

Medical/dental expenses: Mary should follow up with the client regarding the substantial medical expenses in Year 2 relative to Year 1 and confirm that the $5,000 deduction is after any insurance reimbursement and the AGI floor. Alice's Year 2 AGI floor for medical expenses is $7,500 ($100,000 AGI × 7.5%), so her total out-of-pocket expenses must have been $12,500 in Year 2 to have an itemized deduction of $5,000.

Real estate taxes: Alice's Year 2 real estate taxes are significantly higher than the previous year. Home mortgage interest also increased significantly, so this could be an indication that Alice purchased a new, more expensive home. The real estate taxes could also have increased significantly because of a reassessment, either due to home improvements or market increases in the area. Mary should follow up with Alice to try to determine the reason behind the increase in real estate taxes.

Home mortgage interest: Alice's home mortgage interest increased substantially in Year 2. As noted earlier with real estate taxes, the increase in both deductions could indicate that Alice purchased a new, more expensive home. The increase in home mortgage interest could also be due to refinancing or an equity loan for home improvements. Mary should follow up with Alice to determine the cause of the increased home mortgage interest.

Charitable contributions: Alice's charitable contributions increased from $1,000 in Year 1 to $10,000 in Year 2. This could very well be an input error, with an extra zero entered for the Year 2 charitable contributions. Mary should check the source documents to see if Alice's Year 2 charitable contributions are $1,000, rather than $10,000. If not, Mary should follow up with Alice to confirm the Year 2 charitable contributions amount.

NOTES

MODULE 6: Section 199A Qualified Business Income Deduction

REG 1

1 Section 199A Qualified Business Income Deduction for Flow-Through Business Entities

1.1 Section 199A Overview

The Tax Cuts and Jobs Act of 2017 enacted Internal Revenue Code Section 199A, which provides a deduction of up to 20 percent of qualified business income for eligible flow-through entities. The qualified business income (QBI) deduction (also known as the Section 199A deduction) is available to all taxpayers other than a regular C corporation. This includes individuals, trusts, and estates. The deduction is taken "below the line" or from adjusted gross income.

1.2 Definitions

1. **Qualified Business Income (QBI):** Ordinary business income less ordinary business deductions earned from a sole proprietorship, S corporation, limited liability company, or partnership connected to business conducted within the U.S. QBI does not include any wages earned as an employee or guaranteed payments to partners. Dividends, interest, and long-term and short-term capital gains and losses are not included. QBI for a business must be reduced by any adjustments taken to arrive at AGI that relate to that business. This includes the deductible part of the self-employment (SE) tax, deductions for qualified contributions to SE retirement plans, and SE health insurance deductions.

2. **Qualified Property:** Any tangible, depreciable property that is held by the business at the end of the year and is used at any point during the year in the production of QBI.

3. **Qualified Trade or Business (QTB):** Any business other than a Specified Service Trade or Business (SSTB).

4. **Specified Service Trade or Business (SSTB):** An SSTB is a trade or business involving direct services in the fields of health, law, accounting, actuarial science, performing arts, consulting, athletics, financial services, brokerage, including investing and investment management, trading or dealing in securities, partnership interests or commodities, and any trade in which the principal asset is the reputation or skill of one or more of its employees or owners. Engineering and architectural services are specifically excluded from the definition of SSTB.

1.3 Calculating the Deduction

The basic deduction:

$$20\% \times \text{Qualified business income (QBI)}$$

Section 199A Qualified Business Income Deduction

1.4 Limitations to the Section 199A QBI Deduction

Limitations are applied to the QBI deduction based on the taxable income (before the QBI deduction) of the taxpayer and whether the business is a qualified trade or business (QTB) or a specified trade or business (SSTB). SSTBs are only eligible for the deduction if the taxpayer's taxable income before the QBI deduction is below a certain level. There are three types of limitations that may apply.

1.4.1 Limitations Based on Taxable Income Level

2023	
Filing Status	Taxable Income Before QBI Deduction
Single and all other	$182,100–$232,100
Married filing jointly	$364,200–$464,200

1.4.2 W-2 Wage and Property Limitation

When applicable, the QBI deduction is limited to the greater of:

1. 50 percent of W-2 wages for the business; or
2. 25 percent of W-2 wages for the business plus 2.5 percent of the unadjusted basis immediately after acquisition (UBIA) of all qualified property.

The W-2 wage and property limitation does not apply to real estate investment trust (REIT) or publicly traded partnership (PTP) income.

1.4.3 Overall Taxable Income Limitation to Section 199A QBI Deduction

Once the tentative QBI deduction for each qualifying business is calculated, an overall limitation based on the taxpayer's taxable income in excess of net capital gain must be considered. For purposes of the Section 199A overall taxable income limitation, net capital gain includes the excess of net long-term capital gain (LTCG) over net short-term capital loss (STCL) and qualified dividend income. The total Section 199A QBI deduction is the lesser of:

1. Combined QBI deductions for all qualifying businesses; or
2. 20% of the taxpayer's taxable income (before the QBI deduction) in excess of net capital gain.

1.5 Three Categories of Taxpayers

To best understand how to apply the limitations based on taxable income and the W-2 wage and property limitation, taxpayers can be divided into three categories:

- **Category 1:** Taxpayers with taxable income *at or below* $182,100 (single or head of household) or $364,200 (MFJ) (2023).
- **Category 2:** Taxpayers with taxable income *above* $232,100 (single or head of household) or $464,200 (MFJ) (2023).
- **Category 3:** Taxpayers with taxable income *between* $182,100 and $232,100 (single or head of household) or $364,200 and $464,200 (MFJ) (2023). Category 3 is a very complex calculation and is beyond the scope of the exam, therefore, the details are not covered in this text.

1.5.1 Category 1

Taxpayers with taxable income at or below $182,100 (single or head of household) or $364,200 (MFJ) (2023):

> If QTB → Full 20% QBI deduction
> If SSTB → Full 20% QBI deduction

Basically, if a taxpayer's taxable income before the QBI deduction is under the applicable thresholds, neither the restrictive rules for SSTBs nor the W-2 wage and property limit apply. The taxpayer is eligible for the full deduction (20% × QBI). In this taxable income range, an SSTB is treated the same as a QTB.

Example 1 — QTB With Taxable Income Up to $182,100

Facts: A taxpayer filing as single has the following:

Taxable income before QBI deduction = $50,000

Net capital gains = $5,000

QBI = $40,000

Required: Calculate the Section 199A QBI deduction.

Solution:

Tentative QBI deduction = $40,000 × 20% = $8,000

W-2 wage and property limitation does not apply because taxable income before the QBI deduction is less than $182,100.

Overall limit = ($50,000 taxable income − $5,000 net capital gains) × 20% = $9,000, so not limited by overall limit

Section 199A QBI deduction = $8,000

Example 2 — SSTB With Taxable Income Up to $182,100

Facts: A taxpayer filing as single has the following:

Taxable income before QBI deduction = $50,000

Net capital gains = $15,000

QBI = $40,000

Required: Calculate the Section 199A QBI deduction.

Solution:

Tentative QBI deduction = $40,000 × 20% = $8,000

W-2 wage and property limitation and SSTB exclusion do not apply because taxable income before the QBI deduction is less than $182,100.

Overall limit = ($50,000 taxable income − $15,000 net capital gains) × 20% = $7,000, so deduction is limited by overall limit

Section 199A QBI deduction = $7,000

1.5.2 Category 2

Taxpayers with taxable income above $232,100 (single or head of household) or $464,200 (MFJ) (2023):

> If QTB → Full W-2 wage and property limitation applies
>
> If SSTB → No QBI deduction allowed

Example 3 QTB With Taxable Income of $232,100 or More

Facts: A taxpayer filing as single has the following:

Taxable income before QBI deduction = $240,000

Net capital gains = $0

QBI = $100,000

Taxpayer's share of QTB's W-2 wages = $30,000

Taxpayer's share of QTB's UBIA of qualified property = $80,000

Required: Calculate the Section 199A QBI deduction.

Solution: Because the taxpayer's taxable income of $240,000 is greater than the maximum amount of $232,100 and the business is a QTB, the full W-2 wage and property limitation applies.

Tentative QBI deduction = $100,000 QBI × 20% = $20,000

W-2 wage and property limitation:

   Greater of:

   1. $30,000 W-2 wages × 50% = $15,000

   2. ($30,000 W-2 wages × 25%) + ($80,000 UBIA of qualified property × 2.5%) = $9,500

W-2 wage and property limitation of $15,000 is less than the tentative QBI deduction of $20,000, so the QBI deduction is limited to $15,000 by the W-2 wage and property limitation.

Overall limit = $240,000 taxable income × 20% = $48,000, so not limited by the overall limit

Section 199A QBI deduction = $15,000

Example 4 — SSTB With Taxable Income of $232,100 or More

Facts: A taxpayer filing as single has the following:

Taxable income before QBI deduction = $240,000

Net capital gains = $0

QBI = $100,000

Taxpayer's share of SSTB's W-2 wages = $30,000

Taxpayer's share of SSTB's UBIA of qualified property = $80,000

Required: Calculate the Section 199A QBI deduction.

Solution: Because the business is an SSTB and the taxpayer's taxable income exceeds $232,100, the taxpayer is not eligible for the QBI deduction.

Section 199A QBI deduction = $0

NOTES

MODULE 7

Tax Computations and Credits

REG 1

1 Individual Ordinary Income Tax Calculation and Limitations

1.1 Individual Ordinary Income Tax Rate Structure

The ordinary income tax rates for individuals are 10, 12, 22, 24, 32, 35, and 37 percent.

2023 Tax Rate	Single	Head of Household	Married Filing Jointly	Married Filing Separately
10%	$0–$11,000	$0–$15,700	$0–$22,000	$0–$11,000
12%	$11,001–$44,725	$15,701–$59,850	$22,001–$89,450	$11,001–$44,725
22%	$44,726–$95,375	$59,851–$95,350	$89,451–$190,750	$44,726–$95,375
24%	$95,376–$182,100	$95,351–$182,100	$190,751–$364,200	$95,376–$182,100
32%	$182,101–$231,250	$182,101–$231,250	$364,201–$462,500	$182,101–$231,250
35%	$231,251–$578,125	$231,251–$578,100	$462,501–$693,750	$231,251–$346,875
37%	Over $578,125	Over $578,100	Over $693,750	Over $346,875

1.2 Individual Preferential Income Tax Rates

Long-term capital gains and qualified dividends are taxed at preferential income tax rates, as shown in the table below.

| Tax Rate | 2023 Taxable Income | | | |
	Single	Head of Household	Married Filing Jointly	Married Filing Separately
0%	$0–$44,625	$0–$59,750	$0–$89,250	$0–$44,625
15%	$44,626–$492,300	$59,751–$523,050	$89,251–$553,850	$44,626–$276,900
20%	Over $492,300	Over $523,050	Over $553,850	Over $276,900

Tax Computations and Credits

> ### Example 1   Calculating Individual Income Tax Liability
>
> 1. **Facts:** A taxpayer with single filing status has $100,000 of taxable income.
>   **Required:** Calculate the income tax liability in 2023.
>   **Solution:**
>   ($11,000 − $0) × 10% = $1,100
>   ($44,725 − $11,000) × 12% = $4,047
>   ($95,375 − $44,725) × 22% = $11,143
>   ($100,000 − $95,375) × 24% = $1,110
> $1,100 + $4,047 + $11,143 + $1,110 = **$17,400**
>
> 2. **Facts:** A taxpayer with head of household filing status has $60,000 of taxable income.
>   **Required:** Calculate the income tax liability in 2023.
>   **Solution:**
>   ($15,700 − $0) × 10% = $1,570
>   ($59,850 − $15,700) × 12% = $5,298
>   ($60,000 − $59,850) × 22% = $33
> $1,570 + $5,298 + $33 = **$6,901**
>
> 3. **Facts:** A taxpayer with married filing jointly filing status has $75,000 of taxable income.
>   **Required:** Calculate the income tax liability in 2023.
>   **Solution:**
>   ($22,000 − $0) × 10% = $2,200
>   ($75,000 − $22,000) × 12% = $6,360
> $2,200 + $6,360 = **$8,560**
>
> 4. **Facts:** A taxpayer with married filing separately filing status has $50,000 of taxable income.
>   **Required:** Calculate the income tax liability in 2023.
>   **Solution:**
>   ($11,000 − $0) × 10% = $1,100
>   ($44,725 − $11,000) × 12% = $4,047
>   ($50,000 − $44,725) × 22% = $1,160.50
> $1,100 + $4,047 + $1,160.50 = **$6,307.50**

1.3 Progressive Tax Rate Structure

- The individual income tax rate structure is a progressive tax rate structure.
- With a progressive tax rate structure, the marginal tax rate increases as taxable income increases.

- The tax rate applied to the next amount of incremental taxable income or deductions is the marginal tax rate.
- It is calculated as the change in tax divided by the change in taxable income.

> **Example 2 — Increasing Marginal Tax Rate**
>
> **Facts:** Mark, a married taxpayer filing jointly, has discovered that he will receive an additional consulting check in December 2023 that he did not expect until next year. Before the additional income, his taxable income is $75,000. After the receipt of the additional consulting income, his taxable income is $90,000.
>
> **Required:** Determine Mark's marginal tax rate on the additional taxable income.
>
> **Solution:**
>
> **Tax calculated on $75,000 for married filing jointly:**
>
> ($22,000 − $0) × 10% = $2,200
> ($75,000 − $22,000) × 12% = $6,360
> $2,200 + $6,360 = **$8,560**
>
> **Tax calculated on $90,000 for married filing jointly:**
>
> ($22,000 − $0) × 10% = $2,200
> ($89,450 − $22,000) × 12% = $8,094
> ($90,000 − $89,450) × 22% = $121
> $2,200 + $8,094 + $121 = **$10,415**
>
> **The marginal tax rate is calculated as follows:**
>
> $10,415 − $8,560 = $1,855 change in tax liability / $15,000 change in taxable income = **12.4%**

2 Tax Credits

2.1 Tax Credits in General

Tax credits reduce personal tax liability. There are two basic types of tax credits.

2.1.1 Nonrefundable Personal Tax Credits

Personal tax credits may reduce personal tax liability to zero, but they may not result in a refund. Personal tax credits include:

- Child and dependent care credit
- Elderly and permanently disabled credit
- Education credits
    - Lifetime learning credit
    - American opportunity credit (60 percent nonrefundable)

- Retirement savings contribution credit
- Foreign tax credit
- General business credit
- Adoption credit

2.1.2 Refundable Credits

Refundable credits are subtracted from income tax liability. They may result in a cash refund when the credit exceeds tax liability owed even if no tax is withheld from wages. Refundable credits and refundable payments include:

- Child tax credit (refund is limited)
- Earned income credit
- Federal income tax withheld (Form W-2)
- Excess Social Security tax paid
- American opportunity credit (40 percent refundable)

2.2 Child and Dependent Care Credit

The child and dependent care credit is 20 percent to 35 percent of work-related expenses to care for qualifying persons. The maximum allowable expenses are $3,000 for one qualifying person and $6,000 for two or more qualifying people.

Maximum Expenditures	
One dependent	$3,000
Two or more dependents	$6,000

2.2.1 Qualifying Persons

The child and dependent care credit is available to taxpayers who maintain a household, work, and incur eligible expenses for the care of the following qualifying persons:

- A dependent qualifying child who is under age 13 when the care is provided.
- A disabled dependent of any age who is unable to care for himself, whether or not he can be claimed as a dependent, but who must meet the support test of a dependent (half of support provided by the taxpayer).
- A spouse who is disabled and not able to take care of himself or herself.

2.2.2 Earned Income Requirement

Married taxpayers must both produce earned income from wages, salary, or self-employment net income to be eligible for the child and dependent care credit (unless one is a full-time student or physically or mentally incapacitated).

2.2.3 Eligible Expenses

Eligible expenditures must be for the purpose of enabling the taxpayer to be gainfully employed (i.e., allowing that person to work or look for work).

- Babysitter
- Nursery school
- Day care
- Not elementary school

2.2.4 Calculation of Credit

The amount that is eligible for the credit is the lesser of: (1) the earned income of the lesser-earning spouse, (2) the actual expenses incurred, or (3) the maximum allowable amount ($3,000 or $6,000). The credit is the qualifying amount multiplied by the applicable percentage, which is based on the taxpayer's adjusted gross income (AGI).

- **Maximum 35 Percent:** The maximum child or dependent care credit is $1,050 ($3,000 × 35%) if the taxpayer has one qualifying dependent, or $2,100 ($6,000 × 35%) if the taxpayer has two or more qualifying dependents. In order to obtain the maximum credit, the taxpayer's AGI must be $15,000 or less.

- **Phase-out From 35 Percent to 20 Percent:** The credit decreases by 1 percent for each $2,000 (or fraction thereof) of AGI over $15,000, but is not reduced below 20 percent.

- **Minimum 20 Percent:** The maximum child care credit at the lowest rate of 20 percent for taxpayers with AGI of more than $43,000 is $600 ($3,000 × 20%) if the taxpayer has one qualifying dependent, or $1,200 ($6,000 × 20%) if the taxpayer has two or more qualifying dependents.

Example 3 — Child and Dependent Care Credit

Facts: JoAnn Veiga is a widow with two dependent children. Her current year AGI is $50,000, for which the applicable child and dependent care credit rate is 20 percent. Her work-related expenses for a home caregiver for the children are $3,600 and $3,800 for child care at a nursery school.

Required: Calculate the amount of the child and dependent care credit for JoAnn.

Solution: JoAnn can take a child care credit of $1,200, calculated as follows:

Work-related expenses (home caregiver)	$3,600
Nursery school expenses	3,800
Total qualifying expenses	$7,400
Maximum allowable for two dependents	$6,000
Applicable credit percentage	× 20%
Amount of credit	$1,200

2.3 Credit for the Elderly and/or Permanently Disabled

2.3.1 Eligibility

This credit of 15 percent of eligible income is available to individuals who are:

1. 65 years of age or older; or
2. under age 65, retired due to total and permanent disability, and received taxable disability income for the year.

2.3.2 Base Amount

The base amount used to figure the credit is as follows:

- $5,000 for a single person, widow, or widower.
- $5,000 if married filing jointly and only one spouse is a qualified individual.
- $7,500 if married filing jointly and both are qualified individuals.
- $3,750 for a qualified individual who is married filing separately.

If a qualified individual is under age 65 and has disability income of less than $5,000, the base amount is limited to $5,000.

2.3.3 Adjusted Gross Income Limit

Eligible income is reduced by:

1. any Social Security payments and other excludable pensions or annuities received by the taxpayer; and
2. one half of the taxpayer's adjusted gross income that exceeds the following levels:

Single taxpayers	$ 7,500
Married persons filing jointly	$10,000
Married persons filing separately	$ 5,000

2.3.4 Summary of Credit Calculation

A taxpayer who is 65 or older starts with a tax credit for the elderly based on a specified amount that is reduced first by any Social Security payments and other excludable pensions and second by one half (50 percent) of any adjusted gross income over the stated maximum. The results, if any, are multiplied by 15 percent to arrive at the allowable tax credit. The credit is limited to the amount of tax.

Single		**Joint**
5,000	Base Amount	7,500
(ALL)	(Social Security)	(ALL)
(½ over $7,500)	(½ Excess AGI)	(½ over $10,000)
Balance		Balance
× 15%	Rate	× 15%
Credit		Credit

> **Example 4** — **Credit for the Elderly and/or Permanently Disabled**
>
> **Facts:** Peter is single and 68 years old. He received the following income for the year:
>
> | | |
> |---|---|
> | Social Security received | $3,120 |
> | Taxable interest | 215 |
> | Taxable retirement distributions | 3,600 |
> | Wages from a part-time job | 4,245 |
>
> **Required:** Calculate Peter's credit for the elderly and/or permanently disabled.
>
> **Solution:** His credit will be $240, computed as follows:
>
> Peter's adjusted gross income is $8,060, calculated as follows:
>
> | | |
> |---|---|
> | Wages from part-time job | $4,245 |
> | Taxable retirement distributions | 3,600 |
> | Taxable interest | 215 |
> | | $8,060 |
>
> To calculate credit:
>
> | | | | |
> |---|---|---|---|
> | Base amount | | | $5,000 |
> | Less: | | | |
> | Social Security | | $3,120 | |
> | Excess AGI: | $8,060 | | |
> | | (7,500) | | |
> | | 560 × 50% | 280 | (3,400) |
> | | | | $1,600 |
> | Balance | | | 15% |
> | Credit | | | $ 240 |

2.4 Education Tax Incentives

Assuming the requirements are met, a taxpayer has the opportunity to reduce taxes by taking advantage of the American opportunity credit (AOC), the lifetime learning credit, and/or a nontaxable distribution from a Coverdell education savings account used to pay higher education costs.

2.4.1 American Opportunity Tax Credit (AOTC)

The American opportunity tax credit is available against federal income taxes for qualified tuition, fees, and course materials (including books) paid for a student's first four years of postsecondary (college) education at an eligible educational institution.

- The maximum AOTC credit is $2,500:
  - 100 percent of the first $2,000 of qualified expenses; plus
  - 25 percent of the next $2,000 of expenses paid during the year.

- The qualified expenses are on a "per student" basis and must be incurred on behalf of the:
  - taxpayer;
  - taxpayer's spouse; or
  - taxpayer's dependent.
- If a child is claimed as a dependent by a parent, expenses paid by both the parent and the child are deemed to have been made by the parent for this purpose.
- The student must be at least half-time for at least one academic period during the year.
- The credit is not available for the expenses of a student convicted of a federal or state felony drug offense in the calendar year for which expenses are incurred.
- The credit phase-out begins with modified AGI exceeding $80,000 ($160,000 MFJ), with full phase-out at $90,000 ($180,000 MFJ).
- Refundable portion: Subject to certain restrictions, 40 percent of the American opportunity tax credit is refundable. This means that up to $1,000 ($2,500 maximum credit × 40%) may be refunded.

2.4.2 Lifetime Learning Credit (LLC)

The lifetime learning credit is available for an unlimited number of years for qualified tuition and related course fees at eligible educational institutions.

- The credit is equal to 20 percent of qualified expenses up to $10,000.
- Qualified expenses include tuition and course fees (not course materials) for undergraduate courses, graduate-level courses, certain professional degree courses, and courses to acquire or improve job skills.
- The qualified expenses are on a "per taxpayer" basis, rather than a "per student" basis, so the maximum credit is $2,000 regardless of the number of qualifying students.
- As with the American opportunity tax credit, expenses paid by a dependent child are treated as if made by the parent.
- The credit is phased out when modified AGI is $80,000 ($160,000 MFJ) and is fully phased out when modified AGI is $90,000 ($180,000 MFJ).

2.4.3 Not Limited to One Type of Credit per Tax Return

The taxpayer does not have to choose one type of credit on his or her income tax return for the year. For example, a parent may claim a lifetime learning credit for the expenses of one child and an American opportunity credit for the expenses of another child in the same taxable year. However, more than one credit cannot be claimed for the same student in the same year.

2.4.4 Coverdell Education Savings Accounts

A separate education savings account may be set up to pay the qualified education expenses of a designated beneficiary.

- Contributions are nondeductible; maximum contribution per beneficiary is $2,000 annually.
- The designated beneficiary may be any child under age 18. There is no limit to the number of beneficiaries (each beneficiary has a separate account).

- The maximum allowable contribution amount is phased out for taxpayers with modified adjusted gross income between these amounts:

AGI Phase-out Ranges	
Unmarried	$95,000–$110,000
Married	$190,000–$220,000

- Earnings accumulate tax-free while in an education savings account.
- Distributions, both of principal and interest, are tax-free to the extent that they are used for qualified elementary, secondary, or higher education expenses of the designated beneficiary.
- Qualified education expenses include tuition, fees, tutoring, books, room and board, supplies, and equipment.
- Any amounts remaining when the beneficiary reaches 30 years of age must be distributed (except in the case of a special needs beneficiary). If the distribution is made directly to the beneficiary, the distributed amount is taxable to the beneficiary and subject to a 10 percent penalty. Alternatively, the balance can be rolled over tax free to another family member of the taxpayer with no penalty.
- A taxpayer can claim the American opportunity tax credit or lifetime learning credit for a tax year and also exclude from gross income amounts distributed from a Coverdell education savings account. However, the distribution cannot be used for the same educational expenses for which either the American opportunity tax credit or the lifetime learning credit was claimed.

2.4.5 Section 529 Qualified Tuition Programs (QTP)

- A QTP is a program under which a person may purchase tuition credits or make cash contributions to an account on behalf of a beneficiary for payment of qualified higher education expenses. The program must be established and maintained by a state, state agency, or by an eligible educational institution. Eligible educational institutions generally include any accredited postsecondary educational institution, so long as contributions made to the program are held in a "qualified trust."
- Qualified higher education expenses include tuition, fees, books, supplies, and equipment required by an educational institution for enrollment or attendance. These expenses also include the reasonable cost of room and board if the beneficiary is enrolled at least half-time.
- Distributions from a QTP, including cash, earnings, and in-kind distributions, may be excluded from a designated beneficiary's gross income to the extent that the distribution is used to pay for qualified higher education expenses.

2023 Education Tax Incentives: Summary

Item	General Rule	Limit	Income Phase-out
Income Exclusion			
U.S. Savings Bond—Series EE	Exclude interest income	Must pay educational expense	AGI $91,850–$106,850 (MFJ $137,800–$167,800) (2023)
Employer-paid education expenses	Exclude from income	Up to $5,250 per year	No income limit
Scholarships	Exclude from income	Only tuition, books, and fees, not room and board	No income limit
Adjustments			
Educator expenses	Deduct as above-the-line adjustment	$300	No income limit
Coverdell education savings account	Nondeductible	$2,000	AGI $95,000–$110,000 (MFJ $190,000–$220,000)
Student loan interest deduction	Deduct as above-the-line adjustment	$2,500	AGI $75,000–$90,000 (MFJ $155,000–$185,000)
Credits			
American opportunity tax credit	First four years; partially refundable	$2,500 per person; tuition, fees, and course materials	AGI $80,000–$90,000 (MFJ $160,000–$180,000)
Lifetime learning credit	After first four years; nonrefundable	$2,000 per taxpayer; tuition and fees, not course materials	AGI $80,000–$90,000 (MFJ $160,000–$180,000)
Miscellaneous			
529 plan (qualified tuition program)	No deduction No income	Vary by state	None

2.5 Adoption Credit

A credit for qualifying expenses of adopting a child is available. For 2023, the maximum credit allowed is the amount of qualified adoption expenses up to $15,950.

The adoption credit is nonrefundable, but any credit in excess of your tax liability may be carried forward for up to five years.

- **Phase-out**

    The available adoption credit begins to phase out for taxpayers with modified adjusted gross income (MAGI) over $239,230 and is completely phased out with MAGI of $279,230 (2023).

- **Eligible Expenses**
    - All reasonable and necessary expenses, costs, and fees are available for the credit.
    - The credit is not available for adopting the child of a spouse or for a surrogate parenting arrangement.
    - Medical expenses do not qualify as eligible expenses.

- **Timing**

    The credit is claimed for years after the payment is made until the adoption is final, at which point expenses paid in the year it becomes final are claimed in that year. For foreign children adopted, no credit can be claimed until the year it becomes final. In either case, expenses paid in later years can be claimed in the year paid.

2.6 Retirement Savings Contributions Credit

A nonrefundable tax credit is available for low- and moderate-income taxpayers for contributions to a qualified employer-sponsored retirement plan or IRA.

- **Eligible Taxpayers**
    - At least 18 years old by the close of the tax year
    - Not a full-time student
    - Not a dependent of another taxpayer

- **Allowable Credit**

    The tax credit is 10 percent, 20 percent, or 50 percent of the taxpayer's contribution to a qualified retirement plan for the year. The credit rate depends on the taxpayer's filing status and AGI. The maximum contribution eligible for the credit is $2,000 per taxpayer.
    No carryover is allowed.

	2023 Adjusted Gross Income (AGI)			
Credit Rate	Single or MFS	Head of Household	Married Filing Jointly	Maximum Credit
50%	$0–$21,750	$0–$32,625	$0–$43,500	$2,000 × 50% = $1,000
20%	$21,751–$23,750	$32,626–$35,625	$43,501–$47,500	$2,000 × 20% = $400
10%	$23,751–$36,500	$35,626–$54,750	$47,501–$73,000	$2,000 × 10% = $200
0%	Over $36,500	Over $54,750	Over $73,000	$2,000 × 0% = $0

2.7 Foreign Tax Credit

A taxpayer may claim a credit for foreign income taxes paid to a foreign country or United States possession. There is a limitation on the amount of the credit an individual can obtain. In lieu of this credit, an individual can deduct the taxes as an itemized deduction.

- **Allowable Credit**

    There is no limit on foreign taxes used as a deduction; however, foreign tax credits are limited to the lesser of:

    - Foreign taxes paid, or

    - $$\frac{\text{Taxable income from all foreign operations}}{\text{Total taxable worldwide income}} \times \text{U.S. tax} = \text{Foreign tax credit limit}$$

- **Carryover of Excess (Disallowed) Credit**

    Any disallowed foreign tax credit may be carried over as follows:
    - Carry back one year
    - Carry forward 10 years

2.8 General Business Credit

2.8.1 Included Credits

The general business credit is a combination of:

- Investment credit
- Work opportunity tax credit
- Alternative fuels credit
- Increased research credit (generally 20 percent of the increase in qualified research expenditures over the base amount for the year)
- Low-income housing credit

- Qualified child care expenditures;
- Welfare-to-work credit;
- Employer-provided child care credit;
- Small employer retirement plan start-up costs credit;
- Alternative motor vehicle credit
- Other infrequent (on exam) credits

2.8.2 Calculation of Credit

The credit is limited to regular tax liability after other tax credits, minus 25 percent of regular tax liability (after other tax credits) over $25,000.

Tax Liability		Allowable Percentages		Allowable Amount
$0–$25,000	×	100%	=	×
Excess	×	75%	=	×
Maximum credit permitted				Total

2.8.3 Unused Credit Carryover

Although some limits must be applied separately, unused credits generally may be carried back one year and forward 20 years.

2.9 Work Opportunity Credit

The work opportunity credit is available to employers who hire employees from a targeted group. This credit is part of the general business credit.

2.9.1 Credit

- 40 percent of first $6,000 of first year's wages
- 40 percent of first $3,000 to certain summer youth

2.9.2 Qualified Groups

- Disabled
- 18- to- 24-year-olds from poor families
- Vietnam veterans from economically disadvantaged areas
- Certain food stamp recipients

2.10 "Child" Tax Credit

For tax years 2018–2025, taxpayers may claim a $2,000 tax credit for each "qualifying child."

Tax Computations and Credits

2.10.1 Qualifying Child

The "**CARES**" rules on dependency definitions apply here, except that a child must be under the age of 17 (not the 19-year or 24-year age limits that "**CARES**" implies). The qualifying child must be a citizen, a national, or a resident of the United States.

2.10.2 Phase-out of Child Tax Credit

Higher-income taxpayers must reduce the $2,000 allowable child tax credit by $50 for each $1,000 (or fraction thereof) by which modified adjusted gross income (AGI) exceeds:

- $400,000 for a married filing jointly return;
- $200,000 for an unmarried individual; or
- $200,000 for married individuals filing a separate return.

2.10.3 Refundable Amount

The child tax credit is refundable to the extent of the lesser of:

- excess of child tax credit over tax liability;
- earned income in excess of $2,500 multiplied by 15 percent; or
- $1,600 per qualifying child (2023).

2.10.4 Due Diligence Requirements

To help prevent improper claims, paid preparers are subject to due diligence requirements for returns that claim the child tax credit (similar due diligence requirements apply to returns that claim the earned income tax credit).

2.10.5 Non-child Dependent Credit

A taxpayer may claim an additional non-child dependent tax credit of $500 for each dependent who is not a qualifying child under age 17. This may include children who are age 17 and above or other dependents who meet the requirements of a qualifying relative. The non-child dependent credit is subject to the same AGI phase-out amounts and is not refundable.

2.11 Earned Income Credit (Refundable)

2.11.1 Eligibility

To be eligible for the earned income credit, a taxpayer must:

- live in the U.S. (main home) for more than half the taxable year;
- meet certain earned low-income thresholds;
- not have more than a specified amount of disqualified income;
- if there are no qualifying children, be over age 25 and under age 65 (applies to both taxpayer and spouse); and
- file a joint return with one's spouse with certain exceptions (which means that the spouse cannot be a dependent of another).

2.11.2 Earned Income

Earned income is wages, salaries, tips, other employee compensation, and earnings from self-employment. It does not include pension and annuity income.

Pass Key

The most frequently tested issue involving the *earned income credit* is that it is a refundable credit.

2.11.3 Qualifying Child

A qualifying child is not a requirement in order to be eligible for the earned income credit. However, if the taxpayer has a qualifying child, the earned income credit percentage and allowable earned income level is higher. A qualifying child is a child who:

- is the taxpayer's son, daughter, adopted child, grandchild, stepchild, foster child, brother, sister, stepbrother, stepsister, or descendant of those individuals;
- was (at the end of the year) either under age 19 or under age 24 and a full-time student, or any age and permanently and totally disabled;
- lived with the taxpayer in the taxpayer's main home in the U.S. for more than half of the taxable year; and
- is the taxpayer's dependent (if the child is married).

2.11.4 Earned Income Credit Calculation

For 2023, the earned income credit table is as follows:

	No Children	One Child	Two Children	Three or More Children
Maximum earned income credit	$600	$3,995	$6,604	$7,430
Earned income required to receive maximum credit	$7,840	$11,750	$16,510	$16,510
Credit rate percentage	7.65%	34%	40%	45%
Phase-out percentage	7.65%	15.98%	21.06%	21.06%
Credit phase-out for AGI or earned income (if greater) over this amount *(all taxpayers except married filing jointly)*	$9,800	$21,560	$21,560	$21,560
Credit phase-out for AGI or earned income (if greater) over this amount *(for married filing jointly)*	$16,370	$28,120	$28,120	$28,120

Tax Computations and Credits   REG 1

> **Example 5   Earned Income Tax Credit**
>
> **Facts:** Karen is 26 years old. In 2023, she had gross income of $12,000 from her job at the local university. She is single with no dependents.
>
> **Required:** Calculate the amount of earned income credit Karen can take in the current year.
>
> **Solution:** Karen is eligible to take an earned income credit in the amount of $432 after phase-out.
>
> | | |
> |---|---|
> | Earned income | $12,000 |
> | Maximum income eligible for credit | $7,840 |
> | × 7.65% | $600 [maximum credit] |
> | $12,000 earned income − $9,800 phase-out threshold | $2,200 |
> | × 7.65% phase-out percentage | $168 [phase-out amount] |
> | $600 maximum credit − $168 phase-out amount | $432 |

2.11.5 Investment Income

An individual cannot claim the credit if the individual has investment income exceeding $11,000 (2023). Investment income includes taxable and nontaxable interest, dividends, net rental and royalty income, net capital gains income, and net passive income.

2.11.6 Due Diligence Requirements

To increase the prevention of improper claims, paid preparers are subject to due diligence requirements for returns that claim the earned income tax credit.

2.12 Taxes Withheld (W-2)

All income taxes withheld from a taxpayer's paycheck are treated as a "credit" against the taxpayer's tax liability. When this credit exceeds the tax liability, a refund is provided to the taxpayer.

2.13 Excess FICA (Social Security Tax Withheld)

Excess Social Security tax withheld is treated as additional tax payments withheld.

- **Two or More Employers:** An employee who has had Social Security tax withheld in an amount greater than the maximum for a particular year may claim the excess as a credit against income tax (in the payment section), if that excess resulted from correct withholding by two or more employers.

- **One Employer:** If the excess was withheld by only one employer, the employer must refund the excess to the employee. No credit is allowed.

2.14 Small Employer Retirement Plan Start-up Costs Credit

Eligible small businesses are allowed a tax credit related to the start-up costs of establishing a new qualified retirement plan. The credit is available for the first three years of the plan (may elect to start claiming the credit in the tax year before the year the plan becomes effective).

2.14.1 Eligible Employers

- No more than 100 employees who received at least $5,000 in compensation in the preceding year; and
- At least one plan participant is a non-highly compensated employee

2.14.2 Eligible Start-up Costs

Eligible start-up costs include the ordinary and necessary costs to set up and administer the plan, and to educate employees about the plan.

An employer can choose to either deduct the start-up costs or claim the credit for those costs, but cannot do both.

2.14.3 Amount of the Credit

The credit is the greater of:

- 100 percent of the first $1,000 of eligible start-up costs for employers with 50 or fewer employees (50 percent for employers with 51 to 100 employees); or
- The lesser of:
  - $250 for each employee who is eligible for the plan and not a highly compensated employee; or
  - $5,000.

Example 6 — Small Employer Retirement Plan Start-up Costs Credit

Facts: Alice started a SEP IRA for her business in the current year that includes herself and two employees. The eligible start-up costs were $1,200. Alice is not a highly compensated employee.

Required: Calculate the amount of Alice's small employer retirement plan start-up costs credit.

Solution: The amount of the credit is $1,000, which is the greater of:

- 100 percent of the first $1,000 of eligible start-up costs: $1,000 × 100% = $1,000; or
- Lesser of: $250 × 3 employee-participants = **$750**, or $5,000.

2.15 Small Business Health Care Tax Credit

- A credit of up to 50 percent of the employer's costs of the plan premiums (or the average of the group's premium for small businesses within the taxpayer's state) is allowed as a credit for eligible employers, provided the employer contributes at least 50 percent of the costs of health coverage on behalf of employees enrolled in a qualified health plan offered through a Small Business Health Options Program (SHOP).
- Smaller businesses receive the better tax benefits.

- The credit is not refundable, and the unused amount is carried back one year and then carried forward for 20 years. (Tax-exempt organizations, however, will receive a refund of the tax credit.)
- The costs for family members, sole-proprietors, partners, S corporation owners with greater than two percent ownership, and shareholders owning more than five percent of corporations are excluded.
- If the expenses were used to qualify for the credit, they are not allowable as tax deductions for employee benefits expense.

2.16 Residential Energy Credits

2.16.1 Residential Clean Energy Credit

A credit of 30 percent of the installation costs for qualifying solar, wind, and geothermal energy-generating systems in 2022 through 2032 is allowed. A reduced credit percentage is allowed in 2033 (26%) and 2034 (22%).

2.16.2 Energy Efficient Home Improvement Credit

A credit for the costs of qualified energy efficiency improvements.

- If placed in service in 2022, the credit is 10 percent of qualified costs with a lifetime credit limit of $500.
- If placed in service after December 31, 2022, the credit is 30 percent of qualified costs with an annual credit limit of $1,200.

2.17 Vehicle and Fuel-Related Credits

2.17.1 Clean Vehicle Credit

A credit of up to $7,500 for new electric vehicles ($4,000 for previously owned electric vehicles) placed in service after December 31, 2022. The credit is subject to modified AGI limitations.

2.17.2 Alternative Fuel Refueling Property Credit

A credit of 30 percent of the installation costs of "qualified alternative fuel vehicle refueling property" installed in the home (e.g., electric vehicle recharging station). Maximum credit of $1,000.

2.18 Premium Tax Credit (PTC)

The premium tax credit is a refundable credit that helps eligible individuals and families with low or moderate income afford health insurance purchased through a Health Insurance Marketplace. The "credits" are available immediately when the insurance is purchased to help eligible individuals pay for their monthly health insurance premiums.

3 Estimated Tax and Inadequate Withholding

3.1 Tax Payments

A taxpayer typically makes prepayments of tax during the year. These payments reduce the amount shown as "total tax" on the tax return and result in the calculation of tax owed to the IRS or a refund owed to the taxpayer at the bottom of Form 1040. Payments include:

- Taxes withheld from paychecks (W-2 or 1099)
- Estimated taxes paid (quarterly, with extension, or applied from a prior year)
- Excess Social Security tax withheld (from two or more employers)

3.2 Estimated Taxes (Required Minimum)

A taxpayer is required to make estimated quarterly tax payments if both of the following conditions are met:

- **$1,000 or More Tax Liability**

    One condition is met if the amount of taxes owed (excess of tax liability over withholding) is expected to be $1,000 or more.

- **Inadequate Tax Estimates**

    The other condition is met if the taxpayer's withholding is less than the lesser of:
    - 90 percent of the current year's tax; or
    - 100 percent of last year's tax.
        —This applies even if an individual files a tax return with a zero tax liability in the prior year.
        —Exception: If a taxpayer had adjusted gross income in excess of $150,000 ($75,000 for married filing separately) in the prior year, 110 percent of the prior year's tax liability is used to compute the safe harbor for estimate payments.

3.3 Failure to Pay Estimated Taxes (Penalty)

If the taxpayer does not make proper quarterly estimated payments, a penalty may be assessed. There is no penalty due under any circumstances if the balance of tax owed at filing is under $1,000. The Internal Revenue Service may waive the penalty if the failure to pay was the result of casualty, disaster, illness, or death of the taxpayer.

3.4 Withholding Tax Treated as Estimated Payments

If, toward the end of the taxable year, a taxpayer determines that estimated payments have been insufficient to avoid a penalty, a taxpayer can increase withholding from wages, and the withholdings will be considered to have been paid evenly during the year. Such action will usually reduce or eliminate any penalty. A new W-4 will have to be completed and submitted to the taxpayer's employer.

4 Other Taxes

4.1 Self-Employment Tax

The self-employment tax represents the employer portion and the employee portion of FICA taxes (Social Security and Medicare) imposed on self-employment income. 100 percent of self-employment tax is collected as an "other tax" and reported in the "other taxes" section of the Form 1040. (Note that 50 percent of this amount is reported as an adjustment to arrive at AGI.)

4.2 Additional Medicare Tax

An additional Medicare tax of 0.9 percent is imposed on wages in excess of $250,000 for married filing jointly; $125,000 for married filing separately; and $200,000 for all other taxpayers.

- Employers are responsible for withholding this additional tax on all wages paid to an employee that exceed $200,000 in a calendar year.
- Any amounts withheld in excess can be claimed as a credit on the taxpayer's individual income tax return.

4.3 Net Investment Income Tax

The net investment income (NII) tax applies a rate of 3.8 percent to certain net investment income of individuals who have income above statutory threshold AGI amounts. The statutory threshold amounts are $250,000 for a filing status of married filing jointly, and $200,000 for taxpayers with a single or head of household filing status. The 3.8 percent tax is imposed on the lesser of net investment income or the excess AGI over the threshold amount.

Generally, investment income includes, but is not limited to: interest, dividends, capital gains, rental and royalty income, nonqualified annuities, income from businesses involved in the trading of financial instruments or commodities, and businesses that are passive activities to the taxpayer. Expenses allocable to the income can be deducted.

Example 7 — Net Investment Income Tax

Facts: Susie is a single taxpayer with AGI of $210,000 and taxable income of $190,000. Susie's income includes $400 interest on a savings account at the local bank, $500 in qualified dividends, and $10,000 of rental income. The tax for a single taxpayer earning over $182,100 but not over $231,250 is equal to $37,104 plus 32 percent of the excess over $182,100.

Required: Calculate Susie's net investment income tax and total income tax liability.

Solution: Susie's net investment income tax equals $380 and her total tax liability is $39,927.

Susie's net investment income is $10,900 ($400 interest + $500 dividends + $10,000 rental income)

Adjusted gross income	$210,000
Threshold amount for a single taxpayer	200,000
Excess AGI over the threshold	$ 10,000

The net investment income tax is 3.8 percent of the lesser of the net investment income ($10,900) or the excess AGI ($10,000). The tax on net investment income equals 3.8 percent × $10,000 = $380.

Susie's total tax is calculated below:

Taxable income	$190,000
Less: income taxed at preferential rates (qualified dividends)	(500)
Income taxed at ordinary rates	$189,500
Ordinary income tax calculation for single filers [$37,104 + 32% × (189,500 − 182,100)]	39,472
Tax on income at 15% preferential rate* ($500 qualified dividends × 15%)	75
Net investment income tax ($10,000 × 3.8%)	380
Total income tax + net investment income tax	$ 39,927

*The preferential rate for single taxpayers with taxable income between $44,625–$492,300 is 15 percent.

4.4 Kiddie Tax

The net unearned income of a dependent child under 18 years of age (or a child age 18 to under 24 who does not provide over half of his/her own support and is a full-time student) is taxed at the parent's rate. Net unearned income is calculated by taking the child's total unearned income (from dividends, interest, rents, royalties, etc.) and subtracting $2,500: the child's allowable 2023 standard deduction of $1,250 plus an additional $1,250 (which is taxed at the child's regular income tax rate). If the child also has earned income of more than $1,250, the standard deduction is earned income plus $400 (maximum of $13,850, the 2023 single standard deduction amount).

Parents may elect to include on their own return the unearned income of the applicable child provided that the income is between $1,250 and $12,500 and consists solely of interest, dividends, and capital gains distributions.

2023 Child's Unearned Income	Tax Rate
$0–$1,250	0%
$1,251–$2,500	Child's rate
Over $2,500	Parent's rate

Property Taxation

Module

1. Basis and Holding Period of Assets — 3
2. Gains and Losses — 15
3. Cost Recovery — 23

NOTES

MODULE 1
Basis and Holding Period of Assets

1 Adjusted Basis and Holding Period of Assets Sold

1.1 Purchased Tangible Property

1.1.1 Basis

Generally, the initial basis of property is the cost of such property to the taxpayer. The cost of property includes all amounts to purchase the property, prepare the property for use, and place the property into service. Examples include shipping costs, installation costs, sales taxes, and testing costs.

- Real property is land and all items permanently affixed to the land (e.g., buildings, paving, etc.).
- Personal property is all property not classified as real property.

> **Example 1   Calculating Basis**
>
> **Facts:** A taxpayer purchases a piece of equipment that will be used in a business. The cost of the equipment is $5,000. The shipping cost for the equipment is $500, and the cost to install the equipment is $200.
>
> **Required:** Determine the basis of the equipment.
>
> **Solution:** The tax basis of the piece of equipment is $5,700 ($5,000 + $500 + $200).

1.1.2 Holding Period

The holding period of purchased property begins on the date the property is acquired.

1.1.3 Reduce Basis for Accumulated Depreciation

The basis is adjusted downward for the amount of any depreciation, allowed or allowable, taken by the taxpayer with respect to that asset. The basis that has been adjusted downward by accumulated depreciation is referred to as the adjusted basis of the asset.

> **Example 2   Calculating Adjusted Basis**
>
> **Facts:** A taxpayer has a milling machine that was purchased for $10,000. In both Year 1 and Year 2, the taxpayer deducted $1,000 from gross income for depreciation of the machine.
>
> **Required:** Determine the adjusted basis of the milling machine at the end of Year 2.
>
> **Solution:** Accumulated depreciation at the end of Year 2 is $2,000 ($1,000 depreciation deduction taken in Year 1 + $1,000 depreciation deduction taken in Year 2). Accordingly, the adjusted basis at the end of Year 2 would be $8,000 ($10,000 minus $2,000).

1.1.4 Basis Spreading Adjustments

Although most adjustments to basis involve an increase or decrease in the basis of property, some spread the basis.

> **Illustration 1 Basis "Spreading"**
>
> Under the tax law, the receipt of a nontaxable stock dividend or stock split requires the shareholder to spread the basis of his or her original shares over both the original shares and the new shares received, resulting in the same total basis in the stock but a lower basis per share of stock held.
>
> For example, a taxpayer purchased 100 shares of stock at $11/share, so the total cost basis is $1,100 (100 × $11). The taxpayer then receives 10 additional shares of the stock as a result of a 10 percent nontaxable stock dividend (100 shares × 10%). The $1,100 basis of the original shares is spread over the 110 total shares owned, so the basis per share is now $10/share.

1.2 Gifted Property Basis for Gain/Loss Purposes

1.2.1 General Rule: Donor's Rollover Cost Basis

Property acquired as a gift generally retains the cost basis it had in the hands of the donor at the time of the gift. Basis is increased by any gift tax paid that is attributable to the net appreciation in the value of the gift. Gains and losses are calculated using this rollover cost basis (subject to the exception noted below).

1.2.2 Exception: Lower FMV at Date of Gift

If the fair market value at the date of the gift is lower than the rollover cost basis from the donor, the basis for the donee depends on the donee's future selling price of the asset.

- **Sale of Gifts at Price Greater Than Donor's Rollover Basis (Gain Basis):** When a taxpayer sells a gift for greater than the rollover basis, the gain shall be the difference between the sale price and that rollover basis.

> **Example 3 Sale of Gift at Price Greater Than Donor's Basis**
>
> **Facts:** Donor gives non-depreciable property worth $3,000 with an adjusted basis of $5,000 to taxpayer, who subsequently sells the property for $6,500.
>
> **Required:** Determine the basis used and the gain on the sale of the property.
>
> **Solution:** The taxpayer's gain will be $1,500 ($6,500 proceeds minus $5,000 basis).

- **Sale of Gift at Price Less Than Lower Fair Market Value (Loss Basis):** When a taxpayer sells the gift for less than the lower FMV at the date of the gift, the basis of the gift for purposes of determining the loss is the fair market value of the gift at the time the gift was given.

Example 4 — Sale of Gift at Price Less Than Lower FMV

Facts: Donor gives property worth $3,000 having an adjusted basis of $5,000 to taxpayer, who subsequently sells the property for $1,000.

Required: Determine the basis used and the loss on the sale of the property.

Solution: The taxpayer's loss will be $2,000 ($3,000 FMV at date of gift minus $1,000). (Note that the loss may or may not be deductible on the taxpayer's income tax return, depending on the situation.)

- **Sale Less Than Rollover Cost Basis but Greater Than Lower Fair Market Value (in the Middle):** When a taxpayer sells a gift for a price less than the donor's rollover cost basis, but more than the lower fair market value at the date of gift, neither gain nor loss is recognized. The basis to the donee is the "middle" selling price.

1.2.3 Gifted Property Basis for Depreciation

- Regardless of the basis for the gain/loss (which may not be known at the time depreciation is to begin), the basis for depreciation purposes (if applicable) is the lesser of:
  - the donor's adjusted basis at the date of the gift; or
  - the fair market value at the date of the gift.
- The amount of accumulated depreciation will then reduce the taxpayer's basis calculated for gain/loss purposes (per above) before the actual gain or loss on the sale is determined.

Example 5 — Determining Basis

Facts: A donor gives property worth $3,000 with an adjusted basis of $5,000 to a taxpayer.

Required: Determine the basis of the property:
- if the property is in a gain situation on sale;
- if the property is in a loss situation on sale;
- if the property is in a zero gain/loss situation on sale;
- for calculating depreciation prior to the sale.

Solution:
- For purposes of determining gain on the sale, the taxpayer's basis is $5,000.
- For purposes of determining loss on the sale, the taxpayer's basis is $3,000.
- If the taxpayer subsequently sells the property for $3,500, there is no gain or loss on the sale, and the basis is $3,500.
- For purposes of calculating depreciation on the asset (if applicable) prior to the sale, the depreciable basis is $3,000.

Pass Key

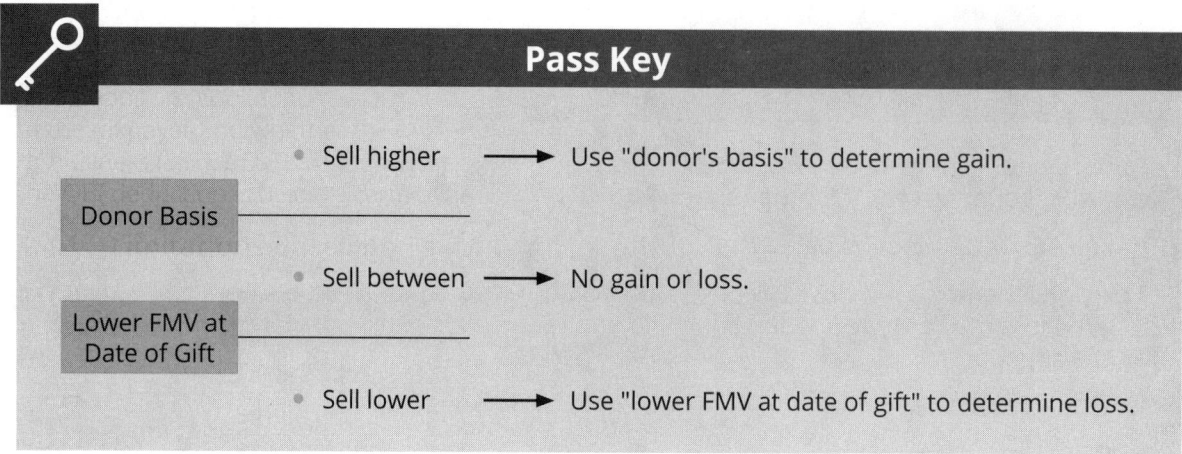

1.2.4 Holding Period

The recipient of the gift normally assumes the donor's holding period. However, under the exception above, if fair market value at the time of the gift is used (loss basis) as the basis of the gift, the holding period starts as of the date of the gift.

Illustration 2 Basis of Gifted Stock and Gain or Loss on Resale

	General Rule: FMV Higher	Exception: FMV Lower		
	1	2	3	4
Donor's (rich uncle) basis	$20,000	$20,000	$20,000	$20,000
FMV at date of gift	40,000	13,000	13,000	13,000
Donee's (nephew) selling price	30,000	25,000	10,000	15,000
Donee's basis for gain/loss purposes	20,000	20,000	13,000	15,000
Taxable gain (if any)	10,000	5,000	-0-	-0-
Deductible loss (if any)	-0-	-0-	3,000	-0-

1.3 Inherited Property Basis

1.3.1 General Rule: FMV at Date of Death

Property acquired by bequest or inheritance generally takes as its basis the step-up (or step-down) to the fair market value at the date of the decedent's death.

1.3.2 Alternate Valuation Date

If validly elected by the executor, the fair market value on the alternate valuation date (the earlier of six months later or the date of distribution/sale) may be used to value all of the estate property. The alternate valuation date is only available if its use lowers the entire gross estate and estate tax (although individual assets may go up or down during the period).

If the alternate valuation date is validly elected, the basis of the asset is the FMV at the earlier of:
- distribution date of asset; or
- six months after death.

> **Example 6 Sale of Inherited Property**
>
> **Facts:** A decedent died owning property worth $60,000 and in which he had a cost basis of $20,000. His son inherited the property and subsequently sold it for $55,000.
>
> **Required:** Determine the loss on the sale of property.
>
> **Solution:** The son will recognize a loss of $5,000 ($55,000 selling price − $60,000 basis). The built-in gain in the property at the time of the decedent's death is never recognized because his son takes a basis in the land equal to the FMV at the date of death.

1.3.3 Holding Period

Inherited property is automatically considered to be long-term property regardless of how long it has actually been held.

> **Example 7 Basis of Inherited Property**
>
> **Facts:** Assume that a taxpayer inherited property from a decedent. The FMV at the date of death was $20,000. The property was worth $15,000 six months later and was worth $22,000 when it was distributed to the taxpayer eight months later. It had a cost basis to the deceased of $5,000.
>
> 1. **Required:** What is the basis of inherited property to the taxpayer:
>   a. if the alternate valuation date was not elected?
>   b. if the alternate valuation date was elected?
>
>   **Solution:**
>   a. $20,000 (FMV at date of death)
>   b. $15,000 (FMV at earlier of six months after death or date of distribution)
>
> 2. **Required:** Assuming that the beneficiary sold this property for $25,000, compute the capital gain:
>   a. assuming that the alternate valuation date was not elected.
>   b. assuming that the alternate valuation date was elected.
>
>   **Solution:**
>   a. $5,000 = 25,000 − 20,000
>   b. $10,000 = 25,000 − 15,000

1.4 Property Converted From Personal to Business Use

If property is held for personal use and later converted to business use, the basis for depreciation is calculated in a similar manner as calculating the basis on gifted property.

1.4.1 Tax Basis for Depreciation

The basis of the property converted from personal to business use for depreciation purposes is the lesser of:

- the original cost basis, as adjusted for any improvements to the property; or
- the fair market value (FMV) of the property on the date of conversion.

> **Example 8 Converted Property: Tax Basis for Depreciation**
>
> **Facts:** Sue Smith converted the following personal use assets to business use when she started her consulting business:
>
> Computer equipment (cost $2,000, FMV $1,200)
>
> Office furniture (cost $1,500, FMV $1,800)
>
> **Required:** What is Sue's tax basis in each of the assets for depreciation purposes?
>
> **Solution:** The tax basis for depreciation purposes in property converted from personal use to business use is the lesser of: (1) the cost basis of the asset; or (2) the FMV of the asset on the date of conversion.
>
> Basis of computer equipment: $1,200 (FMV)
>
> Basis of office furniture: $1,500 (cost)

1.4.2 Tax Basis for Gain/Loss Purposes

If the property converted to business use is later sold or disposed of, the tax basis of the property will depend on whether the property is sold at a gain or loss. The tax basis used for the purpose may be different from the basis used for depreciation.

To determine if a gain or loss occurred upon the sale of the asset, compare the sales price to the adjusted basis at the date of the sale, which is the original cost basis less any depreciation taken.

The tax basis for determining a gain is the adjusted basis of the property at the date of the sale.

The basis for determining a deductible loss is as follows:

1. First, considering the amounts at the time of conversion to business use, take the lesser of:
    - the adjusted cost basis; or
    - the FMV of the property.
2. Then, reduce the lesser amount by any depreciation deductions taken after the conversion to business use.

Example 9 — Converted Property: Tax Basis for Gain

Facts: Sue Smith converted her personal use office furniture to business use when she started her consulting business. The office furniture cost $1,500, and its FMV at the time of conversion was $1,800.

Sue sold the office furniture two years later for $2,000. Sue has deducted $400 in depreciation for the office furniture since conversion.

Required: What is Sue's tax basis in the office furniture for purposes of calculating gain or loss?

Solution: Tax basis of office furniture for calculating gain or loss = $1,100

The first step is to determine whether there is a gain or loss by comparing the $2,000 sales price to the $1,100 adjusted basis ($1,500 cost less the $400 depreciation taken) at the date of the sale.

Because the $2,000 sales price is greater than the $1,100 adjusted basis at the time of the sale, the property is sold at a gain. Therefore, the tax basis for determining the gain is the adjusted basis of the property at the date of the sale ($1,500 cost basis less the $400 depreciation taken after conversion), which equals a tax basis of $1,100.

Example 10 — Converted Property: Tax Basis for Loss

Facts: Sue Smith converted her personal use computer equipment to business use when she started her consulting business. The computer equipment cost $2,000, and its FMV at the time of conversion was $1,200. Sue sold the computer equipment two years later for $500, after she had deducted $400 in depreciation for the equipment.

Required: What is Sue's tax basis in the computer equipment for purposes of calculating the loss?

Solution: Tax basis of computer equipment for calculating gain or loss = $800

The first step is to determine whether there is a gain or loss by comparing the $500 sales price to the $1,600 adjusted basis ($2,000 cost less the $400 depreciation taken) at the date of the sale.

Because the $500 sales price is less than the $1,600 adjusted basis at the time of the sale, the property is sold at a loss. Therefore, to determine the tax basis for calculating the deductible loss, we take the lesser of the $2,000 adjusted basis at the time of the conversion or the $1,200 FMV of the property at the time of the conversion and then reduce that amount by the $400 depreciation taken, which equals a tax basis of $800.

1.5 Intangible Property

The initial tax basis of an intangible asset is generally the cost or purchase price. The initial basis is adjusted downward by amortization deductions taken on the asset (adjusted basis).

1.5.1 Section 197 Purchased Intangibles

Section 197 intangible assets are intangible assets acquired in connection with the purchase of an existing business. A portion of the lump-sum purchase price of the business' assets is allocated to Section 197 intangible assets. These include intangibles such as:

- Goodwill
- Going-concern value
- Covenant not to compete
- Licenses and permits
- Customer or supplier lists
- Franchises, trademarks, and trade names
- Patents, copyrights, etc. owned by the purchased business

1.5.2 Research and Experimental Costs

Research and experimental costs can be immediately expensed or capitalized and amortized. If the costs are capitalized, any unamortized costs remaining when a patent is obtained are added to the basis of the patent intangible.

1.5.3 Patents and Copyrights

The initial basis of patents and copyrights that are purchased directly (other than those acquired as part of a lump-sum purchase of an existing business) is the purchase price of the patent or copyright.

The basis of self-created patents and copyrights include the costs of development, legal costs, and government fees. The value of the inventor or author's time is not included in basis. Research and experimental costs that are not immediately expensed can be included in the basis of the patent.

1.5.4 Loan Costs

Loan closing costs, such as loan origination fees, are capitalized as an intangible asset and amortized.

1.5.5 Organizational Costs and Start-up Costs

Taxpayers are allowed to immediately expense the first $5,000 of business organization costs and the first $5,000 of business start-up costs. The $5,000 allowance is reduced dollar-for-dollar when total costs exceed $50,000 for each item. The costs that are not immediately expensed are capitalized as intangible assets and amortized.

- **Business Organizational Costs**
  - Applies to the formation and organization of a partnership, LLC, or corporation
  - *Qualifying costs:* costs of forming and organizing a partnership, LLC, or corporation, such as:
    —legal fees;
    —accounting fees;
    —filing fees; and
    —costs of organizational meetings.
  - *Nonqualifying costs:* costs associated with:
    —issuing and selling stocks or partnership interests; and
    —transferring assets to the corporation or partnership.
- **Business Start-up Costs**
  - Applies to the start-up of a business organized as a sole proprietorship, partnership, or corporation
  - *Qualifying costs:* costs to investigate and create the business that are incurred before the business begins operations:
    —Investigation of potential markets, locations, products, etc.
    —Marketing and advertising for the opening of the business
    —Costs to secure prospective distributors, suppliers, or customers
    —Worker hiring and training costs
    —Facility and equipment set-up costs

Example 11 — Qualifying Organizational and Start-up Costs

Facts: ABC Company, a calendar-year C corporation, was incorporated on June 30, Year 1, and started doing business on July 1, Year 1. ABC Company incurred the following costs in organizing and starting up the business:

Legal fees for drafting corporate charter and bylaws	$14,000
Accounting fees for setting up accounting books	10,000
State incorporation filing fees	2,000
Brokerage costs of issuing and selling stock	12,000
Travel costs to investigate possible locations in May, Year 1	24,000
Costs to recruit, interview, and hire employees incurred in June, Year 1	28,000
Costs to train employees incurred in July, Year 1	15,000

(continued)

(continued)

Required: What are ABC Company's total qualifying organization costs and start-up costs?

Solution:

Qualifying organizational costs

Legal fees	$14,000
Accounting fees	10,000
Filing fees	2,000
Total qualifying organizational costs	$26,000

The $12,000 costs of issuing and selling stock do not qualify as amortizable organizational costs.

Qualifying start-up costs

Travel costs to investigate possible locations	$24,000
Costs to recruit, interview, and hire employees	28,000
Total qualifying start-up costs	$52,000

Only the qualifying costs incurred before the business begins operations are capitalized as start-up costs. The costs to train employees were incurred after the start of business operations on July 1, Year 1, so these costs are deductible business expenses, rather than amortizable start-up costs.

2 Capitalize or Expense

2.1 Capital Expenditures

The general rule is that the cost of all tangible and intangible property with a useful life of more than one year must be capitalized. There are, however, several exceptions to this rule.

2.2 Repairs and Maintenance vs. Improvements

2.2.1 Repairs and Maintenance

Repairs and maintenance are those costs incurred to maintain property in working condition and do not add significant value to the property or extend the life of the property. Repair and maintenance costs are immediately expensed (deducted).

2.2.2 Improvements

Improvements to property must be capitalized. An expenditure is an improvement if it:

- results in a betterment to the property (enlarges, expands, or increases the quality of the property);
- substantially extends the useful life of the property;
- restores the property's value or use; or
- adapts the property to a new or different use.

2.3 Materials and Supplies

Incidental materials and supplies that cost $200 or less, or that are consumed in one year or less, are immediately expensed (deducted).

2.4 De Minimis Safe Harbor

Businesses that have a policy of immediately expensing low-cost personal property items for financial accounting purposes are allowed to immediately expense (deduct) up to a certain amount of those costs for income tax purposes under the de minimis safe harbor provision. The amount the taxpayer is allowed to deduct for each item depends on whether the taxpayer has an applicable financial statement (AFS), which generally means an audited financial statement. A taxpayer with an AFS can deduct the amount paid for items costing up to $5,000. For a taxpayer who does not have an AFS, the amount is $2,500 per item. If the cost of the item is more than the allowable amount, the entire cost of the item must be capitalized.

Example 12 Capitalize vs. Expense

Facts: Center Corp. has an applicable financial statement and at the beginning of Year 1 has a written accounting policy to expense amounts paid for tangible personal property costing up to $10,000. During Year 1, Center pays $50,000 for eight desks.

Required: Determine Center Corp.'s amount expensed and/or capitalized for the desks for federal tax purposes.

Solution: For financial reporting purposes, Center can expense the entire $50,000 paid for the eight desks because each desk costs less than the $10,000 limit ($50,000/8 = $6,250 per desk). However, for tax purposes, Center must capitalize all of the purchases unless their economic life is less than 12 months because the de minimis rule is not met. The de minimis rule is not met because the purchases exceed $5,000 per asset.

NOTES

MODULE 2 Gains and Losses

REG 2

1 Calculation of Gain or Loss on Disposition

Generally, gain or loss realized on the sale of an asset is calculated by comparing the amount realized on the disposition to the adjusted basis of the asset being relinquished in the transaction. For certain types of transactions, the gain or loss is realized but not recognized.

Illustration 1 Calculating Gain or Loss at Disposition

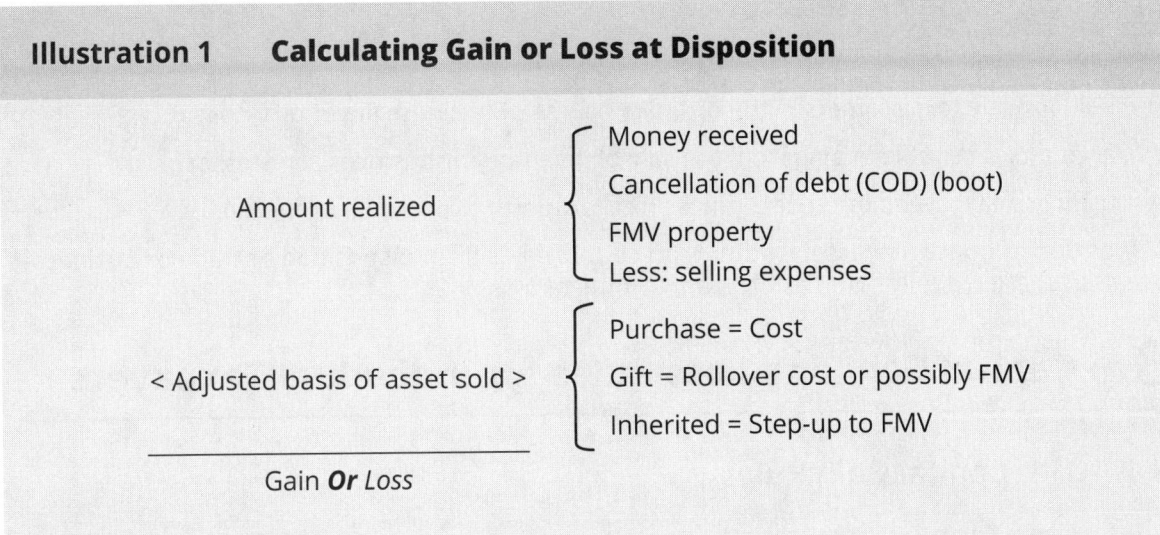

Amount realized
- Money received
- Cancellation of debt (COD) (boot)
- FMV property
- Less: selling expenses

< Adjusted basis of asset sold >
- Purchase = Cost
- Gift = Rollover cost or possibly FMV
- Inherited = Step-up to FMV

Gain *Or* Loss

Example 1 Realized Gain

Facts: A taxpayer conveys commercial property in which the taxpayer has a basis of $70,000 and which is subject to a mortgage of $45,000 to X for $60,000 in cash, and X's assumption of the mortgage on the property.

Required: Determine the amount realized on the sale and the gain or loss realized.

Solution: The amount realized by the taxpayer is $105,000 (Debt relief of $45,000 + Cash of $60,000), and the taxpayer realizes a gain of $35,000 ($105,000 amount realized − $70,000 basis in the property).

2 Character of Gain or Loss

When a taxpayer disposes of property, the gain or loss recognized is classified as either capital or ordinary, depending on how the asset disposed of was used by the taxpayer.

2.1 Capital Assets

Capital assets include assets that are held or used for:

- investment (e.g., stocks, bonds, virtual currency); or
- personal use (e.g., personal car, home, furniture).

Dispositions of capital assets are typically taxed as capital gains/losses.

2.2 Noncapital Assets

Noncapital assets include assets that are:

- held for sale to customers in the ordinary course of business (inventory); or
- accounts receivable arising from the sale of inventory or business services; or
- used in a taxpayer's trade or business (real property or personal property).

Disposition of noncapital assets (other than certain gains from disposition of trade or business-use assets) are typically taxed as ordinary income or loss.

3 Capital Gain and Loss Rules for Individual Taxpayers

3.1 Net Capital Gain Rules

3.1.1 Long-Term

- **Holding Period:** More than one year.
- **Tax Rate:** The tax rate is dependent on the taxpayer's taxable income and filing status:

	2023 Taxable Income			
Tax Rate	Single	Head of Household	Married Filing Jointly	Married Filing Separately
0%	$0–$44,625	$0–$59,750	$0–$89,250	$0–$44,625
15%	$44,626–$492,300	$59,751–$523,050	$89,251–$553,850	$44,626–$276,900
20%	Over $492,300	Over $523,050	Over $553,850	Over $276,900

3.1.2 Short-Term

- **Holding Period:** One year or less.
- **Tax Rate:** Treated as ordinary income.

3.1.3 Collectibles and Qualified Small Business Stock (28 Percent Rate Group)

Long-term gains on the sale of collectibles (e.g., works of art, stamp or coin collections, antiques) and Section 1202 qualified small business stock (QSBS) in excess of the Section 1202 exclusion amount are taxed at a maximum rate of 28 percent.

QSBS is original issue C corporation stock that is held for more than five years. The C corporation's tax basis in its assets must be no more than $50 million. A taxpayer is allowed to exclude part of the gain on the sale of QSBS. The exclusion amount is the greater of $10 million or ten times the taxpayer's basis in the stock. Any gain in excess of the excluded amount is taxed at a maximum rate of 28 percent.

3.2 Net Capital Loss Deduction and Loss Carryover Rules

3.2.1 $3,000 Maximum Deduction

Individual taxpayers realizing a net long-term or short-term capital loss may only recognize (deduct) a maximum of $3,000 of the realized loss from other types of gross income (ordinary income, passive income, or portfolio income). A joint return of spouses is treated as one person. If the spouses file separately, the loss deduction is limited to half ($1,500). If the taxpayer has both net short-term capital losses and net long-term capital losses, the net short-term capital losses are deducted first.

3.2.2 Excess Net Capital Loss

Carry forward for an unlimited period of time until exhausted. The loss maintains its character as long-term or short-term in future years.

3.2.3 Personal (Nonbusiness) Bad Debt

A personal (nonbusiness) bad debt loss is treated as a short-term capital loss in the year the debt becomes totally worthless.

3.2.4 Worthless Stock and Securities

The cost (or other basis) of worthless stock or securities is treated as a capital loss, as if they were sold on the last day of the taxable year in which they became totally worthless.

3.2.5 Short Sales

A short sale of stock results in a capital gain or loss. The holding period is based on the date the short sale is executed, not the closing date of the short sale when the stock is delivered.

3.3 Netting Process for Individuals

Gains and losses, including any capital loss carryforwards, are netted within each tax rate group, resulting in a net gain or loss for the group.

- Short-term ordinary tax rate group
- Long-term 0/15/20 percent tax rate group
- Long-term 28 percent tax rate group (collectibles and QSBS)

Gains and Losses

If every group has a net gain, or if every group has a net loss, then each maintains its own character. The net gains are taxed at the appropriate tax rate. Up to $3,000 of net capital losses are deducted (short-term first), and any remaining losses are carried forward.

If some of the groups have net gains and some of the groups have net losses, the netting process becomes more complicated. Basically, the net capital gain or loss from each of the three long-term tax rate groups are netted together. A net long-term capital loss (LTCL) offsets a net short-term capital gain (STCG), and a net short-term capital loss (STCL) offsets a net long-term capital gain (LTCG).

- Net STCL is offset against net LTCGs, starting with the 28 percent tax rate group, then the 0/15/20 percent tax rate group.

- Net LTCL from the 0/15/20 percent tax rate group is offset against other LTCGs in the 28 percent tax rate group. Any remaining net LTCL from the 0/15/20 percent tax rate group is offset against any net STCG.

- Net LTCL from the 28 percent tax rate group is offset against other LTCGs in the 0/15/20 percent rate group. Any remaining net LTCL from the 28 percent group is offset against any net STCG.

Example 2 Individual Capital Gains and Losses Netting Process

Facts: Jessica Jones, a single individual taxpayer, had the following capital gains and losses for the current tax year:

Capital Asset	Holding Period	Selling Price	Tax Basis	Capital Gain (Loss)
A Stock	6 months	$10,000	$ 9,000	$ 1,000
B Stock	9 months	5,000	9,000	(4,000)
C Stock	2 years	20,000	25,000	(5,000)
D Stock	5 years	30,000	18,000	12,000
Sculpture	3 years	8,000	7,000	1,000

Required: Calculate the amount and character of Jessica's net capital gain or loss for the year.

Solution:

$5,000 net LTCG taxed at the 0/15/20 percent preferential tax rate.

Net STCG(L) = A stock STCG 1,000 + B stock STCL (4,000) = (3,000) net STCL

Net 0/15/20 percent group LTCG(L) = C stock LTCL (5,000) + D stock LTCG 12,000 = 7,000 net LTCG

Net 28 percent group = Sculpture (collectible held long-term) 1,000 LTCG

The $3,000 net STCL is first offset against the $1,000 LTCG from the 28 percent group. The remaining $2,000 net STCL is offset against the $7,000 net LTCG from the 0/15/20 percent group. The remaining $5,000 of net LTCG is taxed at the 0/15/20 percent tax rate.

4 Capital Gain and Loss Rules for C Corporations

4.1 Net Capital Gains

Net capital gains of a corporation are added to ordinary income and taxed at the regular tax rate.

- There is no distinction between short-term and long-term capital gains and losses for C corporations.
- C Corporations do not get the benefit of lower capital gains rates.

4.2 Net Capital Losses

Corporations may not deduct any net capital losses from ordinary income.

- Net capital losses are carried back three years and forward five years.
- Net capital losses can offset net capital gains in other years within the carryback/carryforward window.

Pass Key

	Offset Income or Gains	Excess Carryback	Excess Carryforward
Individual capital losses	$3,000	No	Indefinitely
Corporate capital losses	No	3 years	5 years

5 Losses (Nondeductible)

"**WRaP**" up these losses and throw them away because they are nondeductible.

- **W**ash sale losses
- **R**elated party losses
- **a**nd
- **P**ersonal losses

5.1 Wash Sale Loss

A wash sale exists when a security (stock or bond) is sold for a loss and is repurchased within 30 days before or after the sale date. Dealers in securities are excluded from wash sale rules if the loss occurs from a transaction made in the ordinary course of business.

5.1.1 Disallowed Loss

The loss on the wash sale is disallowed for tax purposes. The wash sale disallowance only applies to losses, not gains.

5.1.2 Basis of Repurchased Security

The basis of the repurchased security is equal to the purchase price of the new security plus the disallowed loss on the wash sale (or, alternatively, the basis of the old security, less the proceeds from the sale, plus the purchase price of the new security).

5.1.3 Date of Acquisition

The date of acquisition of the repurchased security is the date of acquisition of the original security.

5.1.4 Gain

If a security is sold resulting in a gain and it is repurchased within 30 days, the taxpayer cannot use "substituted basis." Instead, the taxpayer must pay capital gains tax and use the new purchase price as the basis.

Example 3 — Wash Sale

Facts: Bob DeFilippis entered into the following transactions in April:

Item	Cost	Selling Price
(A) 100 shares of XYZ stock	$22,000	$21,000
(B) 100 shares of XYZ stock	21,500	

The shares sold during the year were purchased 15 years ago. These shares were sold on April 1 and the new shares were purchased on April 25.

Required: Determine if the sale qualifies as a wash sale, the amount of any loss allowed, and the basis of the purchased stock.

Solution: Although there is a loss on the sale of $1,000 ($21,000 sales price − $22,000 cost basis), the realized loss will be disallowed because the same stock (XYZ) was purchased within 30 days of the sale. The basis of the stock in the second purchase on April 25 is now $22,500, as the disallowed wash sale loss is added to the basis ($21,500 cost + $1,000 disallowed wash sale loss).

Pass Key

The CPA Examination has often tested the wash sale rules by having the taxpayer purchase shares of the same stock 30 days *before* the sale of the stock that resulted in a loss. This is still a wash sale, and the loss is disallowed. For example, on January 4 you buy one share for $100. On March 5 you buy another share for $40. Then, on March 15, the first share is sold for $41. Although you have "realized" a $59 loss, it will not be recognized because of the wash sale rules.

5.2 Related Party Losses

Sales between related parties are not considered "arm's-length," and the loss is generally disallowed.

5.3 Personal Losses

No deduction is allowed for a loss on the disposal of a personal-use asset. An itemized deduction may be available for a casualty loss attributable to a federally declared disaster.

NOTES

MODULE 3
Cost Recovery

REG 2

1 Depreciation

Depreciation is an annual allowance given to a trade or business for exhaustion, wear and tear, and normal obsolescence of assets used in trade or business. An asset's basis must be reduced by the depreciation allowed (or allowable) for a particular year, even if depreciation was not claimed by the taxpayer for that particular year. The depreciation method typically used for federal income tax purposes is the Modified Accelerated Cost Recovery System (MACRS).

1.1 Definitions

- **Real Property (Land and Buildings):** Real property is defined as land and all items permanently affixed to the land (e.g., buildings, paving, etc.).
- **Personal Property (Machinery, Equipment, Computers, and Automobiles):** Personal property is defined as tangible, movable property not affixed to the land.

1.2 MACRS: Personal Property

1.2.1 Types of Property

3-year Class:	Includes special tools and certain racehorses.
5-year Class:	Includes automobiles, light trucks, computers, and copiers.
7-year Class:	Includes furniture and fixtures, machinery, and equipment.
10-year Class:	Includes boats and water transportation equipment.
15-year Class:	Includes qualified improvements to the interior of existing nonresidential buildings and certain improvements made directly to land.
20-year Class:	Includes certain farm buildings and municipal sewers.

The vast majority of personal property assets fall into the 5-year and 7-year classes.

1.2.2 MACRS Depreciation Rules Method

For 3-, 5-, 7-, and 10-year MACRS property (other than real property) placed in service after January 1, 1987, MACRS is computed using the 200 percent declining balance method. For 15- and 20-year property, MACRS is computed using the 150 percent declining balance method.

1.2.3 Salvage Value (Ignored)

Salvage value is ignored under MACRS.

1.2.4 Half-Year Convention

In general, a *half-year convention* applies to personal property, under which such property placed in service or disposed of during a taxable year is treated as having been placed in service or disposed of halfway through the year. A personal property asset is allowed six months of depreciation in the year of acquisition and disposition, regardless of the date on which it is acquired or disposed.

The MACRS depreciation table below provides the MACRS rates for each year for the five-year and seven-year classes of depreciable personal property. The half-year convention is built into the first-year and last-year MACRS rates. If personal property is disposed of before the last year, the full-year MACRS rate must be multiplied by one-half for the half-year convention in the year of disposition.

	MACRS Rates: Half-Year Convention	
	Recovery Period	
Recovery Year	*5 Years*	*7 Years*
1	20.00%	14.29%
2	32.00%	24.49%
3	19.20%	17.49%
4	11.52%	12.49%
5	11.52%	8.93%
6	5.76%	8.92%
7	—	8.93%
8	—	4.46%
Total	**100%**	**100%**

1.2.5 Straight-Line in Lieu of Accelerated Depreciation Election

A taxpayer may choose to depreciate property on a straight-line basis, rather than use the more accelerated MACRS. A taxpayer who chooses straight-line may choose the regular recovery period or a longer alternative depreciation system (ADS) recovery period (provided in the tax law).

> ### Example 1   MACRS Depreciation: Half-Year Convention
>
> **Facts:** Acme Co., a calendar year sole proprietorship, purchased office furniture on February 14, Year 1, for $10,000. No other purchases were made in Year 1. The company disposed of the office furniture on March 20, Year 3.
>
> **Required:** Calculate MACRS depreciation for the office furniture in Years 1, 2, and 3.
>
> **Solution:** The office furniture is MACRS seven-year property. The MACRS depreciation rates for Years 1, 2, and 3 are provided in the MACRS depreciation table. The half-year convention for the first year is built into the first-year rate from the table. The Year 3 rate is for a full year, so it must be multiplied by one-half for the half-year convention in the year of disposition.
>
> Year 1 depreciation = $10,000 cost × 14.29% (7-year, Year 1 rate) = $1,429
>
> Year 2 depreciation = $10,000 × 24.49% (7-year, Year 2 rate) = $2,449
>
> Year 3 depreciation = $10,000 × 17.49% (7-year, Year 3 rate) × 1/2 year = $874.50
>
> **Required:** Calculate Acme's Year 1 depreciation if Acme instead elects to depreciate the office furniture using straight-line over the ADS recovery period, which is 10 years for office furniture.
>
> **Solution:** The annual straight-line rate is 10 percent (1/10 years). The half-year convention still applies in the year of acquisition and disposition.
>
> Year 1 depreciation = $10,000 × 10% × 1/2 year = $500

1.2.6 Mid-quarter Convention

If more than 40 percent of depreciable personal property is placed in service in the last quarter of the year, a mid-quarter, rather than a half-year, convention applies, and the mid-quarter MACRS tables are used to calculate depreciation. With a mid-quarter convention, personal property placed in service or disposed of during a taxable year is treated as having been placed in service or disposed of halfway through the quarter in which it was disposed.

The mid-quarter MACRS rates for assets placed in service in each quarter are provided in four depreciation tables (one for each quarter). The partial tables below include the MACRS rates for the first three years for five-year and seven-year property. The mid-quarter convention is built into the first-year and last-year MACRS rates in the mid-quarter MACRS tables. If personal property is disposed of before the last year, the full-year MACRS rate must be multiplied by a mid-quarter ratio for the mid-quarter convention in the year of disposition.

- Quarter 1 (disposed of January–March): 0.5 of a quarter out of 4.0 quarters = 12.5%
- Quarter 2 (disposed of April–June): 1.5 quarters out of 4.0 quarters = 37.5%
- Quarter 3 (disposed of July–September): 2.5 quarters out of 4.0 quarters = 62.5%
- Quarter 4 (disposed of October–December): 3.5 quarters out of 4.0 quarters = 87.5%

MACRS Rates: Mid-quarter Convention—First Quarter

Recovery Year	Recovery Period	
	5 Years	7 Years
1	35.00%	25.00%
2	26.00%	21.43%
3	15.60%	15.31%
4–8	⋮	⋮

MACRS Rates: Mid-quarter Convention—Second Quarter

Recovery Year	Recovery Period	
	5 Years	7 Years
1	25.00%	17.85%
2	30.00%	23.47%
3	18.00%	16.76%
4–8	⋮	⋮

MACRS Rates: Mid-quarter Convention—Third Quarter

Recovery Year	Recovery Period	
	5 Years	7 Years
1	15.00%	10.71%
2	34.00%	25.51%
3	20.40%	18.22%
4–8	⋮	⋮

MACRS Rates: Mid-quarter Convention—Fourth Quarter

Recovery Year	Recovery Period	
	5 Years	7 Years
1	5.00%	3.57%
2	38.00%	27.55%
3	22.80%	19.68%
4–8	⋮	⋮

> ### Example 2 — MACRS Depreciation: Mid-quarter Convention
>
> **Facts:** Acme Co., a calendar year sole proprietorship, purchased office furniture on February 14, Year 1, for $10,000, and computers on October 30, Year 1, for $8,500. No other purchases were made in Year 1. The company disposed of the office furniture on March 20, Year 3.
>
> **Required:** Calculate MACRS depreciation for the office furniture and computers in Years 1, 2, and 3.
>
> **Solution:** Because personal property was acquired in the fourth quarter, first do the 40 percent test to determine whether the half-year or mid-quarter convention applies:
>
> Fourth-quarter personal property acquired ÷ Total personal property acquired = $8,500 ÷ $18,500 = 46%, which is more than 40 percent, so the mid-quarter convention applies.
>
> The MACRS depreciation rates for Years 1, 2, and 3 are provided in the MACRS depreciation table for the quarter in which each asset was acquired and placed in service. The office furniture, which is seven-year property, was acquired in February so the rates from the first-quarter table apply. The computers, which are five-year property, were acquired in the fourth quarter so the rates from the fourth-quarter table apply. The mid-quarter convention for the first year is built into the first-year rate from the table. The Year 3 rate is for a full year, so it must be multiplied by the mid-quarter ratio for the mid-quarter convention in the year of disposition. The office furniture was disposed of in March, Year 3, so the appropriate mid-quarter ratio is 0.5 quarter out of 4.0 quarters, or 12.5 percent.
>
> *Year 1 depreciation:*
> - Computers: $8,500 cost × 5% (5-year, fourth quarter, Year 1 rate) = $425
> - Furniture: $10,000 cost × 25% (7-year, first quarter, Year 1 rate) = $2,500
>
> *Year 2 depreciation:*
> - Computers: $8,500 × 38% (5-year, fourth quarter, Year 2 rate) = $3,230
> - Furniture: $10,000 × 21.43% (7-year, first quarter, Year 2 rate) = $2,143
>
> *Year 3 depreciation:*
> - Computers: $8,500 × 22.8% (5-year, fourth quarter, Year 3 rate) = $1,938
> - Furniture: $10,000 × 15.31% (7-year, first quarter, Year 3 rate) × 12.5% (mid-quarter convention) = $191

1.3 MACRS: Real Property

Salvage value should be ignored when computing MACRS depreciation on real property.

1.3.1 Residential Rental Property (27.5-Year Straight-Line)

Examples of *residential rental property* include apartment buildings and rental homes.

1.3.2 Nonresidential Real Property (39-Year Straight-Line)

Examples of *nonresidential real property* (real property that is not residential rental property) include office buildings and warehouses.

1.3.3 Land

Land is not depreciable and should be removed from the total cost of real property when calculating depreciation.

1.3.4 Mid-month Convention

Straight-line depreciation is computed based on the number of months the property was in service. One half month is taken in the month the property is placed in service. One half month is taken for the month in which the property is disposed of.

> **Example 3 — MACRS Depreciation: Mid-month Convention**
>
> **Facts:** Acme Co., a calendar year sole proprietorship, purchased an office building on April 6, Year 1, for $100,000. The company disposed of the office building on March 20, Year 3.
>
> **Required:** Calculate MACRS depreciation for the office building in Years 1, 2, and 3.
>
> **Solution:** The office building is 39-year nonresidential real property, and is depreciated straight-line using a mid-month convention. The straight-line depreciation rate is 2.564 percent (1/39 years). Under the mid-month convention, the property is treated as being placed in service in the middle of April, allowing 8.5 months of depreciation for Year 1. The building was disposed of in March, Year 3, so 2.5 months of depreciation is allowed for Year 3.
>
> Year 1 depreciation: $100,000 cost × 2.564% × 8.5 months ÷ 12 months = $1,816
>
> Year 2 depreciation: $100,000 × 2.564% = $2,564
>
> Year 3 depreciation: $100,000 × 2.564% × 2.5 months ÷ 12 months = $534

> **Pass Key**
>
> It is important for CPA Examination candidates to remember the following concepts:
>
> | Personal Property | Real Property |
> |---|---|
> | • Half-year convention
• Mid-quarter convention | • Mid-month convention |

1.4 Section 179 Expense Deduction

In lieu of depreciation, a taxpayer can elect to immediately expense a fixed amount of the cost of qualified business-use property purchased and placed in service during the year.

1.4.1 Eligible Property

- Tangible personal property
- Off-the-shelf computer software Qualified real property: qualified improvements to the interior portion of a nonresidential building after the date the building was first placed in service, including:
  - Roofs
  - Heating, ventilation, and air-conditioning
  - Fire protection and alarm systems
  - Security systems

1.4.2 Ineligible Property

- Intangible assets
- Land and improvements
- Elevator or escalator
- Real property that is not "qualified real property"
- Tangible personal property that is used less than 50 percent for business
- Property not acquired by purchase (gift, inheritance, exchange, or conversion from personal to business use)
- Property acquired from a related party

1.4.3 Limitations on Immediate Expensing

The 2023 allowance is $1,160,000 for qualified property that is purchased and placed in service during the year.

- The maximum amount is reduced dollar for dollar by the amount of property placed in service during the taxable year that exceeds $2,890,000 (2023).
- The deduction is limited to taxable income (before the deduction).

Example 4   Section 179 Expense Deduction

Facts: Nicholas Inc. placed into service $50,000 of five-year property in Year 1. Assume that Nicholas Inc. is not subject to the taxable income limitation for a Section 179 expense deduction. Year 1 MACRS rate for five-year property from MACRS depreciation tables = 20%.

Required: Compare Nicholas' MACRS depreciation expense to its Section 179 expense if Nicholas elects to take the full amount of Section 179 expense against the property.

Solution: MACRS: $50,000 × 20% = $10,000 depreciation deduction. Section 179: $50,000. The property placed into service is within Section 179 expensing and property limits, so the entire amount is deductible this year (given that Nicholas is not in a net loss situation). Electing Section 179 yields the greatest deduction. (Note that if the taxpayer is in a loss position or sees the need for greater deductions in the future, depreciating the asset under normal MACRS convention would be best).

1.5 Bonus Depreciation

Under bonus depreciation rules, a taxpayer can expense an additional percentage of qualified property that is placed into service in the current year.

- Qualified property is personal property with a recovery period of 20 years or less, including qualified improvement property. A property is only qualified if the acquiring taxpayer had not previously used the acquired property and the property is not acquired from a related party.

- The bonus depreciation percentage was 100 percent for property placed in service during years 2018 through 2022, but phases down to 80 percent in 2023, 60 percent in 2024, 40 percent in 2025, and 20 percent in 2026.

- An $8,000 additional first-year depreciation for vehicles on which bonus depreciation is claimed is allowed.

- Bonus depreciation is claimed after the Section 179 expense deduction, if elected, but before the regular MACRS depreciation expense deduction.

Example 5 — Bonus Depreciation and Section 179 Expense

Facts: Company A places into service $3,000,000 of seven-year MACRS property in 2023 (all qualified under the rules of Section 179 and bonus depreciation).

Required: Determine the total cost recovery deduction for the year on the property, assuming that Company A wants to elect the maximum Section 179 allowed and take the maximum cost recovery deduction allowed for the current year (2023).

Solution: The order is Section 179 first, then bonus depreciation, then regular MACRS depreciation:

Section 179: $1,050,000 Section 179 expense deduction (the $1,160,000 allowance is reduced dollar for dollar by qualified property placed into service in excess of $2,890,000; Qualified property $3,000,000 − $2,890,000 threshold = $110,000 reduction in allowance). $1,160,000 allowance − $110,000 reduction = $1,050,000 reduced allowance.

Bonus: $1,560,000 ($3,000,000 − $1,050,000 Section 179 expense deduction = $1,950,000 available for bonus. $1,950,000 × 80% bonus rate = $1,560,000).

MACRS: $3,000,000 − $1,050,000 Section 179 − $1,560,000 bonus depreciation = $390,000 remaining basis to be recovered under MACRS. $390,000 × 14.29% (Year 1, seven-year MACRS rate) = $55,731.

Total cost recovery deduction for the year: $2,665,731 ($1,050,000 Section 179 + $1,560,000 bonus depreciation + $55,731 MACRS).

2 Amortization

2.1 Amortization Method

Intangible assets are amortized using the straight-line method with a full-month convention, which means that a full month of amortization is taken in the month of acquisition and disposition.

2.2 Recovery Period

The most common recovery period for intangible assets is 180 months (15 years).

Pass Key

It is important to know the difference in the treatment of intangibles for GAAP (financial statements) and tax (income tax returns).

Tax Rule: Generally, amortize straight-line over 180 months (15 years)

GAAP Rule: Subject to impairment test

- *Intangibles With Finite Lives:* Amortize over the life of the asset
- *Intangibles With Infinite Lives:* Not amortized

- **Section 197 Purchased Intangibles (Goodwill):** Amortize over 180 months, beginning with month purchased.
- **Capitalized Research and Experimental Costs:** Amortize over no less than 60 months, beginning with the month an economic benefit from the costs is first received; no longer amortized once patent is obtained.
- **Patents and Copyrights**
  - **Purchased:** Amortize over the remaining life of the patent or copyright
  - **Self-created:** Amortize over the life of the patent or copyright
- **Loan Costs:** Amortize debt-issuance costs over the term of the loan
- **Capitalized Organizational Costs and Start-up Costs:** Amortize any remaining costs after the $5,000 expense allowance (as adjusted for phase-out, if any) over 180 months, beginning with the month in which business operations start.

Example 6 — Deduction for Organizational and Start-up Costs

Facts: ABC Company, a calendar-year C corporation, was incorporated on June 30, Year 1, and started doing business on July 1, Year 1. ABC Company had total qualifying organizational costs of $26,000 and total qualifying start-up costs of $52,000.

Required: Determine ABC Company's Year 1 deduction for organizational costs and start-up costs.

Solution: The total deduction for organizational and start-up costs in Year 1 is $10,333 ($5,700 + $4,633):

Organizational Costs

Total qualifying organizational costs	$26,000
Immediate expensing allowed in Year 1	(5,000)
Remaining organizational costs capitalized	21,000
Amortization months in Year 1	× 6
Total months of amortization	÷ 180
Year 1 amortization of capitalized costs	700
Immediate expensing allowed in Year 1	5,000
Total Year 1 deduction for organizational costs	$ 5,700

Start-up Costs

Total qualifying start-up costs	$52,000
Immediate expensing allowed in Year 1 ($5,000 − $2,000 costs in excess of $50,000)	(3,000)
Remaining start-up costs capitalized	49,000
Amortization months in Year 1	× 6
Total months of amortization	÷ 180
Year 1 amortization of capitalized costs	1,633
Immediate expensing allowed in Year 1	3,000
Total Year 1 deduction for start-up costs	$ 4,633

Illustration 1   Automated Diagnostic and Validation Check: Cost Recovery

Mary, a CPA, is preparing the Year 1 federal income tax return for her client, Kay Jones. Kay, a self-employed, calendar-year taxpayer, owns depreciable property for her consulting business and rental property. Mary received the following message in a software diagnostic report when she was preparing Kay's Year 1 federal income tax return:

Form 4562 Depreciation

A box was checked to elect Section 179 immediate expensing for the following assets acquired in Year 1. Please review the assets identified to confirm whether they are eligible for Section 179 and remove the Section 179 code for assets that are ineligible. If the Section 179 code is removed, MACRS depreciation will be calculated for the asset based on the classification identified (residential real property, nonresidential real property, tangible personal property, etc.).

Asset number 225, Apartment Building Security System

Asset number 230, Office Building Security System

Asset number 236, Office Building Elevator

Asset number 242, Office Building Parking Lot

Mary should remove the Section 179 expense election code for all of the assets identified except Asset 230, Office Building Security System. A security system installed in an existing nonresidential building is a qualified improvement that is eligible for Section 179 immediate expensing.

Asset 225, Apartment Building Security System: A security system installed in an existing residential building is not a Section 179 qualified improvement.

Asset 236, Office Building Elevator: Although the elevator was installed in an existing nonresidential building, elevators and escalators are not Section 179 qualified improvements.

Asset 242, Office Building Parking Lot: Land and land improvements are not eligible for Section 179 immediate expensing.

NOTES

Entity Taxation

Module

1	C Corporation Overview	3
2	Differences Between Book and Tax	13
3	C Corporation Tax Computations and Credits	21
4	Calculating Loss Limitations for C Corporations	27
5	S Corporation Overview	29
6	Partnership Overview	41
7	Tax-Exempt Organization Overview	51
8	State and Local Tax Issues	55

REG 3

NOTES

MODULE 1: C Corporation Overview

REG 3

1 C Corporation Taxable Income

1.1 Gross Income

The concept of *gross income* is very similar for both corporations and individuals. The general rule is that income is recognized when received.

- Cash received in advance of accrual GAAP income is taxed, such as:
  - Interest income received in advance.
  - Rental income received in advance. (Nonrefundable rent deposits and lease cancellation payments are rental income when received.)
  - Royalty income received in advance.
- Some GAAP income items are not included in taxable income, such as:
  - Interest income from municipal or state obligations/bonds.
  - Certain proceeds from life insurance on the life of a corporate officer ("key person" policy) when the corporation is the beneficiary.
    —For life insurance contracts that were issued after August 17, 2006, limitations exist regarding the amount of proceeds that are excluded from income relating to company-owned life insurance (COLI) contracts, unless certain requirements are met. The general rule is that the portion of the proceeds that equals the previously paid premiums and other nondeductible amounts paid in is tax-free, and the balance is generally taxable.
- In contrast to individual taxpayers, corporate capital gains are taxed at the same rate as ordinary corporate income (i.e., no special capital gains rates apply).

1.2 Accrual Basis vs. Cash Basis

While the cash basis of accounting is used for tax purposes by most individuals, qualified personal service corporations (which are treated as individuals for purposes of these rules), and taxpayers whose average annual gross receipts do not exceed $29 million (2023) for the prior three-year period, the accrual basis method of accounting for tax purposes is required for the following:

- The accounting for purchases and sales of inventory (and inventories must be maintained), provided the business has greater than $29 million of average annual gross receipts for the three-year period ending with the preceding tax year.
- Tax shelters.
- Certain farming corporations (other farming or tree-raising businesses may generally use the cash basis), provided the business has greater than $29 million of average annual gross receipts for the three-year period ending with the preceding tax year.
- C corporations, trusts with unrelated trade or business income, and partnerships having a C corporation as a partner, provided the business has greater than $29 million of average annual gross receipts for the three-year period ending with the preceding tax year.

1.3 Trade or Business Deductions (Ordinary and Necessary Expenses)

All of the ordinary and necessary expenses paid or incurred during the taxable year in carrying on a business are deductible. "Ordinary and necessary" means that the expenses are common (or accepted) in the particular business or profession and that they relate to the production of the current year's income. Reasonable salaries, office rentals, office supplies, and traveling expenses are all deductible when incurred for business purposes.

1.3.1 Executive Compensation

A publicly held corporation may not deduct compensation expenses in excess of $1,000,000 paid to covered employees, which includes the CEO, CFO, and the three other most-highly compensated officers. Covered employees remain covered employees for all future years.

Entertainment expenses for officers, directors, and 10-percent-or-greater shareholders may be deducted only to the extent that they are included in the individual's gross income.

Corporations are allowed to deduct reasonable compensation paid to shareholder-employees. If the IRS determines that part of a shareholder's salary is unreasonable, it may reclassify part of the salary as a dividend distribution. A salary is a deductible business expense for the corporation, and is subject to various payroll taxes; a dividend is not deductible. From the shareholder-employee perspective, a salary is taxed as ordinary income, and is subject to Social Security and Medicare taxes, and a dividend is generally taxed at preferential tax rates.

1.3.2 Bonus Accruals (Non-shareholder/Employees)

Bonuses paid by an accrual basis taxpayer are deductible in the tax year when all events have occurred that establish a liability with reasonable accuracy, and provided they are paid within 2.5 months of the taxpayer's year-end.

1.3.3 Bad Debts: Specific Charge-off Method

- **Accrual Basis:** *Accrual method* taxpayers must use the specific charge-off method (direct write-off method) for tax purposes. Thus, most taxpayers will write off bad debts as they become worthless or partially worthless. (The allowance method is still required for financial accounting purposes, but it is not allowed for calculating the income tax deduction.)

- **Cash Basis:** A very important point for purposes of the CPA Exam is to be aware of bad debts of cash basis taxpayers. Because a cash basis taxpayer has not included the amount in gross income, a bad debt is not deductible, except in the case of an uncollectible check that has been deposited and recorded as income.

1.3.4 Business Interest Expense

Most *interest* paid or accrued during the taxable year on indebtedness incurred for business purposes is deductible, although limitations may apply.

The business interest expense deduction is limited to the sum of (1) business interest income; (2) 30 percent of adjusted taxable income (ATI); and (3) floor plan financing interest expense.

ATI is taxable business income for the year excluding all interest income and interest expense. Floor plan financing is debt that is typically used to acquire motor vehicles held for sale or lease where the debt is secured by the acquired inventory.

Disallowed business interest expense can be carried forward indefinitely. The limitation does not apply if the taxpayer's average annual gross receipts are $29 million or less (2023) for the prior three taxable years.

Prepaid interest expense must be allocated to the proper period to which it is related. Interest expense on debt incurred to purchase "tax-free" bonds is not deductible.

1.3.5 Charitable Contributions (10 Percent of Adjusted Taxable Income Limitation)

Corporations making contributions to qualifying charitable organizations are allowed a maximum deduction of 10 percent of their taxable income, as defined below. Any disallowed charitable contribution may be carried forward for five years. Any accrual must be paid within 3.5 months of the taxable year-end to be deductible. Total taxable income for purposes of the charitable contributions limit is calculated before the deduction of:

- any charitable contribution deduction;
- the dividends-received deduction; or
- any capital loss carryback.

1.3.6 Business Losses or Casualty Losses Related to Business

Generally, any loss sustained during the taxable year and not compensated for by insurance or otherwise is deductible. The loss may be treated as an ordinary loss or a capital loss, depending upon the type of asset involved in the casualty. Business casualty losses are treated differently from losses by individuals in a federally declared disaster.

- **Partially Destroyed:** For property only partially destroyed, the loss is limited to the lesser of:
  - the decline in value of the property; or
  - the adjusted basis of the property immediately before the casualty.
- **Fully Destroyed (NBV):** For property that has been fully destroyed (i.e., a total loss), the amount of the loss is the adjusted basis of the property.

Example 1 — Casualty Loss

1. **Facts:** Bad Luck Inc. had a major casualty loss in Year 1. A warehouse building was seriously damaged by a storm, and the federal government declared a major disaster for the area. The fair market value of the building before the storm was $850,000; the fair market value after the storm was $400,000. The adjusted basis of the property was $600,000. Insurance reimbursements amounted to $300,000.

    Required: Determine the amount of casualty loss that can be deducted for tax purposes.

    Solution: The amount of the casualty loss before insurance reimbursements is $450,000, which is the decline in value of the property and is less than the adjusted basis of the property. Subtracting the insurance reimbursement of $300,000, Bad Luck's deductible loss would be $150,000.

2. **Facts:** Assume the same facts above except that the property was totally destroyed.

    Required: Determine the amount of casualty loss that can be deducted for tax purposes.

    Solution: The deductible casualty loss would be $300,000 ($600,000 − $300,000). Note that the adjusted basis is used to determine the casualty loss, not the decline in value.

1.3.7 Organizational and Start-up Costs

- **Calculation**

    A corporation may elect to deduct up to $5,000 of organizational costs and $5,000 of start-up costs. Each $5,000 amount is reduced by the amount by which the organizational or start-up costs exceed $50,000, respectively. Any excess organizational or start-up costs are amortized over 180 months (beginning with the month in which active trade or business begins).

C Corporation Overview

- **Included Costs**

    Allowable organizational costs and start-up costs include fees paid for legal services in drafting the corporate charter, bylaws, minutes of organization meetings, fees paid for accounting services, and fees paid to the state of incorporation.

- **Excluded Costs**

    The costs do not include costs of issuing and selling the stock, commissions, underwriter's fees, and costs incurred in the transfer of assets to a corporation.

Pass Key

It is important for CPA candidates to remember the difference in the GAAP (financial statement) and the tax (income tax return) rule for organizational and start-up costs.

Organizational and Start-up Costs

- Tax rule: $5,000 expense maximum/180 months amortization of remainder
- GAAP rule: Expense

Example 2 Organizational Costs

Facts: Kristi Co., a newly organized corporation, was formed on June 30, Year 1, and began doing business on July 1, Year 1. The corporation will have a December 31 year-end. Kristi Co. incurred the following expenses in organizing the business:

Legal fees for drafting corporate charter	$15,000
Fees paid for accounting services	5,000
Fees paid to state of incorporation	3,000
Costs of selling shares of stock	10,000
	$33,000

Required: Determine the deduction for organizational costs in Year 1.

Solution: Amortization for the six months (July 1 to December 31, Year 1) will be $5,600, calculated as follows:

Legal fees for corporate charter	$15,000
Accounting fees	5,000
Fees paid to state	3,000
Organization expenses	$23,000

$23,000
<5,000> ──────────────────→ $5,000
$18,000 ÷ 180 mo. = $100 per mo. × 6 mo. =   600
                                            $5,600

The deduction for organizational costs in Year 1 is $5,600. The cost of selling the shares may not be amortized; it is a reduction in the capital stock account.

1.3.8 Amortization, Depreciation, and Depletion

Goodwill, covenants not-to-compete, franchises, trademarks, and trade names must be amortized on a straight-line basis over a 15-year period beginning with the month such intangible was acquired. For depreciation and depletion, corporations use the same rules as other trades and businesses.

> **Pass Key**
>
> The CPA Examination often tests the candidate's ability to distinguish the GAAP (financial statements) and tax (income tax returns) rules. The difference in the treatment of purchased goodwill (years 2002 and forward) should be noted:
>
> **Purchased Goodwill**
> - Tax rule: Amortized on a straight-line basis over 15 years
> - GAAP rule: Not amortized; test for impairment

1.3.9 Life Insurance Premiums (Expense)

- **Corporation Named as Beneficiary—Corporation Owns the Policy (Key Person):** Premiums paid by the corporation for life insurance policies on key employees are not deductible when the corporation is directly or indirectly the beneficiary.

- **Insured Employee Named as Beneficiary—Employee Owns the Policy (Fringe Benefit):** If the premiums are paid on insurance policies where the beneficiary is named by the insured employee, such premiums are deductible by the corporation as an employee benefit.

1.3.10 Business Gifts

Business gifts are deductible up to a maximum deduction of $25 per recipient per year.

1.3.11 Business Meals

Business meals are 50 percent deductible to the corporation. This includes employee travel meals, meals provided as a de minimis fringe benefit, and meals provided for the convenience of the employer.

1.3.12 Business Entertainment Expenses Not Deductible

Business entertainment expenses are not deductible.

1.3.13 Penalties and Illegal Activities Not Deductible

Bribes, kickbacks, fines, penalties, and other payments that are illegal under federal law or under a generally enforced state law are not deductible. Similarly, the top two thirds of a treble damage payment are not deductible if the taxpayer has been convicted of an antitrust violation.

1.3.14 Payments Made Related to Sexual Harassment or Sexual Abuse

Any settlement, payment, or related attorney fees related to sexual harassment or sexual abuse are not deductible if the settlement or payment is subject to a nondisclosure agreement.

1.3.15 Taxes

All state and local taxes and federal payroll taxes are deductible when incurred on property or income relating to business. Federal income taxes are not deductible. Foreign income taxes may be used as a credit.

1.3.16 Lobbying and Political Expenditures

Lobbying expenses incurred in attempting to influence local, state, or federal legislation are not deductible. Political contributions are not deductible.

1.3.17 Capital Loss Deduction Not Allowed

The $3,000 deduction for net capital losses available to individuals is not allowed to corporations. Thus, a corporation can only use capital losses to offset capital gains. Excess capital losses may be carried back three years or carried forward five years.

1.3.18 Inventory Valuation Methods

In general, the tax method used for accounting purposes can be used for income tax purposes; provided the method clearly reflects income and is consistent in application (i.e., opening and closing inventories must use the same valuation method). Furthermore, all taxpayers who have inventory are required to use the accrual basis of accounting for purchases and sales unless the taxpayer has average annual gross receipts of $29 million or less during the three preceding years. A change in inventory method is considered a change in accounting method and must be approved by the IRS.

- **Basic Valuation Methods**

  - **Cost Method:** Inventories are valued at cost (including direct labor, direct materials, and attributable indirect costs), less discounts, plus freight-in. The cost methods of "prime cost" (no overhead) and "direct cost" (which includes variable overhead only) are not allowable for tax purposes.

  - **Lower of Cost or Market Method:** Inventories are valued at the lower of cost (per above) or market, which for normal goods is generally the current bid price at the date of inventory for each item in inventory (i.e., the lower amount is determined based on each item, not on the aggregate value of the inventory).

  - **Rolling-Average Method:** This method will generally not be allowed when inventories are held for long periods of time or when costs tend to fluctuate significantly (unless the taxpayer regularly recomputes costs and makes certain adjustments), as the method may not clearly reflect income in certain cases.

  - **Retail Method:** In general, the retail method will approximate the cost or the market of items in inventory by subtracting the mark-up percentage to retail from the retail price, typically from inventory that has a large volume of items.

- **Common Inventory Identification Methods (Cost-Flow Assumptions)**

  - **FIFO (First In, First Out) Method:** FIFO is the most commonly used method, unless the inventory can be specifically identified.

  - **LIFO (Last In, First Out) Method:** LIFO must be elected by the taxpayer in the first year it is used, and the taxpayer must use the same method for its financial statement purposes. Significant adjustments to inventory valuations may be required to use LIFO.

Uniform Capitalization Rules Impact

IRC Section 263A details the uniform capitalization rules that require certain costs normally expensed be capitalized as part of inventory for tax purposes. This may cause the corporation to make an M-1/M-3 adjustment on their tax return to conform to the rules. Certain methods of accounting for inventory do not provide for the capitalization of the inventory costs that are required by the uniform capitalization rules. Thus, taxpayers who are subject to the uniform capitalization rules may not use certain valuation methods. Taxpayers with average annual gross receipts of $29 million or less (2023) during the three preceding years are not subject to the uniform capitalization rules and may treat these costs as supplies.

Unsalable or Unusable Goods

When inventories are deemed to be unsalable or unusable, they must be valued at their expected selling price ("bona fide selling price") within 30 days less the costs to dispose of them.

1.4 Dividends-Received Deduction

Domestic corporations are allowed a *dividends-received deduction (DRD)* based on qualified dividend income. The purpose of this deduction is to prevent triple taxation of earnings (as illustrated in the diagram below). The amount of the dividends-received deduction allowed depends on the percentage of the investee corporation owned by the investor corporation. The percentage allowed may be either 50, 65, or 100 percent. The corporate shareholder must own the investee stock for at least 46 days during the 91-day period beginning on the date 45 days before the ex-dividend date of the stock to qualify for the dividends-received deduction. Below is the percentage deductions based upon stock ownership:

Percentage Ownership	Dividends-Received Deduction
0% to < 20%	50%
20% to < 80%	65%
80% or more	100%

1.4.1 DRD Taxable Income Limitation

The *dividends-received deduction (DRD)* equals the lesser of:

- 50 percent (or 65 percent) dividends received; or
- 50 percent (or 65 percent) of taxable income computed without regard to the DRD, any NOL carryforward, or any capital loss carryback.

1.4.2 Exception to DRD Taxable Income Limitation

The *taxable income limitation* above does not apply if taking the full dividends-received deduction results in a net operating loss (NOL).

Illustration 1 Dividends-Received Deduction

The Duffy Corp. owns 30 percent of the Fox Corp. (so the 65 percent dividends-received deduction, or DRD, applies). Below are alternative situations for the year. The dividends-received deduction and taxable income would be calculated as follows:

	Scenario 1	Scenario 2	Scenario 3
Gross Income			
Operating revenue	250	250	250
Dividend income	100	100	100
Total revenue	350	350	350
Less: deductions			
Total deductions, including charitable contributions	(200)	(260)	(290)
Taxable Income (TI) before DRD	150	90	60
Tentative DRD (65% × $100)	65	65	65
Limitation (65% of TI before DRD)	98	59	39
DRD	(65)	(59)*	(65)**
Taxable income	85	31	(5)

*Limited to lesser of 65 percent of dividends received ($100) or TI before DRD ($90) and no NOL created.

**When subtracting the full 65 percent DRD, an NOL is created, thus 65 percent of TI before DRD limitation does not apply.

1.4.3 Entities Not Eligible for the DRD

The dividends-received deduction is not available to:

- personal service corporations;
- personal holding companies; or
- (personally taxed) S corporations.

Pass Key

An easy way to remember the entities not eligible for the dividends-received deduction:

Don't take it *personally*. In addition, the DRD does not apply to dividends received from certain banks and savings institutions, RICs, REITs, public utilities, tax exempt corporations, cooperatives, or DISCs.

1.4.4 100 Percent Dividends-Received Deduction

- **Affiliated Corporations—100 Percent:** Dividends from affiliated corporations (80 percent or more common ownership) that file consolidated returns qualify for a 100 percent deduction.

- **Small Business Investment Corporations (SBICs)—100 Percent:** A 100 percent deduction is allowed for dividends received by a small business investment company. An SBIC makes equity and long-term credit available to small business concerns.

Pass Key

Don't forget the DRD percentages.

- Ownership 0% to < 20%; DRD is 50%
- Ownership 20% to < 80%; DRD is 65%
- Ownership 80% or more; DRD is 100%

1.4.5 C Corporation Taxable Income and Limitations

Gross Income (Includes dividend income)

< Deductions >
- **Special Deductions (Not Included)**
  - Charitable contributions (CC) deduction
  - Dividends-received deduction (DRD)
  - Capital loss carryback

A

< Charitable Contributions Deduction >
- Not gifts ($25 for business gifts)
- Not political contributions
- Maximum allowed is 10% of A*
- 5-year carryforward
- Accrued amounts are deductible if paid within 3½ months after year-end

B

< Dividends-Received Deduction >
- **Requirements**
  1. First corporation is taxed
  2. Owned 45 days before or after
- **Dividend Income**
  - 100% (own 80%–100%) (consolidate)
  - 65% (own 20%–79%) (large investment)
  - 50% (own under 20%) (small investment)
  - Limited to DRD % (50% or 65%) of B
  - Exception: If DRD creates or adds to NOL, DRD is not limited to DRD % of B

Taxable Income Or Loss
- **Net Operating Loss**
  - Carryback five years, carryforward indefinitely (2018–2020)
  - No carryback, carryforward indefinitely; 80% of taxable income limit (2021 and beyond)

*The chart indicates that the corporate charitable deduction is limited to 10 percent of "A." "A" is defined here as gross income minus all deductions other than special deductions. This is the same definition as that presented earlier in this module; the material is simply shown differently.

MODULE 2: Differences Between Book and Tax

REG 3

1 Book Income vs. Taxable Income

Differences between net income per a company's financial statements and taxable income reported on a tax return exist because of the difference between GAAP and tax law. The following chart illustrates book (or financial statement) income versus taxable income.

	Financial Statement	Tax Return
Income from continuing operations before taxes	Income < Expense > NIBT* < Tax > NIAT**	Gross income
Discontinued operations, net of tax	Income < expense > − Tax = NIAT NIBT	< Deductions > A < Charity > B
Accounting adjustment and changes, net of tax (to retained earnings)	Net income ← M-1/M-3 Reconcile →	< Div. rec. ded. > Taxable income

*NIBT = Net income before tax
**NIAT = Net income after tax

Note: Schedule M-1 does not distinguish between temporary and permanent differences. Part II of Schedule M-3 does, however.

2 Temporary vs. Permanent Differences

- Temporary differences are items of income or expense that are recognized in one period for book but in a different period for tax. These cause timing differences between the two incomes but, in the long run, there is no difference between book and tax.

- Permanent differences are items of income or expense that are recognized for book but never recognized for tax, or vice versa. These cause permanent differences between book and taxable income.

Differences Between Book and Tax

For example, depreciation is typically calculated using a straight-line method for books but an accelerated method for tax. The difference between these two methods will create a difference in depreciation expense from year to year, but ultimately will result in the same total deduction for both book and tax. This is a temporary difference. An example of a permanent difference is municipal bond interest income, which is recognized as income for books but is always excluded for tax. This difference will never reverse.

Example 1 — Temporary vs. Permanent Differences

Facts: Barnette Corporation recorded book income of $560,000 for Year 6, which included the following items of income and expense:

Straight-line depreciation expense	$8,000
Municipal bond interest	4,000

Accelerated depreciation for the year per MACRS is $12,000. In addition, royalty income of $17,000 was received in advance of being earned and appropriately not recorded for books.

Required: Reconcile book income to taxable income.

Solution:

Temporary book/tax differences:

Royalty income per tax (when received)	$ 17,000	
Royalty income per book (when earned)	0	
Difference		17,000
MACRS depreciation expense (per tax)	(12,000)	
Straight-line depreciation expense (per books)	(8,000)	
Difference		(4,000)
Total temporary differences		$13,000

Permanent book/tax differences:

Municipal bond interest recognized for tax	$ 0	
Municipal bond interest recognized for book	4,000	
Difference		(4,000)
Total permanent differences		$(4,000)

Reconciliation of book income to taxable income:

Book income	$560,000
Income for tax but not book	17,000
Income for book but not tax	(4,000)
Deduction for tax but not book	(4,000)
Taxable income	$569,000

3 Schedules M-1 and M-3

The IRS requires that a company reconcile book/tax differences on either Schedule M-1 or Schedule M-3 (this determination is made based on the total assets of the company).

- Schedule M-1 does not distinguish between temporary and permanent differences.
- If the total assets of the company are $10 million or greater, the company is required to reconcile book and taxable income (loss) on Schedule M-3.
- The M-3 breaks out items of book income/expense in more detail, and distinguishes between temporary and permanent differences.

Illustration 1   Schedule M-1

Schedule M-1
Reconciliation of Income (Loss) per Books to Taxable Income

1	Net income (or loss) per books	$ 875,000
2	+ Federal income tax (per books)	384,500
3	+ Excess capital losses over gains	5,000
4	+ Income subject to tax not recorded on books this year:	
	+ Installment sale income	8,500
	+ Rents received in advance	15,000
5	+ Expenses recorded on books this year not on the tax return:	
	+ Book depreciation	14,000
	+ Meals in excess of 50% allowance	4,200
	+ Allowance for doubtful accounts (increase)	15,000
	+ Warranty accrual	8,500
	+ Goodwill impairment per books	5,000
	+ Pension expense accrued	12,000
	+ Penalties	1,000
6	Add lines 1 through 5	$1,347,700

(continued)

(continued)

7	– Income recorded on books this year not included on this return:		
	– Tax-exempt interest	$	3,500
	– Life insurance proceeds		100,000
8	– Deductions on this return not charged against book income this year:		
	– Tax depreciation		28,000
	– Contribution carryover		0
	– Section 179 deduction		20,000
	– Direct bad debt write-offs		8,650
	– Actual warranty costs		7,500
	– Amortization of organizational cost		500
	– Goodwill amortization per return		9,200
	– Pensions paid		11,350
9	Add lines 7 and 8	$	188,700
10	Taxable income (line 28 page 1 of Form 1120) line 6 minus line 9		$1,159,000

This is taxable income per page 1 of the tax return, before the dividends-received deduction and the NOL carryforward deduction.

Example 2 — Book/Tax Reconciliation

Facts: Batson Corp. is a calendar year C corporation that began doing business on January 1, Year 1. The company provided the following trial balance.

	DR	CR
Cash	$ 850,000	
Accounts receivable	950,000	
Machinery and equipment	1,500,000	
Accumulated depreciation		$ 880,000
Land	1,000,000	
Accounts payable		900,000
Common stock		100,000
Retained earnings		1,500,000
Revenue		2,200,000
Interest income—corporate bonds		105,000
Interest income—municipal bonds		10,000
Depreciation expense	150,000	
Fines expense—EPA violation	50,000	
Wages and salaries expense	1,100,000	
Federal income tax expense	80,000	
State income tax expense	15,000	

In addition to the trial balance, Batson Corp. also furnished depreciation schedules showing that the MACRS depreciation for the year on the machinery and equipment is $200,000. The company also provided a schedule of wages and salaries showing its officers were compensated $350,000, which is included in the wages and salaries expense.

Required:

1. Prepare a book-tax reconciliation for Batson Corp.
2. Prepare the form Schedule M-1 Reconciliation of Income (Loss) per books with income per return for Batson Corp.

(continued)

(continued)

Solution:

1. Batson Corp.'s book-tax reconciliation is as follows:

Revenue	$ 2,200,000
Interest income—corporate bonds	105,000
Interest income—municipal bonds	10,000
Depreciation expense	(150,000)
Fines expense—EPA violation	(50,000)
Wages and salaries expense	(1,100,000)
Federal income tax expense	(80,000)
State income tax expense	(15,000)
Book income	**$ 920,000**
Permanent differences	
Federal income tax expense per books	80,000
Interest income from municipal bonds	(10,000)
EPA fines expense	50,000
Temporary differences	
Depreciation	(50,000)
Taxable income	**$ 990,000**

Permanent differences:

- Federal income tax is always added back to book income as a permanent difference.
- Interest income from municipal bonds is not taxable and should be excluded from taxable income. Interest income from other sources, including interest paid by the federal government, is taxable and creates no difference between book and tax income.
- Fines and penalties are not deductible for tax purposes.

Temporary differences:

- Per the depreciation schedules for tax purposes provided by Batson Corp., the MACRS depreciation on the depreciable property is $200,000. The books reflect $150,000 of depreciation expense, meaning that book income should be reduced by an additional $50,000 to arrive at the tax depreciation figure.

Wages and salaries do not create a book-tax difference because none of the officers' salaries exceeded $1 million. State income tax expense generally never creates a book-tax difference.

(continued)

(continued)

2. Batson Corp.'s Schedule M-1 appears as follows (*income as reconciled on Schedule M-1 matches Page 1 of Form 1120*):

Schedule M-1 — Reconciliation of Income (Loss) per Books With Income per Return

Note: The corporation may be required to file Schedule M-3. See instructions.

1	Net income (loss) per books	920,000	7	Income recorded on books this year not included on this return (itemize):	
2	Federal income tax per books	80,000		Tax-exempt interest $ 10,000	
3	Excess of capital losses over capital gains				
4	Income subject to tax not recorded on books this year (itemize):				10,000
			8	Deductions on this return not charged against book income this year (itemize):	
5	Expenses recorded on books this year not deducted on this return (itemize):		a	Depreciation $ 50,000	
a	Depreciation $		b	Charitable contributions $	
b	Charitable contributions $				
c	Travel and entertainment $				50,000
	Fines Expense -- EPA Violations	50,000	9	Add lines 7 and 8	60,000
6	Add lines 1 through 5	1,050,000	10	Income (page 1, line 28)—line 6 less line 9	990,000

3.1 Corporation Tax Summary

The following chart lists common items of income/expense on an income statement and tax return, indicating which items will result in a book/tax difference.

Corporation Tax Summary	GAAP: Financial Statements	IRC: Tax Return	Temp.	Perm.	None
Gross Income					
Gross sales	Income	Income			✓
Installment sales	Income	Income when received	✓		
Rents and royalties in advance	Income when earned	Income when received	✓		
State tax refund	Income	Income			✓
Dividends:					
equity method	Income is subsidiary's earnings	Income is dividends-received	✓		
100/65/50% exclusion	No exclusion	Excluded forever		✓	
Items Not Includable in "Taxable Income"					
State and municipal bond interest	Income	Not taxable income		✓	
Life insurance proceeds	Income	Generally not taxable income		✓	
Gain/loss on treasury stock	Not reported	Not reported			✓
Ordinary Expenses					
Cost of goods sold	Currently expensed	Uniform capitalization rules			✓
Officers' compensation (top)	Expense	$1,000,000 limit			✓
Bad debt	Allowance (estimated)	Direct write-off	✓		
Estimated liability for contingency (e.g., warranty)	Expense (accrue estimated)	No deduction until paid	✓		
Interest expense: business loan	Expense	Deduct (up to limit)	✓		✓
Tax-free investment	Expense	Not deductible		✓	
Charitable contributions	All expensed	Limited to 10% of adjusted taxable income	✓	✓	✓
Loss on abandonment/casualty	Expense	Deduct			✓
Loss on worthless securities	Expense	Deduct			✓
Depreciation: MACRS vs. straight-line	Slow depreciation	Fast depreciation	✓		
Section 179 depreciation	Not allowed (must depreciate)	$1,160,000 (2023)	✓		
Different basis of asset	Use GAAP basis	Use tax basis	✓		
Amortization: start-up/organizational expenses	Expense	$5,000 maximum/amortize excess over 15 years	✓		
Franchise	Amortize	Amortize over 15 years	✓		
Goodwill	Impairment test	Amortize over 15 years	✓		
Depletion: percentage vs. straight-line (cost)	Cost over years	Percentage of sales	✓		
Percentage in excess of cost	Not allowed	Percentage of sales		✓	
Profit sharing and pension expense	Expense accrued	No deduction until paid	✓		
Accrued expense (50% owner/family)	Expense accrued	No deduction until paid	✓		
State taxes (paid)	Expense	Deduct			✓
Meals	Expense	Generally 50% deductible		✓	
GAAP Expense Items That Are Not Tax Deductions					
Life insurance expense (corporation)	Expense	Not deductible		✓	
Penalties	Expense	Not deductible		✓	
Entertainment	Expense	Not deductible		✓	
Lobbying/political expense	Expense	Not deductible		✓	
Federal income taxes	Expense	Not deductible		✓	
Special Items					
Net capital gain (NCG)	Income	Income			✓
Net capital loss (NCL)	Report as loss	Not deductible	✓		
Carryback/carryover (3 years back/5 years forward)	Not applicable	Offset NCGs in other years	✓		
Related shareholder	Report as a loss	Not deductible		✓	
Net operating loss	Report as a loss	Carryover indefinitely	✓		
Research and development	Expense	Expense/amortize/capitalize	✓	✓	✓

MODULE 3 C Corporation Tax Computations and Credits

REG 3

1 Taxation of a C Corporation

1.1 Filing Requirements

A C corporation is required to file a U.S. Corporation Income Tax Return, Form 1120, by the 15th day of the fourth month after the close of its tax year (for a December 31 corporation, the return is due by April 15). For C corporations with fiscal years ending on June 30, the tax return is due by the 15th day of the third month after the close of the tax year (changing to the 15th day of the fourth month for tax years beginning after December 31, 2025).

1.1.1 Legal Holiday or Weekend

When the due date falls on a legal holiday or weekend, the tax return is due on the next business day.

1.1.2 Extension (Form 7004)

An extension of six months is available by filing Form 7004. C corporations with a June 30 year-end have a seven-month extension.

1.2 Estimated Payments of Corporate Tax

Corporations are required to pay estimated taxes on the 15th day of the fourth, sixth, ninth, and 12th months of their tax year. One-fourth of the estimated tax is due with each payment. Unequal quarterly payments may be made using the annualized income method. An underpayment penalty will be assessed if these payments are not made on a timely basis and the amount owed on the return is $500 or more.

1.2.1 Corporations Other Than Large Corporations

Corporations not classified as large corporations are required to pay the lesser of:

- 100 percent of the tax shown on the return for the current year; or
- 100 percent of the tax shown on the return for the preceding year.

Note: This alternative cannot be used if the corporation owed no tax for the preceding year or the preceding tax year was less than 12 months.

1.2.2 Large Corporations

A large corporation (a corporation for which taxable income was $1 million or more in any of its three preceding tax years) must pay 100 percent of the tax as shown on the current year return.

1.3 Flat Tax Rate and Taxable Income

The taxable income of a corporation is arrived at by taking gross income (basically the same items that would be included in an individual's gross income) and deducting the same business expenses that an individual would deduct. A corporation's taxable income is subject to a flat tax of 21 percent. Personal service corporations are also subject to a flat tax of 21 percent.

1.4 Tax Credits

1.4.1 General Business Credit

- **Included Credits**

  The general business credit consists of a combination of any of the following:
  - Investment credit
  - Work opportunity tax credit
  - Alternative fuels credit
  - Research and development tax credit (generally 20 percent of the increase in qualified research expenditures over the base amount for the year)
  - Low-income housing credit
  - Small employer pension plan start-up costs credit
  - Other infrequent credits

- **Limitation**

  The credit may not exceed "net income tax" (regular tax less nonrefundable tax credits) less 25 percent of net regular tax liability above $25,000.

- **Unused Credit Carryover**

  Although some limits must be applied separately, unused credits may generally be carried back one year and forward 20 years.

1.4.2 Research and Development Tax Credit (Part of General Business Credit)

- The research and development (R&D) tax credit is designed to stimulate research and development activity of U.S. companies by reducing their after-tax cost.
- The credit is generally calculated as 20 percent of the increase in qualified research expenditures over a defined base amount.
- The research tax credit can also be calculated using the alternative simplified credit.
- The R&D tax credit is first computed separately and then is subject to the limitations of the general business credit because it is a component of the general business credit.
- "Qualified small businesses," defined as businesses with less than $5 million in annual gross receipts and having gross receipts for no more than five years, are able to use the R&D tax credit to offset the FICA employer portion of payroll tax. The amount of credit that can be used to offset payroll tax is capped at $250,000 for each eligible year.

1.4.3 Foreign Tax Credit

- Domestic corporations that have paid or accrued qualified foreign income taxes to a foreign country or U.S. possession may generally credit those taxes against their U.S. income tax liability on foreign source income.

- A corporation may choose annually to take either a credit or a deduction for eligible foreign taxes paid or accrued. Generally, if a corporation elects the benefits of the foreign tax credit for any tax year, no portion of the foreign taxes will be allowed as a deduction in that year or any subsequent tax year.

- The goal of the foreign tax credit is to keep a U.S. taxpayer's worldwide effective tax rate from exceeding the U.S. statutory tax rate, which is accomplished through the foreign tax credit limitation.

- The foreign tax credit is calculated as follows:
  - **Step 1:** Determine the qualified foreign income taxes paid or accrued for the tax year. To be eligible for the credit, the foreign levy must predominantly have the nature of an income tax in the U.S. sense (taxes on wages, interest, dividends, and royalties generally qualify). The foreign levy must also meet the jurisdictional nexus ("attribution") requirement, meaning that it generally is only allowed as a credit if it is attributable to the foreign jurisdiction that imposes the tax.
  - **Step 2:** Compute the foreign tax credit limitation. This is done by multiplying the amount of pre-credit U.S. tax paid in a year by the ratio of foreign source taxable income earned to income earned from both foreign and domestic sources (worldwide taxable income).
  - **Step 3:** Determine the lesser of qualified foreign taxes paid (step 1) or the foreign tax credit limitation (step 2).

- Any unused foreign tax credits can be carried back for one year and then carried forward for 10 years.

Example 1   Foreign Tax Credit

Facts: Rowe Co., a domestic corporation, has $20 million of worldwide taxable income, including $5 million of income from foreign sources. Rowe Co. paid $2.5 million of qualified foreign taxes during the year. Assume that the U.S. corporate income tax rate is 21 percent.

Required: Determine the amount of foreign tax credit for Rowe Co.

Solution:

Step 1 (Qualified foreign taxes): $2.5 million

Step 2 (Foreign tax credit limitation): U.S. tax liability is $20 million × 21% = $4.2 million
   Ratio of foreign source/total taxable income is $5 million / $20 million = 25%
   Foreign tax credit limitation is $4.2 million × 25% = $1,050,000

Step 3 (Lesser of steps 1 and 2): $1,050,000

Rowe Co. can carry its excess unused credits ($2.5 million − $1,050,000 = $1,450,000) back one year and forward 10 years.

1.5 Accumulated Earnings Tax

- The accumulated earnings tax is a penalty tax imposed on regular C corporations whose accumulated (retained) earnings are in excess of $250,000 if the earnings are considered to be improperly retained instead of being distributed as dividends to (high tax bracket) shareholders. The accumulated earnings tax is only paid when the IRS assesses the tax because, during an audit, it concluded that insufficient dividends were paid out compared with the amount of earnings accumulated by the corporation.
  - Regular C corporations are entitled to $250,000 of (lifetime) accumulated earnings.
  - Personal service corporations are entitled to only $150,000 of (lifetime) accumulated earnings.
  - The accumulated earnings tax is not imposed on personal holding companies (PHCs), tax-exempt corporations, or passive foreign investment corporations.
- The additional accumulated earnings tax rate is a flat 20 percent.
- To avoid accumulation of earnings being considered unreasonable by the IRS, there must be:
  - a demonstrated specific, definite, and feasible plan for the use of accumulated earnings (reasonable needs); or
  - a need to redeem the corporate stock included in a deceased stockholder's gross estate.
- Just because the stock is widely held does not exempt it from the accumulated earnings tax. The accumulated earnings tax is not self-assessed by the corporation; it is IRS-assessed as a result of an IRS audit of the corporation.
- A dividend paid by the due date of the tax return or hypothetical "consent" dividends may reduce or eliminate the tax.
- Calculation:

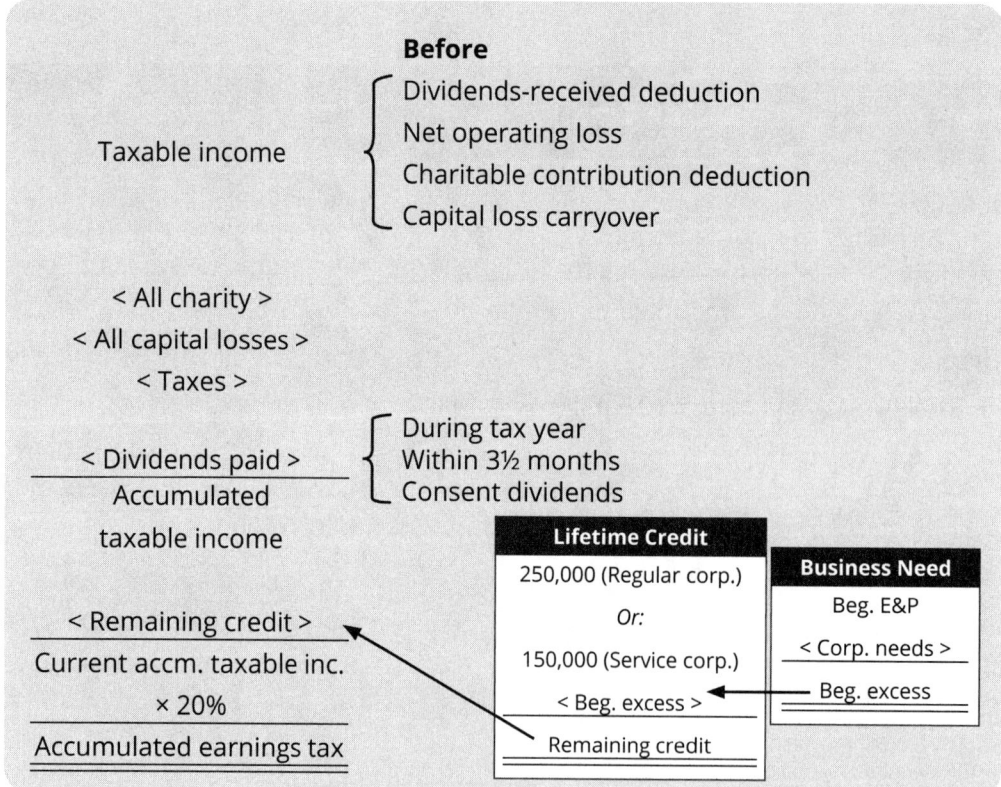

1.6 Personal Holding Company Tax

Personal holding companies (PHCs) are really corporations set up by high tax bracket taxpayers to channel their investment income into a corporation and shelter that income through the lower regular tax rate (21 percent) of the corporation, instead of paying their higher individual tax rates on that income.

- **Definition of Personal Holding Company:** The tax law criteria define personal holding companies as corporations more than 50 percent owned by five or fewer individuals (either directly or indirectly at any time during the last half of the tax year) and having 60 percent of adjusted ordinary gross income consisting of:
  - **Net** rent (if less than 50 percent of ordinary gross income);
  - **Interest** that is taxable (nontaxable is excluded);
  - **Royalties** (but not mineral, oil, gas, or copyright royalties); or
  - **Dividends** from an unrelated domestic corporation.

- **Additional Tax Assessed:** Corporations deemed to be personal holding companies are taxed an additional 20 percent on personal holding company net income not distributed.
  - Taxable income must be reduced by federal income taxes and net long-term capital gain (net of tax) to determine the undistributed personal holding company income prior to the dividend paid deduction.
  - There is no penalty if net income is distributed (i.e., in the form of actual dividends or consent dividends).
  - PHCs are not subject to the accumulated earnings tax.

- **Self-Assessed Tax:** The tax is self-assessed by filing a separate Schedule 1120 PH along with Form 1120.

NOTES

MODULE 4
Calculating Loss Limitations for C Corporations

REG 3

1 Net Operating Losses

C corporations are entitled to the same net operating loss (NOL) rules as individuals. NOLs that arise in tax years beginning after December 31, 2017, and before January 1, 2021, can be carried back five years and carried forward indefinitely. An NOL is carried back to the oldest year in the carryback period first. A taxpayer can elect not to carry back and just carry forward. NOLs arising in 2021 and beyond cannot be carried back but can be carried forward indefinitely.

NOL carryforwards from pre-2018 tax years can offset 100 percent of a future year's taxable income. NOL carryforwards from post-2017 tax years can offset 100 percent of taxable income in 2018, 2019, and 2020. Starting in 2021, any NOL carryforwards from post-2017 tax years can only offset 80 percent of the future year's taxable income after deducting any pre-2018 NOL carryforwards.

The following additional points should be noted when calculating the corporate NOL:

1. No charitable contribution deduction is allowed in calculating the NOL.
2. The taxable income limitation normally imposed on the dividends-received deduction does not apply if, after taking into account the full dividends-received deduction, the corporation has an NOL for the year.
3. The NOL deduction for an NOL carryover from another year is not allowed in determining a current year NOL.
4. A corporation may deduct a capital loss carryover from a current year capital gain in calculating an NOL, yet it cannot deduct a capital loss carryback against a net capital gain in determining a current year NOL.

Pass Key

	Offset Other Income	Carryback	Carryforward
Net operating loss (for tax years ending on or before December 31, 2017)	N/A	2	20
Net operating loss (for tax years ending after December 31, 2017, and on or before December 31, 2020)	N/A	5	Indefinitely*
Net operating loss (for tax years ending after December 31, 2020)	N/A	0	Indefinitely*
Corporate net capital loss	-0-	3	5
Individual net capital loss	$3,000 maximum	0	Indefinitely

*NOLs that are being carried forward can offset 100 percent of taxable income in 2018–2020, and 80 percent of taxable income for 2021 and later.

Calculating Loss Limitations for C Corporations

Example 1 — Net Operating Losses

Facts: Reichel Corp. is a calendar year C corporation that began doing business in 2021. The company incurred a net operating loss of $100,000 in 2021. Reichel Corp.'s taxable income was $90,000 in 2022 and $50,000 in 2023.

Required: Calculate Reichel Corp.'s taxable income in 2022 and 2023 after utilizing the available NOL.

Solution:

	2022	2023
Taxable income before NOL	$90,000	$50,000
NOL utilized in current year	(72,000)*	(28,000)
Taxable income after NOL	$18,000	$22,000

*NOLs that are being carried forward from 2018 and later can only offset up to 80 percent of taxable income. The deduction of the $100,000 NOL from 2021 carried forward to 2022 is limited to 80 percent of Reichel Corp.'s taxable income ($90,000 × 80% = $72,000). If the NOL had originated prior to 2018, the 80 percent limitation would not apply.

Reichel Corp.'s taxable income in 2022 after available NOL utilization is $18,000. Because the remaining $28,000 NOL ($100,000 NOL from 2021 less the $72,000 NOL carryforward utilized in 2022) does not exceed the 80 percent limitation in 2023 ($50,000 × 80% = $40,000), Reichel Corp. may use the full amount of the remaining NOL to reduce taxable income in 2023 to $22,000.

2 Capital Losses

The $3,000 deduction for net capital losses available to individuals is not allowed to corporations. Thus, a corporation can only use capital losses to offset capital gains.

- **Capital Loss Carryover:** Net capital losses are carried back three years and forward five years. They are carried over as short-term capital losses and are applied only against capital gains.

Example 2 — Capital Loss Carryover With NOL

Facts: Lane Corp. has gross income of $400,000 (including a $150,000 capital gain) and operating expenses of $500,000. Lane Corp. has an unexpired capital loss carryover of $20,000.

Required: Determine Lane Corp.'s NOL.

Solution: Lane Corp. is able to offset its capital gain of $150,000 by the capital loss carryover of $20,000. Gross income after deducting the capital loss carryover will now be $380,000. The current year NOL is calculated as $380,000 of gross income less operating expenses of $500,000, which is ($120,000). Effectively, the capital loss carryover increased the current year NOL.

MODULE 5: S Corporation Overview

1 Overview

When a corporation is formed, it is by default taxed as a C corporation. Small, closely held corporations, if eligible, may elect to be taxed as an S corporation, a flow-through entity taxed in a manner similar to partnerships. In effect, all the income, gains, losses, and deductions of the corporation are passed (or flowed) through to the shareholders. The individual owners are taxed on their proportionate share of the S corporation earnings regardless of whether the earnings are distributed to them.

2 Eligibility

To qualify as an S corporation, the following requirements must be met:

1. **Qualified Corporation**

    The corporation must be a domestic corporation. An S corporation may own any interest in a C corporation (even 100 percent), but the S corporation may not file a consolidated tax return with the C corporation. An S corporation may also create a qualified S subsidiary in which the S corporation owns 100 percent of the stock; the two S corporations would file as one entity for tax purposes.

2. **Eligible Shareholders**
    - Eligible shareholders must be individuals, estates, or certain types of trusts.
    - An individual shareholder may not be a nonresident alien.
    - Qualified retirement plans and 501(c)(3) charitable organizations may be shareholders.
    - Neither corporations nor partnerships are eligible shareholders.

3. **Shareholder Limit**

    There may be no more than 100 shareholders. Family members may elect to be treated as one shareholder. Family members include common ancestors, lineal descendants of common ancestors, and their current or former spouses.

4. **One Class of Stock**

    There may be no more than one class of stock outstanding. However, differences in common stock voting rights are allowed. Preferred stock is not permitted.

3 Electing S Corporation Status

3.1 When Election Takes Effect

All shareholders (voting and nonvoting) must consent to a valid election on Form 2553, which the company files with the IRS. If the election is filed by the 15th day of third month, it is effective as of the first day of the tax year. For a calendar year corporation, an S election filed by March 15 is effective on January 1 of that year. If the election is filed after March 15, it is effective on January 1 of the following year.

3.2 New Shareholders

After the election is in effect, the consent of a new shareholder is not required. The S corporation status continues until there is a voluntary or involuntary termination.

3.3 S Corporation Tax Year

S corporations file Form 1120S and must adopt the calendar year, unless a valid business purpose for a different taxable year (fiscal year) is established. The return is due by the 15th day of the third month (March 15) after the close of the tax year.

4 Termination of S Election

4.1 Terminating Event

S corporation status will terminate as a result of any of the following:

- Shareholders holding more than 50 percent of the stock (voting and nonvoting) consent to a voluntary revocation.
- The corporation fails to meet any of the qualifications for S status.
- Excess passive investment income: More than 25 percent of the corporation's gross receipts are from passive investment income for three consecutive years (but only if the corporation has prior C corporation E&P).

> **Example 1 — S Corporation Termination**
>
> **Facts:** Small Corporation is a calendar year S corporation, which has maintained a valid S election since the corporation was formed 10 years ago. On February 1 of the current year, Small admits Large Corporation, a C corporation, as a 40 percent shareholder.
>
> **Required:** Determine the impact of Small Corporation's admittance of Large as a shareholder on the S election.
>
> **Solution:** Because Large Corporation is a C corporation, Small would no longer meet the requirements of an S corporation, and its S election would be terminated on February 1, the date Large Corporation is admitted as a shareholder.

4.2 Reelecting S Status

Once an S corporation election has been terminated, the corporation must wait until the beginning of the fifth year after the year of termination before it can elect S corporation status again.

5 S Corporation Income or Loss

5.1 Pass-Through of Income and/or Losses (to Shareholder/K-1)

5.1.1 Overview

Like partnerships, S corporations flow through ordinary business income or loss and separately stated items of income, gain, loss, and deductions to the shareholders. Allocations to shareholders are made on a per-share, per-day basis.

Unlike partnerships, an S corporation shareholder's share of ordinary business income is not subject to self-employment tax, even if the shareholder is actively involved in the operations of the business.

5.1.2 Separately Stated Items

The following S corporation items flow through separately to the shareholder in a manner similar to a partnership (see Schedule K-1 for a complete list):

- Rental real estate income or loss
- Interest income
- Dividend income
- Royalties
- Net short-term capital gain or loss
- Net long-term capital gain or loss
- Net Section 1231 gain or loss
- Charitable contributions
- Section 179 expense deduction

Separately stated items are income and expense items that are:

- subject to special limitations and calculations;
- reported on different tax forms; or
- taxed at different rates.

In general, all other income and expense items would be included as ordinary income or loss. For example, Section 1231 gains are reported on Form 4797, subject to special rules regarding netting and potentially subject to special tax rates.

5.1.3 Section 199A Qualified Business Income (QBI) Deduction

A shareholder may be able to take a below-the-line deduction of 20 percent of qualified business income may be available on ordinary business income flowed-through from an S corporation.

5.2 Fringe Benefits

5.2.1 Deductible Fringe Benefits

Fringe benefits for non-shareholder employees and those employee shareholders owning 2 percent or less of the S corporation are deductible by the S corporation in calculating ordinary business income.

5.2.2 Nondeductible Fringe Benefits

The cost of fringe benefits for shareholders owning over 2 percent is not deductible by the S corporation, unless the corporation includes the benefits in the employee/shareholder's W-2 income.

Example 2   Ordinary Business Income and Separately Stated Items

Facts: Gray Corporation, an S corporation, had the following items of income and deduction for Year 1:

Gross income	$150,000
Cost of goods sold	70,000
Interest income	10,000
Section 1231 gain	5,000
Salary expense	40,000
Depreciation expense (MACRS)	10,000
Charitable contributions	5,000

Required: Calculate Gray Corporation's ordinary business income and separately stated items for Year 1.

Solution: Ordinary business income: $30,000 (gross income of $150,000 less COGS of $70,000, salaries of $40,000, and MACRS depreciation of $10,000)

Separately stated items:

Interest income	$10,000
Section 1231 gain	5,000
Charitable contributions	5,000

Pass Key

Similar to a partnership, shareholders in an S corporation must include on their individual income tax return their distributive share of each separate "pass-through" item.

Shareholders are taxed on these items, regardless of whether or not the items have been distributed (withdrawn) to them during the year.

Illustration 1   Automated Diagnostic and Validation Check: S Corporation

Mary, a CPA, is preparing the Year 2 Form 1120S federal income tax return for her client, Acme Company, a calendar-year corporation. Acme was incorporated on January 1, Year 1, and filed a regular C corporation Form 1120 in Year 1. Acme filed a valid S election effective January 1, Year 2.

Mary received the following messages in a tax preparation software diagnostic report when she was preparing Acme Company's tax return:

Form 1120S, page 1, line 4: net gain (loss) from Form 4797	Box 42

A $15,000 gain was manually entered for line 4 on page 1 of the Form 1120S and included in ordinary business income. The $15,000 amount entered was the total gain on Form 4797, line 9, total long-term gain on the sale of business-use property, not line 17, which is the total ordinary gain (loss) from the sale of business-use property. The software included the $15,000 gain from line 9 of the Form 4797 as a long-term capital gain on Schedule D and a net long-term capital gain on Schedule K, line 8a.

Form 1120S, page 1, line 14: depreciation	Box 54

An amount was entered to manually override the depreciation deducted in calculating ordinary business income on page 1, line 14, of the Form 1120S. The $20,000 amount entered is the total depreciation on Form 4562, which includes both Section 179 deduction and MACRS depreciation.

Schedule K, line 11: Section 179 deduction	Box 77

A code was entered to leave Schedule K, line 11, blank on the return. Form 4562 includes $8,000 of Section 179 deduction.

Form 1120S, page 1, line 18: employee benefit programs	Box 84

Box 84, health insurance benefits for shareholder-employees, was not completed. Please check the box to confirm that the amount entered for employee benefit programs only includes amounts paid for health insurance coverage for employees owning 2 percent or less of the corporation's stock.

(continued)

(continued)

Action Needed:

Mary needs to remove the $15,000 manually entered for line 4 on page 1 of Form 1120S. Form 1120S, page 1 is the calculation of ordinary business income or loss for the S corporation. Form 4797 reports the sales of business-use property. The $15,000 gain was the total long-term capital gain on Form 4797, which was appropriately mapped to Schedule K as a separately stated item. Line 4 on page 1 only includes ordinary gain or loss from line 17 of the Form 4797 in the calculation of ordinary business income.

Mary needs to remove the manual overrides for depreciation and Section 179 deduction, or change the amounts to $12,000 for page 1, line 14 (MACRS depreciation), and $8,000 for Schedule K, line 11 (Section 179 deduction). MACRS depreciation is a deduction in calculating ordinary business income. Section 179 deduction is a separately stated item because the total annual amount each taxpayer can deduct is limited. A taxpayer's Section 179 deduction for the year is limited to the lesser of the allowance amount for the year ($1,160,000 for 2023) or the taxpayer's taxable income (before the deduction). The allowance amount is reduced dollar-for-dollar by the amount of total qualifying property placed in service during the year by the taxpayer that exceeds $2,890,000 (2023).

Mary needs to confirm that the health insurance premiums included in the amount on page 1, line 18, employee benefit programs, are for employees owning 2 percent or less of the corporation's stock. Fringe benefits for employees owning 2 percent or less of the corporation's stock are deductible by the S corporation in calculating ordinary business income. The cost of fringe benefits for shareholders owning over 2 percent is not deductible by the S corporation, unless the corporation includes the benefits in the employee/shareholder's W-2 income.

6 S Corporation Shareholder Stock Basis and Debt Basis

The calculation of a shareholder's basis in S corporation stock is generally the same as partnerships:

```
    Initial stock basis (contributions)
+   Additional contributions
+   Income items (ordinary business income, separately
    stated income/gain items, and tax-exempt income)
−   Distributions to shareholders
−   Nondeductible expenses
−   Loss/deduction items (ordinary business loss, separately
    stated loss/deduction items)
=   Ending basis in S corporation stock
```

Unlike partnerships, S corporation shareholders do not include any S corporation debt in their stock basis. However, an S corporation shareholder does have separate debt basis in loans from the shareholder to the S corporation. When the S corporation repays part or all of the loan, the shareholder's basis in the debt is reduced accordingly.

Stock basis and debt basis cannot be reduced below zero. This affects both the pass-through of S corporation losses/deductions and the tax treatment of distributions to shareholders.

Example 3 — S Corporation Shareholder Stock and Debt Basis

Facts: Jane Gray is a 50 percent shareholder of an S corporation, Gray Corp. Jane's initial tax basis in her Gray Corp. stock in Year 1 was $25,000. Jane also loaned Gray Corp. $20,000 from her personal funds at the beginning of Year 1, and the corporation repaid $2,000 in Year 1. Jane also received a $10,000 cash distribution from Gray Corp. in Year 1.

Gray Corp.'s Year 1 ordinary business income and separately stated items are:

- Ordinary business income: $30,000
- Interest income: $10,000
- Section 1231 gain: $5,000
- Charitable contributions: $5,000

Required: Calculate the amount of Jane's Year 1 ending stock basis and debt basis.

Solution: Year 1 ending basis: Stock $35,000 and debt basis $18,000.

Step 1: Calculate Jane's share of the ordinary business income and separately stated items:

- Ordinary business income: $30,000 × 50% = $15,000
- Interest income: $10,000 × 50% = $5,000
- Section 1231 gain: $5,000 × 50% = $2,500
- Charitable contributions: $5,000 × 50% = $2,500

Step 2: Calculate Jane's stock basis:

Initial stock basis	$25,000
Ordinary business income	15,000
Separately stated interest income	5,000
Separately stated Section 1231 gain	2,500
Cash distributions	(10,000)
Separately stated charitable contributions	(2,500)
Year 1 ending stock basis	$35,000

Step 3: Calculate Jane's debt basis:

Year 1 beginning debt basis (loan from shareholder)	$20,000
Year 1 principal payments by S corporation	(2,000)
Year 1 ending debt basis in loan from shareholder	$18,000

6.1 Tax Basis Limitation

A loss can only be flowed through to an S corporation shareholder's individual income tax return to the extent of the shareholder's tax basis. This includes the shareholder's stock basis and basis in any direct loans from the shareholder to the S corporation.

A loss in excess of the shareholder's tax basis is suspended until tax basis is reinstated in future years. Tax basis can be reinstated by any of the items that increase stock basis: income, gains, and additional contributions. Any increases in future years reinstate the debt basis first, then stock basis.

A suspended loss due to insufficient tax basis can be carried forward indefinitely. However, any suspended losses due to insufficient tax basis remaining when the shareholder disposes of his or her S corporation stock are lost.

Pass Key

An S corporation shareholder is permitted to pass through for deduction on the shareholder's individual income tax return the pro rata share of the S corporation loss subject to the following limitation:

Stock basis (reduced by any distributions) + Debt basis (direct shareholder loans to S corporation)

Example 4 — S Corporation Shareholder Tax Basis Limitation

Facts: Jane Gray is a 50 percent shareholder of an S corporation, Gray Corp. Jane's beginning Year 2 tax basis in her Gray Corp. stock was $35,000. Jane also has debt basis in her direct loan to Gray Corp. of $18,000.

Gray Corp. incurred an ordinary business loss in Year 2 of $120,000. Gray Corp. had ordinary business income in Year 3 of $60,000. There were no separately stated items in Year 2 or Year 3. Gray Corp. did not pay any distributions to shareholders or make any additional payments on the loan in Year 2 or Year 3.

Required: Calculate the amount of ordinary income or loss that flows through to Jane's individual income tax return in Year 2 and Year 3, as well as Jane's Year 2 and Year 3 ending stock basis and debt basis.

(continued)

(continued)

Solution:

Year 2 flow-through of income/loss:

Jane can flow through $53,000 ($35,000 stock basis + $18,000 debt basis) of the ordinary business loss in Year 2, and her Year 2 ending stock basis and debt basis are reduced to zero. There will be a suspended Year 2 loss of $7,000.

Jane's share of Year 2 ordinary business loss: ($120,000 × 50%)	$60,000
Flow-through of loss to the extent of stock basis	(35,000)*
Flow-through of loss to the extent of debt basis	(18,000)**
Remaining loss suspended until basis is reinstated	$ 7,000

*Year 2 ending stock basis is now $0
**Year 2 ending debt basis is now $0

Year 3 flow-through of income/loss:

The $7,000 suspended loss from Year 2 can now be flowed through to her individual income tax return along with the Year 3 ordinary business income.

Jane's share of Year 3 ordinary business income: ($60,000 × 50%)	$30,000
Year 2 suspended loss	(7,000)
Flow-through of income	$23,000

Year 3 ending debt basis in loan from shareholder:

The $30,000 Year 3 ordinary business income reinstates (increases) her debt basis first, then increases stock basis.

Year 2 ending debt basis in loan from shareholder	$ 0
Year 3 ordinary business income (reinstate debt basis first)	18,000
Year 3 ending debt basis in loan from shareholder	$18,000

Year 3 ending stock basis:

Year 2 ending stock basis	$ 0
Jane's share of Year 3 ordinary business income ($60,000 × 50%)	$30,000
Amount used to reinstate debt basis	(18,000)
Amount remaining	12,000
Less: Year 2 suspended loss	(7,000)
Year 3 ending stock basis	$ 5,000

7 Accumulated Adjustments Account (AAA)

The accumulated adjustments account (AAA) is the accumulated earnings and profits during the years the corporation is an S corporation. Distributions may not reduce AAA below zero. However, AAA may be negative due to S corporation losses and deductions.

7.1 Increases to AAA

- Ordinary business income
- Separately stated income and gain items (other than tax-exempt income)

7.2 Decreases to AAA

- Ordinary business losses
- Separately stated losses and deductions
- Nondeductible expenses (other than expenses related to tax-exempt income)
- Distributions (may not reduce AAA below zero)

Example 5   S Corporation Accumulated Adjustments Account (AAA)

Facts: Gray Corp., an S corporation, had the following ordinary business income and separately stated items for Year 1:

- Ordinary business income: $30,000
- Interest income: $10,000
- Section 1231 gain: $5,000
- Charitable contributions: $4,000

Gray Corp. made $21,000 of cash distributions to shareholders in Year 1.

Gray Corp. incurred an ordinary business loss of $120,000 in Year 2, and ordinary business income of $60,000 in Year 3. There were no separately stated items or distributions in Years 2 and 3.

Required: Calculate Gray Corp.'s ending accumulated adjustments account (AAA) balance at the end of Year 3.

(continued)

(continued)

Solution: The Year 3 ending AAA balance is $(40,000).

Year 1 ordinary business income	$ 30,000
Separately stated interest income	10,000
Separately stated Section 1231 gain	5,000
Separately stated charitable contributions	(4,000)
Cash distributions	(21,000)
Year 1 ending AAA balance	20,000
Year 2 ordinary business loss	(120,000)
Year 2 ending AAA balance	(100,000)
Year 3 ordinary business income	60,000
Year 3 ending AAA balance	$(40,000)

NOTES

MODULE 6: Partnership Overview

REG 3

1 Overview

A partnership is a flow-through entity, which means that the income is taxed only once when it "flows through" to the partner. The individual partners, not the partnership, pay tax on the partnership income. Unincorporated business entities such as general partnerships, limited partnerships, and limited liability companies (LLCs) are generally treated as partnerships under the Subchapter K rules of the Internal Revenue Code.

2 Partnership Income or Loss

2.1 Partnership Tax Return

A partnership is not subject to income taxes, but it still must file a partnership tax return (Form 1065). A Form 1065 is an informational return (including Schedules K and K-1) that provides detailed information about partnership income and expenses and indicates the amount and type of each partner's distributive share of ordinary business income (loss) and separately stated income, gain, loss, and deduction items. Each partner is liable only for taxes due on his distributive share of partnership income, as reported on Schedule K-1, regardless of whether the distribution is actually made to the partner.

2.2 Pass-Through of Income or Loss (to Partner/K-1)

A partner must include on an individual income tax return the partner's distributive share of ordinary business income or loss and each separately stated item of income, gain, loss, and deduction. The following chart shows which partnership items will be reported separately on Form 1065 and which will pass through to each individual partner's income tax return as separately stated items to be treated by each individual partner according to his or her own circumstances.

Partnership Overview

		Appears On		
		1065	K	K-1
	Business income	✓		
	< Business expenses >	✓		
	< Guaranteed Payments >			
1.	Ordinary business income or loss	✓	✓	✓
2.	Guaranteed payments to partners	✓	✓	✓
3.	Net rental real estate income or loss		✓	✓
4.	Interest income		✓	✓
5.	Dividend income		✓	✓
6.	Capital gains and losses		✓	✓
7.	Net Section 1231 gain (loss)		✓	✓
8.	Charitable contributions		✓	✓
9.	Section 179 expense deduction		✓	✓
10.	Investment interest expense		✓	✓
11.	Partners' health insurance premiums (included as part of guaranteed payments)	✓	✓	✓
12.	Retirement plan contributions for employees	✓		
13.	Retirement plan contributions for partners		✓	✓
14.	Tax credits (reported by partnership but claimed by partners)		✓	✓

2.3 Guaranteed Payments

Guaranteed payments are reasonable compensation paid to a partner for services provided or use of capital without regard to the partner's profit- or loss-sharing ratio. They are allowable tax deductions to the partnership and taxable income to the partner.

2.3.1 Tax Treatment of Guaranteed Payments

- **Partnership Tax Deduction:** Guaranteed payments are allowable tax deductions to the partnership for services (guaranteed salary) or for the use of capital (guaranteed interest) without regard to partnership income or profit- and loss-sharing ratios (this includes the fair market value of capital partnership interests issued in exchange for services contributed).

- **Partner Taxable Income:** Guaranteed payments are also included on Schedule K-1, to be included as ordinary income to the partner (they may also be included as part of net earnings from self-employment). Guaranteed payments for services are not included in qualified business income (QBI) for purposes of the Section 199A QBI deduction for flow-through business entities.

Example 1 — Ordinary Income Calculation and Other Separately Stated Items

Facts: Acme partnership had the following items of income and deductions for the year:

Gross business income	$250,000
Dividend income	8,000
Salary expense	50,000
Guaranteed payments to partners	35,000
Rent expense	15,000
Depreciation expense (MACRS)	10,000
Section 179 deduction	30,000
Charitable contributions	20,000

Required: Determine the partnership's ordinary business income or loss and separately stated items for the year.

Solution: Ordinary business income for the year is $140,000, calculated as follows:

Gross business income	$250,000
Salary expense	(50,000)
Guaranteed payments to partners	35,000
Rent expense	(15,000)
Depreciation expense (MACRS)	(10,000)
Ordinary business income	$140,000

The separately stated items reported on Schedule K are:

Dividend income	$ 8,000
Section 179 deduction	(30,000)
Charitable contributions	(20,000)
Guaranteed payments to partners	(35,000)

2.4 Organizational Expenditures and Start-up Costs

2.4.1 Calculation

The partnership may elect to deduct up to $5,000 each of organizational expenditures and start-up costs. Each $5,000 amount is reduced by the amount by which the organizational expenditures or start-up costs exceed $50,000, respectively. Any excess organizational expenditures or start-up costs are amortized over 180 months (beginning with the month in which the active trade or business begins).

2.4.2 Costs Included

Allowable organizational expenditures include fees paid for legal services in drafting the partnership agreement, fees paid for accounting services, and fees paid for partnership filings. Start-up costs include training costs, advertising costs, and testing costs incurred prior to the opening of the business.

2.4.3 Syndication Costs (Nondeductible)

Syndication costs (e.g., offering materials) are not deductible.

2.5 Section 199A Qualified Business Income (QBI) Deduction

A partner may be able to take a below-the-line deduction of 20 percent of qualified business income may be available on ordinary business income flowed through from a partnership or LLC.

Illustration 1   Automated Diagnostic and Validation Check: Partnership

Carlos, a CPA, is preparing the Year 2 Form 1065 federal income tax return for her client, Acme Partners, a calendar-year general partnership. The partnership has two equal partners who both actively participate in the operations of the business.

Carlos received the following messages in a tax preparation software diagnostic report when he was preparing Acme Partners' tax return:

Issue 1

Form 1065, page 1, line 7: other income (loss), box 32

Schedule K, line 2: net rental real estate income (loss), box 35

> An amount of $35,000 with a description "net rental real estate income (loss)" was entered in box 32 as other income on page 1 of the Form 1065 and included in the calculation of ordinary business income. No amount was entered in box 35, net rental real estate income (loss). Net rental real estate income (loss) should be entered in box 35 and included as a separately stated item on line 2 of Schedule K.

Carlos needs to move the $35,000 of net rental real estate income from box 32, page 1, other income (loss), to box 35, Schedule K, net rental real estate income (loss). Net rental real estate income (loss) is a separately stated item on Schedule K and is not included on page 1 in calculating ordinary business income (loss).

(continued)

(continued)

Issue 2

Form 1065, page 1, line 9: salaries and wages, box 44

Form 1065, page 1, line 10: guaranteed payments to partners, box 45

Schedule K, line 4a: payments for services

Partner A, Schedule K-1, line 4a: guaranteed payments for services, box 72

Partner B, Schedule K-1, line 4a: guaranteed payments for services, box 73

> An amount of $50,000 was entered in box 44, salaries and wages, and a $0 was entered in box 45, guaranteed payments to partners. No entry was made in boxes 72 and 73 for guaranteed payments for services for each partner. Please confirm that boxes 45, 72, and 73 should be zero.

Carlos needs to check that the $50,000 was employee wages, rather than guaranteed payments to partners. If the amount is actually guaranteed payments to partners, Carlos should move the $50,000 from box 44, salaries and wages, to box 45, guaranteed payments to partners, and enter the amounts for each partner in boxes 72 and 73. Salaries and wages, as well as guaranteed payments to partners, are deductions on page 1 in calculating ordinary business income (loss). However, guaranteed payments to partners are also a separately stated item on Schedule K and included on the recipient partner's Schedule K-1 to be included in the partner's taxable gross income.

Issue 3

Partner A: active participation in business operations, box 9

Partner B: active participation in business operations, box 10

Partner A, Schedule K-1, line 14: self-employment earnings (loss), box 88

Partner B, Schedule K-1, line 14: self-employment earnings (loss), box 89

> A code was entered to leave line 14 blank on both partners' Schedule K-1. Boxes 9 and 10 were checked for Partner A and Partner B indicating that both partners actively participate in the operations of the business. Please confirm both partners' active participation in the business, and that guaranteed payments to partners should be $0.

Carlos should remove the code entered to leave the net earnings from self-employment line on Schedule K blank. Both ordinary business income and guaranteed payments, if any, should be included in net earnings from self-employment. The facts provide that both partners actively participate in the operations of the business, so the boxes indicating that both partners are active were checked correctly. Because both partners are actively involved in the business, both partners' share of ordinary business income should be included in net earnings from self-employment. Any guaranteed payments to partners for services should also be included in net earnings from self-employment.

3 Partner's Tax Basis in Partnership Interest

A partner's basis in his or her partnership interest includes the partner's capital account plus the partner's share of partnership debt. A partner's share of partnership debt includes debt for which the partner has personal liability (recourse debt) and the partner's share of partnership debt secured by property (nonrecourse debt).

A partner's basis in his or her partnership interest is adjusted each year for the partner's share of the following items:

- Increase basis:
  - Additional contributions
  - Income and gain items
  - Increases in partnership debt
- Decrease basis:
  - Distributions
  - Loss and deduction items
  - Decreases in partnership debt

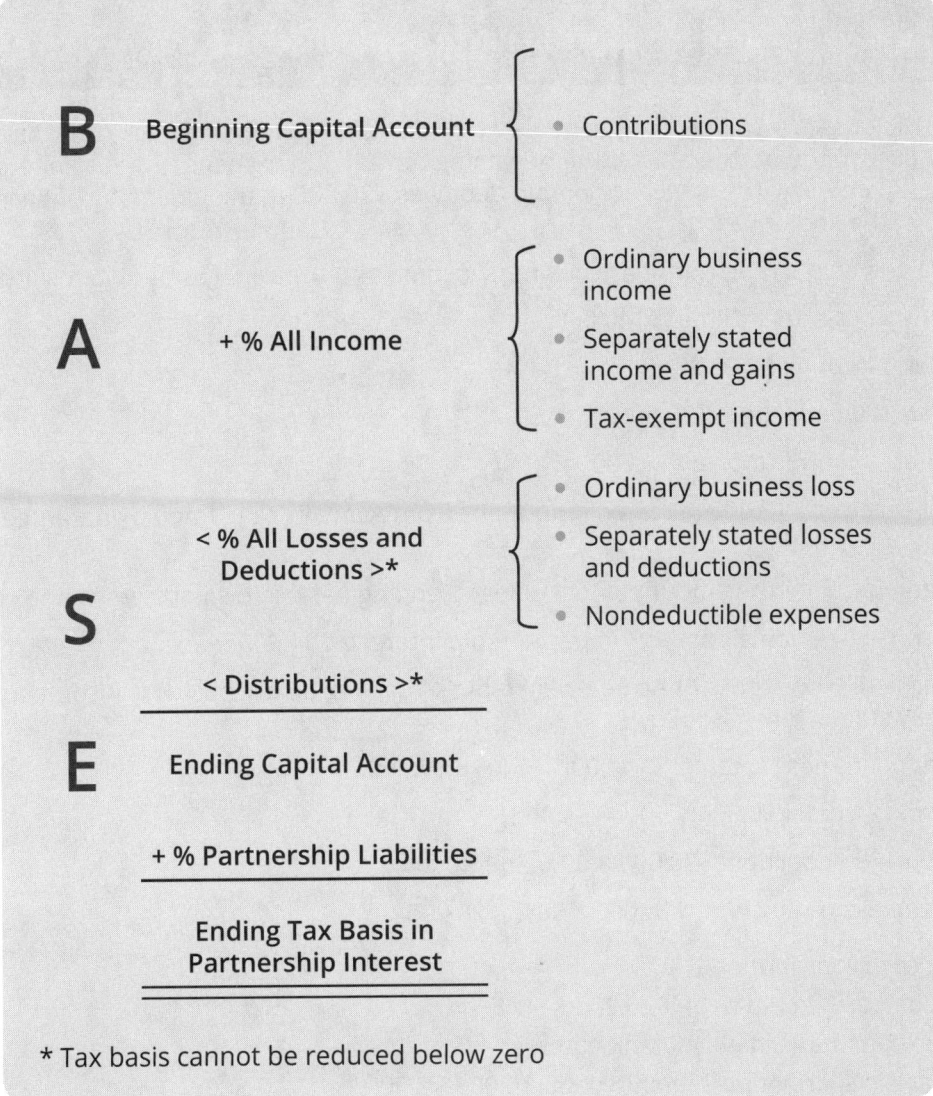

* Tax basis cannot be reduced below zero

Pass Key

It is important to remember the difference between capital account and basis in partnership interest:

Basis in partnership interest = Capital account + Partner's share of partnership liabilities

Example 2 — Partner's Basis in Partnership Interest

Facts: Rick Jones is a 50 percent partner in Acme General Partnership. Rick contributed $50,000 cash to the partnership at the beginning of Year 1 in exchange for his general partnership interest. The total partnership debt was $20,000 at the beginning of Year 1, and $25,000 at the end of Year 1.

Acme Partnership's Year 1 ordinary business income and separately stated items are:

- Ordinary business income: $140,000
- Dividend income: $8,000
- Section 179 deduction: $30,000
- Charitable contributions: $16,000

Rick also received $18,000 in cash distributions from Acme in Year 1 and a guaranteed payment of $15,000.

Required: Calculate the amount of Rick's Year 1 ending basis in his partnership interest.

Solution: Year 1 ending tax basis in partnership interest: $94,000

First, calculate Rick's share of Acme Partnership's Year 1 ordinary business income and separately stated items as follows:

- Ordinary business income: $140,000 × 50% = $70,000
- Dividend income: $8,000 × 50% = $4,000
- Section 179 deduction: $30,000 × 50% = $15,000
- Charitable contributions: $16,000 × 50% = $8,000

Initial cash contribution	$50,000
Share of partnership debt ($20,000 × 50%)	10,000
Initial Year 1 basis in partnership interest	60,000
Increase in share of partnership debt ($5,000* × 50%)	2,500
Ordinary business income	70,000
Separately stated dividend income	4,000
Cash distributions	(18,000)
Separately stated Section 179 deduction	(15,000)
Separately stated charitable contributions	(8,000)
Year 1 ending tax basis in partnership interest	$95,000

*Ending debt of $25,000 − beginning debt $20,000

Pass Key

A frequently tested concept on the CPA Examination is the timing of taxable income to a partner. An easy way to remember the timing of taxable income and basis impact is to associate the partnership interest to a *bank account*:

Event	Tax Consequence	Impact on Basis
Income	Taxable	Increase
Withdrawals	Nontaxable	Decrease

3.1 Tax Basis Limitation

A loss can only be flowed through to a partner's individual income tax return to the extent of the partner's tax basis in his or her partnership interest. A loss in excess of the partner's tax basis in his or her partnership interest is suspended until basis is reinstated in future years.

Basis can be reinstated by any of the items that increase a partner's basis in a partnership interest. This includes the partner's share of:

- Ordinary business income
- Separately stated income and gains
- Additional contributions
- Increase in partnership debt

A partner's share of partnership debt that is included in the partner's basis in his or her partnership interest depends on:

- the type of partner (general partner, limited partner, or LLC member); and
- the type of debt (nonrecourse, or secured; recourse; or personally guaranteed).

A suspended loss due to insufficient tax basis can be carried forward indefinitely. However, any suspended losses due to insufficient tax basis remaining when the partner disposes of his or her partnership interest are lost.

4 Tax Classification of Limited Liability Companies

A limited liability company (LLC) is a separate legal entity from its owners. As with corporate shareholders, LLC "members" are not personally liable for the obligations of the business. All members of an LLC have "limited liability," which is different from a limited partnership, where at least one general partner is personally liable for all partnership debts.

For federal income tax purposes, an LLC is treated as one of the following: a partnership, corporation, or sole proprietorship. The Internal Revenue Code does not specifically address taxation of limited liability companies.

- A limited liability company with at least two owners is taxed as a partnership unless an election is made to have the LLC taxed as a C corporation. Such an election is made on Form 8832, Entity Classification Election.

- A single member LLC is considered a disregarded entity for federal income tax purposes. It is treated as a sole proprietorship if the owner is an individual, and included in the corporation's taxable income if the owner is a C corporation.

NOTES

MODULE 7: Tax-Exempt Organization Overview

REG 3

1 Overview

Tax-exempt organizations are not-for-profit organizations that qualify for exemption from federal income tax. There are over 30 different types of tax-exempt organizations designated in Section 501(c) of the Internal Revenue Code, but by far the most common is Section 501(c)(3) organizations.

2 Section 501(c)(3) Organizations

2.1 Exempt Purpose

A tax-exempt Section 501(c)(3) organization must be organized and operated exclusively for one or more of the following purposes:

- Religious
- Charitable
- Scientific
- Testing for public safety
- Literary
- Educational
- Fostering national or international amateur sports competition (but only if none of its activities involve providing athletic facilities or equipment)
- Prevention of cruelty to children or animals

2.2 Contributions to Section 501(c)(3) Organizations

Unlike almost all other types of tax-exempt organizations, contributions made to Section 501(c)(3) organizations qualify as deductible charitable contributions to the donor.

2.3 Private Foundations and Public Charities

Section 501(c)(3) organizations are classified as either private foundations or public charities.

2.3.1 Private Foundations

A Section 501(c)(3) organization is classified as a private foundation unless it fits into one of the excluded categories provided under the Code. For a private foundation to be tax-exempt and for contributions made to the foundation to be tax-deductible charitable contributions, the foundation's governing instrument must include certain special provisions. These include a requirement that the foundation will distribute income each year as required under the tax law, and that the foundation will not engage in any act of self-dealing or retain any excess business holdings as defined in the tax law.

Private foundations typically receive funding from a single major source, such as a family or corporation, rather than funding from many sources. The primary activity of most private foundations is making grants to other charitable organizations and individuals, rather than directly operating charitable programs.

2.3.2 Public Charities

Section 501(c)(3) organizations that fall into one of the excluded categories under the Code are classified as public charities, rather than private foundations, and are not subject to the rules and restrictions that apply to private foundations. Public charities include:

- Churches, schools, colleges or universities, and hospitals or qualified medical research organizations that are publicly supported
- Other broadly based, publicly supported organizations with limited investment income and unrelated business income
- Not-for-profit organizations that support public charities
- Organizations that test products for public safety

To qualify as publicly supported, at least one-third of the organization's total support must come from governmental units and the general public.

3 Other Tax-Exempt Organizations

3.1 Other Section 501(c) Tax-Exempt Organizations

Some of the more common types of tax-exempt organizations other than Section 501(c)(3) organizations are as follows:

- Corporations organized under an act of Congress as an instrumentality of the United States, including federal credit unions
- Title-holding corporations organized for the sole purpose of holding title to property, collecting income from that property, and turning the income over to a tax-exempt organization
- Civic leagues and social welfare organizations (e.g., Kiwanis or Rotary Club, homeowners' association, volunteer fire department)
- Labor, agricultural, and horticultural organizations
- Business leagues (e.g., chamber of commerce, real estate board)
- Social and recreational clubs
- Beneficiary and domestic fraternal societies
- Mutual insurance companies
- Cemetery companies
- Veterans' organizations of past or present members of the U.S. Armed Forces

3.2 Political Organizations (Section 527)

Political organizations are entities that are organized and operated for the purpose of collecting contributions, or making expenditures, for an exempt function. The exempt function of a political organization is influencing or attempting to influence the selection, election, or appointment of an individual to a federal, state, or local public office or office in a political organization.

Income from contributions, membership dues, political fundraising events, and sale of campaign material is tax-exempt if it is set aside or spent for the exempt function purposes of the political organization.

3.3 Contributions

Although organizations other than Section 501(c)(3) organizations may qualify for exemption from federal income tax under the Internal Revenue Code, contributions to those tax-exempt organizations are generally not tax-deductible charitable contributions to the donors. However, there are a few exceptions, such as contributions to a U.S. instrumentality or volunteer fire department if they are made exclusively for public purposes.

NOTES

MODULE 8
State and Local Tax Issues

REG 3

1 State Income Tax Considerations

In addition to federal income tax, a company is also subject to tax in its state of residence, as well as in any state in which it has nexus.

1.1 Definition of Nexus

Nexus is defined as the minimum level of contact a taxpayer may have with a jurisdiction to be subject to its tax. This is typically caused by a company having property, payroll, or sales within a state, and is determined under the laws of each state, which may vary as to what particular activity will trigger nexus in the state. However, federal law offers some protection to companies where state taxation is concerned.

1.2 Federal Limitations on a State's Right to Impose Income Tax

- Under Public Law No. 86-272, federal law prohibits a state and its political subdivisions (counties, cities, etc.) from imposing a net income tax on a person's net income derived from interstate commerce occurring within the state's borders when the following three circumstances are present:
  - The only business activity of the person within the state consists of the solicitation of orders for sales of tangible personal property;
  - Those orders are sent outside the state for acceptance or rejection; and
  - If those orders are accepted, they are filled by shipment or delivery from a point outside the state.
- "Person" includes individuals, corporations, partnerships, and limited liability companies.
- The prohibition against the state's imposing a net income tax does not apply to the following:
  - Individuals who are domiciled in, or are residents of, the state; and
  - Corporations which are incorporated under the laws of that state (note that the "prohibition-does-not-apply" portion of this federal law does not address either partnerships organized under the laws of that state or limited liability companies organized under the laws of that state).
  - Companies that are soliciting sales of service or other products that do not qualify as tangible personal property.
- The federal law applies only to prohibit a state from imposing a net income tax if the three circumstances above are present. This law does not apply to:
  - sales and use taxes;
  - franchise taxes; and
  - gross receipts taxes (sometimes called business and occupation taxes or commercial activity taxes).

- Because this federal law limits the right of a state to tax net income that a person earns within the state, most, if not all, states:
  - narrowly define "solicitation"; and
  - resolve in favor of the state all ambiguities under the federal law.
- The following are examples of activities that may trigger nexus in a state in which a company operates:
  - Owning or leasing tangible personal or real property.
  - Sending employees into the state for training or work.
  - Soliciting sales in a state.
  - Providing installation, maintenance, etc., to customers within a state (even through a third party).
  - Accepting or rejecting sales orders within the state, or accepting returns.

> **Example 1   Determination of Nexus**
>
> **Facts:** Hundley Corporation sells computers and is incorporated and resides in California. In addition to California, Hundley solicits sales in Oregon, Arizona, and Colorado. It provides installation services to its customers in Arizona, and it conducts employee training at a facility in Colorado.
>
> **Required:** Determine with which states Hundley has nexus.
>
> **Solution:**
> - California (state of residence and incorporation)
> - Arizona (provides installation services to customers)
> - Colorado (conducts employee training)
>
> Hundley likely will be protected from nexus in Oregon by P.L. 86-272, as its only activity in the state is solicitation of sales for tangible personal property.

1.3 State Allocation and Apportionment of Federal Taxable Income

Once nexus is established, the next step is for the company to determine how much of its total federal income or loss should be taxable by each state. This is accomplished through the rules of allocation and apportionment. Although the terms allocation and apportionment are almost always used in the same phrase, they each perform a separate function, and it is important to note the difference between the two. Generally, most states require that corporations (and sometimes, partnerships) use federal taxable income before the NOL deductions and before the dividends-received deduction as the starting point for allocation and apportionment calculations. For corporations, this amount is shown on line 28 on page 1 of the IRS Form 1120.

1.3.1 Allocation of Nonbusiness Income

Generally, allocable items of income are "nonbusiness" income. That is, the income does not relate to the primary business activities of the corporation within the state. "Allocation" refers to the process of removing the nonbusiness income from the line 28 total and assigning it entirely to the state where it should be taxed. Investment income such as interest, dividends, and capital gains from sales of stock are generally allocated entirely to the taxpayer's state of commercial domicile (or residence). Other income such as rental income or capital gains from the sale of rental property is generally entirely sourced to the state where the property is located.

> **Example 2**   **Allocation of Nonbusiness Income**
>
> **Facts:** A corporation selling shoes at retail in two states has invested excess cash, which is not working capital, in high-grade stocks and bonds. The corporation plans to liquidate the investment in 10 years and use the proceeds to pay for the construction in 10 years of a planned distribution center.
>
> **Required:** Determine whether the investment income from the stocks and bonds should be classified as business income or allocated as nonbusiness income.
>
> **Solution:** Because the investment in stocks and bonds does not relate to the primary business activities of the corporation, in this situation, the corporation may be able to allocate entirely to the corporation's home state all dividend income and interest income (and capital gain or loss from the liquidation). No other state would be able to tax these items of nonbusiness income.

1.3.2 Apportionment of Business Income

- The portions of line 28 income which are not allocated entirely to one state are apportioned to all the states in which the corporation does business. Generally, apportionable items of income are "business" income. That is, the income does relate to the primary business activities of the corporation within the state.

- The income apportioned to a state is usually the product of:
  - the apportionment factor (based on the corporation's percentage of property, payroll, and sales in the state); and
  - the portion of line 28 income which is apportionable, business income (line 28 income less allocated income).

1.3.3 Calculation of Apportionment Factor

- Each state dictates exactly how the apportionment factor should be determined in that state, and the methods vary slightly from state to state. However, the standard apportionment factor formula that is used by many states is calculated in the following manner:

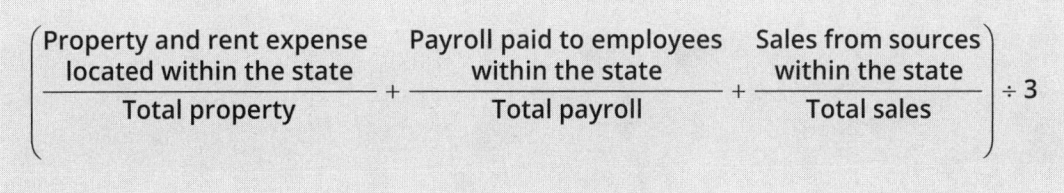

$$\left(\frac{\text{Property and rent expense located within the state}}{\text{Total property}} + \frac{\text{Payroll paid to employees within the state}}{\text{Total payroll}} + \frac{\text{Sales from sources within the state}}{\text{Total sales}} \right) \div 3$$

Example 3: Allocation and Apportionment

Facts: A corporation has commercial domicile in Kansas and has the following breakdown of property, payroll, and sales in the states where it operates:

Property:
Kansas: $400,000
Missouri: $50,000
Oklahoma: $30,000
Nebraska: $20,000
Total: $500,000

Payroll:
Kansas: $40,000
Missouri: $30,000
Oklahoma: $20,000
Nebraska: $10,000
Total: $100,000

Sales:
Kansas: $300,000
Missouri $400,000
Oklahoma: $200,000
Nebraska: $100,000
Total: $1,000,000

The portion of line 28 income representing allocable dividends and interest income (nonbusiness income) described above is $10,000; the remaining portion of line 28 income is $100,000 and relates to business income (and thus is apportionable income). So, total line 28 income is $110,000.

Required: Determine the corporation's taxable income in each state with nexus.

Solution: In order to determine taxable income for each state, first calculate their apportionment factors.

Kansas:
Property factor: 80% ($400,000 / $500,000)
Payroll factor: 40% ($40,000 / $100,000)
Sales factor: 30% ($300,000 / $1,000,000)
Total factor: 50% [(80% + 40% + 30%) / 3]

Missouri:
Property factor: 10% ($50,000 / $500,000)
Payroll factor: 30% ($30,000 / $100,000)
Sales factor: 40% ($400,000 / $1,000,000)
Total factor: 27% [(10% + 30% + 40%] / 3)

Oklahoma:
Property factor: 6% ($30,000 / $500,000)
Payroll factor: 20% ($20,000 / $100,000)
Sales factor: 20% ($200,000 / $1,000,000)
Total factor: 15% [(6% + 20% + 20%] / 3)

Nebraska:
Property factor: 4% ($20,000 / $500,000)
Payroll factor: 10% ($10,000 / $100,000)
Sales factor: 10% ($100,000 / $1,000,000)
Total factor: 8% [(4% + 10% + 10%] / 3)

In this situation, the home state of Kansas could tax $60,000 of the corporation's line 28 amount: (i) $10,000 nonbusiness income allocated entirely to the home state; and (ii) $50,000 apportioned to the home state (50% apportionment factor × $100,000 apportionable business income).

The remaining states have taxable income as follows:
Missouri: $27,000 (27% apportionment factor × $100,000 apportionable business income)
Oklahoma: $15,000 (15% apportionment factor × $100,000 apportionable business income)
Nebraska: $8,000 (8% apportionment factor × $100,000 apportionable business income)

1.4 State Income Taxes and Controlled Taxpayers

Most states do not have a statute similar to the IRC's statute authorizing the IRS to make controlled taxpayer adjustments with respect to transfer pricing issues. However, many states do have a statute allowing the state taxing authority to require a combination of income of related members if such combination will better reflect the extent of business done within the state.

> **Illustration 1 State Taxing Authority Combining Income of Related Members**
>
> Hold Company, located solely in Delaware, owns 100 percent of the stock of OP Company, operating solely in State X. Hold Company's only business is (i) owning the stock of OP Company and (ii) lending money to OP Company. Hold Company and OP Company file a U.S. consolidated income tax return. Because of Hold Company's limited activities, under Delaware law and under State X law, Hold Company is not liable for income tax to either state. Because OP Company operates solely in State X, OP Company is not liable for state income tax in Delaware.
>
> At the end of each business day, OP Company declares and pays a dividend equal to all of OP Company's cash on hand at the end of that day. At the beginning of each next business day, Hold Company lends to OP Company sufficient cash for OP Company's operations for that day. The interest rate is an arm's-length rate. Under the terms of the loan agreement, OP Company does not have to repay any principal for 10 years.
>
> As a result of Hold Company's daily loans to OP Company, each year OP Company incurs deductible interest expenses of $10,000,000. Because Hold Company and OP Company file a U.S. consolidated income tax return, the interest expense incurred by OP Company and the interest income recognized by Hold Company offset each other. Because the interest rate that Hold Company charges OP Company is an arm's-length rate and because the two corporations file a U.S. consolidated income tax return, the IRS makes no transfer pricing, controlled taxpayer adjustments.
>
> Because of the daily dividends paid to Hold Company followed by the daily loan from Hold Company to OP Company, on a "separate return" basis, OP Company's line 28 income has been reduced by OP Company's $10,000,000 interest expense; so OP Company's income subject to tax by State X also has been reduced by $10,000,000 (State X bases its state income tax on the taxpayer's separate return line 28 amount).
>
> However, if State X taxing officials have the authority to combine OP Company and Hold Company, the state tax benefit of OP Company's $10,000,000 interest expense deduction will be offset by Hold Company's $10,000,000 interest income. The combined line 28 amount will now reflect the true income of OP Company, and OP Company will pay to State X the appropriate amount of state income tax.

NOTES

Professional Responsibilities and Federal Tax Procedures

REG 4

Module

1 Circular 230 — 3

2 Professional Responsibilities and Tax Return Preparer Penalties — 11

3 Federal Tax Procedures and Taxpayer Penalties — 21

4 Legal Duties and Responsibilities — 33

NOTES

MODULE 1: Circular 230

1 Overview

Treasury Department Circular 230 is the IRS publication entitled, "Regulations Governing Practice before the Internal Revenue Service." The publication addresses the practice before the IRS with regard to the following:

- rules governing the authority to practice before the IRS;
- the duties and restrictions relating to practice before the IRS;
- the sanctions for violation of the regulations; and
- the rules applicable to disciplinary proceedings.

1.1 Subparts

The publication is divided into subparts addressing such practice as follows:

Subpart A	Rules Governing Authority to Practice
Subpart B	Duties and Restrictions in Practice before the IRS
Subpart C	Sanctions for Violating the Regulations
Subpart D	Rules Applicable to Disciplinary Proceedings
Subpart E	General Provisions

2 Authority to Practice (Subpart A)

The rules governing practice before the IRS apply to:

- Attorneys
- Certified public accountants
- Enrolled agents
- Enrolled actuaries
- Enrolled retirement plan agents
- Registered tax return preparers
- Other persons allowed to represent a taxpayer before the IRS in limited circumstances (e.g., an officer or full-time employee of a corporation or trust may represent that corporation or trust)

3 Duties and Restrictions Relating to Practice Before the IRS (Subpart B)

3.1 Information to Be Furnished to the IRS (Section 10.20)

Information to be furnished includes any IRS requested information or records:

- The practitioner may withhold information or records he believes in good faith and on reasonable grounds to be privileged.
- If the practitioner does not possess the IRS-requested information or records but knows who does, he must so inform the IRS.

3.2 Knowledge of Client Omission (Section 10.21)

A practitioner who knows of a client's noncompliance with federal tax laws or error or omission on a tax return or other document must advise the client of that noncompliance, error, or omission, and the consequences under the tax law of that noncompliance, error, or omission.

3.3 Diligence as to Accuracy (Section 10.22)

A practitioner must exercise due diligence in:

- preparing, approving, and filing tax returns and other documents related to IRS matters; and
- determining the correctness of oral or written representations made by the practitioner to clients or the Treasury Department.

A practitioner is presumed to have exercised due diligence when he or she relies on the work product of another person if the practitioner used reasonable care with respect to such reliance.

3.4 Prompt Disposition of Pending Matters (Section 10.23)

No practitioner may unreasonably delay any matter before the IRS.

3.5 Assistance From or to Disbarred or Suspended Persons and Former IRS Employees (Section 10.24)

With respect to a matter before the IRS, no practitioner can knowingly and directly or indirectly accept help from or assist any person who is under disbarment or suspended from practice before the IRS or accept assistance from any former government employee where either the provisions of Section 10.25 of Circular 230 (below) or any federal law would be violated.

3.6 Practice by Former Government Employees, Their Partners, and Their Associates (Section 10.25)

No member of a firm in which a former government employee works can represent a taxpayer where a conflict of interest may exist, unless the firm isolates the former government employee in such a way to ensure that the former government employee cannot assist in the representation.

- If an individual, while a government employee, "personally and substantially participated" in a particular matter involving specific parties, that individual can never represent or assist those parties with respect to that particular matter.

- If an individual, while a government employee, had "official responsibility" for a particular matter involving specific parties, that individual within two years after leaving government employment cannot represent those parties with respect to that particular matter. Note that the "cannot assist" language above does not apply here.
- Within one year after leaving government employment, the individual cannot appear before the IRS to influence any U.S. Treasury Department employee regarding any rule if either (i) the individual at any time "participated in the development" of the rule; or (ii) within the one year period prior to leaving government employment, the individual has "official responsibility" with respect to that rule.

3.7 Notary (Section 10.26)

A practitioner may not act as a notary public for his or her clients on any tax matter.

3.8 Fees (Section 10.27)

A practitioner may not charge an unconscionable fee in connection with any matter before the IRS.

A contingent fee is allowable only in the following three situations before the IRS:

- IRS examination of, or challenge to, an original tax return (or an amended return or claim for refund or credit that was filed within 120 days of receiving a written notice from the IRS of the examination or challenge to the original tax return)
- Claim solely for a refund of interest and/or penalties
- A judicial proceeding arising under the Internal Revenue Code

3.9 Return of Client's Records (Section 10.28)

In general, a practitioner must, at the request of a client, promptly return any and all client records that are necessary for the client to comply with his or her federal tax obligations. The practitioner may retain copies of the records returned to the client.

If state law allows a practitioner to retain the records in the case of a fee dispute, the practitioner may do so. However, the practitioner must provide the client with reasonable access to review and copy any client records retained by the practitioner that are necessary for the client to comply with his or her federal tax obligations.

Client records include:

- materials prepared by the client or a third party and provided to the practitioner; and
- any return, claim for refund, or other document prepared by the practitioner.

3.10 Conflict of Interest (Section 10.29)

A practitioner may not represent a client before the IRS if it involves a conflict of interest unless:

- the practitioner reasonably believes that he or she can competently represent each of the clients;
- no state or federal law prohibits such representation; and
- each affected client waives the conflict of interest and gives informed consent, and confirms the waiver in writing within 30 days after giving informed consent.

3.11 Solicitation (Section 10.30)

3.11.1 Advertising and Solicitation Restrictions

A practitioner may not, with respect to any Internal Revenue Service matter, in any way use or participate in the use of any form of public communication or private solicitation containing a false, fraudulent, or coercive statement or claim, or a misleading or deceptive statement or claim.

> **Illustration 1 False Advertising**
>
> A small accounting firm with only CPAs advertises on a local television station. The script, which was approved by the partners of the firm, states that "Our talented staff of licensed attorneys and CPAs guarantee you the tax refund you've always wanted." This represents a likely violation of Circular 230 because the firm has falsely advertises it has licensed attorneys when it does not. Also, the advertisement includes a guarantee that could be misleading to clients.

3.11.2 Written Schedule of Fees

Practitioners publishing a written fee schedule must honor those fees for the 30-day period following the last date that the fees were published. If additional fees may be charged for certain matters, the statement must indicate whether clients will be responsible for the costs.

3.11.3 Communicating Fee Information

- In the case of radio and television broadcasting, the broadcast must be recorded and the practitioner must retain a recording of the actual transmission.
- In the case of direct mail and e-commerce communications, the practitioner must retain a copy of the actual communication, along with a list or other description of persons to whom the communication was mailed or otherwise distributed.
- Copies must be retained by the practitioner for a period of at least 36 months from the date of the last transmission or use.

3.12 Negotiation of Taxpayer Checks (Section 10.31)

A practitioner may not endorse or otherwise negotiate any refund check issued to a client.

3.13 Practice of Law (Section 10.32)

Circular 230 may not be construed as authorizing persons not members of the bar to practice law.

3.14 Best Practices for Tax Advisors (Section 10.33)

Tax advisors should provide clients the highest-quality representation by adhering to "best practices" in providing tax preparation advice or assistance in a submission to the IRS. "Best practices" include:

- Communicating with the client regarding the terms of the engagement to determine the client's purpose and use for the advice.
- Establishing the facts and arriving at a conclusion supported by the law and the facts.
- Advising the client about the importance of the conclusions reached (for example, whether the client will be able to avoid penalties).

- Acting fairly and with integrity in practice before the IRS.
- Taking reasonable steps to ensure that all members, associates, and employees of the firm follow procedures that are consistent with the above.

3.15 Competence (Section 10.35)

A practitioner must possess the necessary competence to engage in practice before the IRS. Competent practice requires the appropriate level of knowledge, skill, thoroughness, and preparation necessary for the matter for which the practitioner is engaged. A practitioner may become competent through various methods, such as consulting with experts in the relevant area or studying the relevant law.

4 Standards With Respect to Tax Returns and Documents, Affidavits, and Other Papers (Subpart B, Section 10.34)

4.1 Tax Returns

A practitioner may not willfully or recklessly sign a tax return or advise a client to take a tax position that the practitioner knows or should know lacks a reasonable basis, is an unreasonable position, is a willful attempt to understate tax liability, or recklessly or intentionally disregards the tax rules and regulations.

4.2 Documents, Affidavits, and Other Papers

A practitioner cannot advise a client to take a position on a document, affidavit, or other paper that will be submitted to the IRS unless the position is not frivolous. The practitioner cannot advise a client to submit any document that:

- will delay or impede the administration of federal tax law;
- is frivolous; or
- contains or omits information demonstrating an intentional disregard of a rule or regulation unless the practitioner also advises the client to submit a document evidencing a good faith challenge to the rule or regulation.

4.3 Advising Clients on Potential Penalties

The practitioner must inform the client of the following:

- Any penalties "reasonably likely" to apply with respect to a position taken on a tax return if the practitioner advised the client on the position or prepared or signed the tax return.
- Any penalties "reasonably likely" to apply with respect to any document submitted to the IRS.
- The opportunity to avoid penalties if the client discloses the position taken and the requirements for adequate disclosure.

4.4 Practitioner's Reliance on Information Furnished by Client

Generally, a practitioner who signs the tax return or other document may rely "in good faith without verification" upon information furnished by the client. However, the practitioner cannot ignore the implications of such information or contradictory information known to the practitioner; and must make reasonable inquiries if the information furnished by the client appears to be questionable or incomplete.

5 Written Advice (Subpart B, Section 10.37)

A practitioner may give written advice (including by means of electronic communication) concerning one or more federal tax matters.

The practitioner *must*:

- base the written advice on reasonable factual and legal assumptions (including assumptions as to future events);
- reasonably consider all relevant facts and circumstances that the practitioner knows or reasonably should know;
- use reasonable efforts to identify and ascertain the facts relevant to written advice on each federal tax matter;
- not rely upon representations, statements, findings, or agreements (including projections, financial forecasts, or appraisals) of the taxpayer or any other person if reliance on them would be unreasonable;
- relate applicable law and authorities to facts; and
- must not, in evaluating a federal tax matter, take into account the possibility that a tax return will not be audited or that a matter will not be raised on audit.

5.1 Definition of Federal Tax Matters

A federal tax matter, as used in this section of Circular 230, is any matter concerning the application or interpretation of:

- a revenue provision of the Internal Revenue Code;
- any provision of law impacting a person's obligations under the internal revenue laws and regulations, including but not limited to the person's liability to pay tax or obligation to file returns; or
- any other law or regulation administered by the IRS.

5.2 Reliance on Advice of Others

- A practitioner may only rely on the advice of another person if the advice was reasonable and the reliance is in good faith considering all the facts and circumstances.
- Reliance is not reasonable when:
  - the practitioner knows or reasonably should know that the opinion of the other person should not be relied on;
  - the practitioner knows or reasonably should know that the other person is not competent or lacks the necessary qualifications to provide the advice; or
  - the practitioner knows or reasonably should know that the other person has a conflict of interest in violation of the rules described in this part of Circular 230.

5.3 Standard of Review

- In evaluating whether a practitioner giving written advice concerning one or more federal tax matters complied with these requirements, the commissioner, or delegate, will apply a reasonable practitioner standard, considering all facts and circumstances, including, but not limited to, the scope of the engagement and the type and specificity of the advice sought by the client.

- In the case of an opinion the practitioner knows or has reason to know will be used or referred to by a person other than the practitioner in promoting, marketing, or recommending to one or more taxpayers a partnership or other entity, investment plan or arrangement a significant purpose of which is the avoidance or evasion of any tax imposed by the Internal Revenue Code, the commissioner, or delegate, will apply a reasonable practitioner standard, considering all facts and circumstances.

6 Compliance (Subpart B, Section 10.36)

6.1 Procedures to Ensure Compliance With Circular 230

An individual or individuals who have principal authority for overseeing a firm's federal tax practice must take reasonable steps to ensure that the firm has adequate procedures to ensure compliance with Circular 230.

6.2 Potential Failures to Comply

- The individual *fails* to have adequate procedures to comply with Circular 230; there is a pattern or practice of noncompliance; and this occurs through willfulness, recklessness, or gross incompetence.
- The individual *fails* to ensure the *procedures for compliance are followed*; there is a pattern or practice of noncompliance; and this occurs through willfulness, recklessness, or gross incompetence.
- The individual knows or should know of a pattern of noncompliance and fails to take prompt action to correct the noncompliance.

7 Sanctions for Violations of the Regulations (Subpart C)

The Secretary of the Treasury, after notice and opportunity for a proceeding, may publicly reprimand, suspend, or disbar any practitioner from practice before the IRS if the practitioner:

- is shown to be incompetent or disreputable;
- fails to comply with any regulations in Circular 230; or
- willfully and knowingly misleads or threatens a client or prospective client with intent to defraud.

7.1 Incompetence and Disreputable Conduct

Incompetence and disreputable conduct for which a practitioner may be sanctioned includes:

- Being convicted of (i) any federal tax law crime; (ii) any criminal offense involving dishonesty or breach of conduct; or (iii) any felony under federal or state law for conduct indicating that the practitioner is unfit to practice before the IRS.
- Giving false or misleading information (statements, returns, etc.) to U.S. Department of the Treasury employees or to any tribunal authorized to hear federal tax matters.
- Carrying out any solicitation of business prohibited by Circular 230.
- Willfully failing to make a tax return or willfully evading, or attempting to evade, any assessment or payment of federal tax.

- Willfully counseling or assisting others to evade, or attempt to evade, any assessment or payment of federal tax.
- Failing to timely remit to the IRS any funds received from a client for the purpose of paying any tax or other obligation owed to the U.S. government.
- Using threats or false accusations or offering gifts, inducements, or other favors in order to influence any official action by any IRS employee.
- Being disbarred or suspended from practice as an attorney, CPA, public accountant, or actuary.
- Knowingly helping another person practice before the IRS while that person is suspended, disbarred, or otherwise ineligible to practice before the IRS.
- Being contemptuously abusive, making false accusations or statements, or circulating malicious or libelous matters.
- Knowingly, recklessly, or through gross incompetence giving false opinions on questions arising under the tax laws.
- Willfully failing to sign a tax return when federal tax law requires the practitioner to sign the return (e.g., the practitioner is a "paid preparer") unless the failure is:
    - due to reasonable cause; and
    - not due to willful neglect.
- Willfully disclosing or otherwise using a tax return or tax return information where such disclosure is:
    - not authorized by the Internal Revenue Code;
    - contrary to the order of any court; or
    - contrary to the order of an administrative law judge in connection with a disciplinary proceeding.
- Willfully neglecting to file an e-return when the practitioner is required to do so.
- Willfully preparing or signing a tax return when the practitioner does not have a valid tax preparer ID.
- Willfully representing a taxpayer before the IRS without authorization to do so.

8 Petition for Reinstatement (Subpart D, Section 10.81)

A practitioner disbarred or suspended may petition for reinstatement before the IRS after the expiration of five years following such disbarment or suspension (or immediately following the expiration of the suspension period, if shorter than five years). Reinstatement will not be granted unless the IRS is satisfied that the petitioner is not likely to engage thereafter in conduct contrary to the regulations in Circular 230, and that granting such reinstatement would not be contrary to the public interest.

MODULE 2

Professional Responsibilities and Tax Return Preparer Penalties

REG 4

1 Tax Return Preparer

1.1 Definition of Tax Return Preparer

The term "tax return preparer" means any person who prepares for compensation, or who employs one or more persons to prepare for compensation, any tax return required under the IRC, or any claim for refund of tax imposed by the IRC. The preparation of a substantial portion of a return or claim for refund shall be treated as if it were the preparation of such return or claim for refund. Any tax professional with an IRS preparer tax identification number (PTIN) is authorized to prepare federal tax returns. These individuals are often categorized as enrolled agents, certified public accountants, attorneys, annual filing season program participants, and PTIN holders.

> **Illustration 1   Not a Tax Return Preparer**
>
> A small accounting firm hires two interns each year. The interns review the data provided by the clients and enter the information into the tax return software. The interns also call to request missing information but are not permitted to offer tax advice. The returns are prepared and signed by managers in the firm. In this scenario, the interns would not be regarded as tax return preparers.

1.1.1 Does Not Include

"Tax return preparer" does not include a person who (i) merely furnishes typing, reproducing, or other mechanical assistance; (ii) prepares a return or claim for refund of the employer (or of an officer or employee of the employer); or (iii) prepares as a fiduciary (trustee, executor, etc.) a return or claim for refund for any other person.

1.2 Unlimited Representation Rights

Enrolled agents, certified public accountants, and attorneys have unlimited representation rights before the IRS. Tax professionals with these credentials may represent their clients on any matters including audits, payment/collection issues, and appeals. PTIN holders who are classified as annual filing season program participants and preparers who are PTIN holders but do not have a credential and do not participate in the annual filing season program have limited representation rights.

1.2.1 PTIN Holders With No Credentials

- Tax return preparers who have an active preparer tax identification number but no professional credentials and do not participate in the annual filing season program are authorized only to prepare tax returns.

- Effective January 1, 2016, PTIN holders who do not hold a professional credential and do not participate in the annual filing season program have no authority to represent clients before the IRS (except regarding returns they prepared and filed December 31, 2015, and prior).

1.3 Obtaining a PTIN

The IRS requires all paid tax return preparers to register with the IRS and obtain a preparer tax identification number (PTIN).

1.4 Signing and Nonsigning Tax Return Preparer

- **Signing Tax Return Preparer:** The individual tax return preparer who has the primary responsibility for the overall substantive accuracy of the preparation of such return or claim for refund.

- **Nonsigning Tax Return Preparer:** Any tax return preparer who is not a signing tax return preparer but who prepares all or a substantial portion of a return or claim for refund or offers advice (written or oral) to a taxpayer (or to another tax return preparer) when that advice leads to a position or entry that constitutes a substantial portion of the return. Factors to consider in determining whether a schedule, entry, or other portion of a return or claim for refund is a substantial portion include but are not limited to (i) the size and complexity of the item relative to the taxpayer's gross income; and (ii) the size of the understatement attributable to the item compared to the taxpayer's reported tax liability.

> **Illustration 2 — Nonsigning Tax Return Preparer**
>
> An attorney, who is a PTIN holder, provides a spreadsheet to a CPA that shows the calculation of income to be reported on the income tax return of an estate. The income represents a substantial portion of the return, yet the attorney does not prepare any other portion of the tax return and does not sign the tax return. The attorney could be regarded as a nonsigning preparer for the return for the purpose of assessing tax return preparer penalties.

2 Tax Return Preparer Compliance Penalties

Individuals who meet the qualification of tax return preparers are subject to certain penalties under the Internal Revenue Code. The assessments under IRC Section 6694 are intended to ensure that the tax return preparers are in compliance with federal tax laws.

2.1 Key Terms

2.1.1 Authority

Only the following are authority for purposes of determining whether there is substantial authority (defined below) for the tax treatment of an item (note that conclusions reached in treatises, legal periodicals, legal opinions, or opinions rendered by tax professionals are not "authority"):

- Applicable provisions of the Internal Revenue Code and other statutory provisions.
- Proposed, temporary, and final regulations construing such statutes.
- Revenue rulings and revenue procedures, tax treaties and regulations thereunder, and U.S. Treasury Department and other official explanations of such treaties.
- Court cases.
- Congressional intent as reflected in committee reports, joint explanatory statements of managers included in conference committee reports, and floor statements made prior to enactment by one of a bill's managers.

- "General Explanations" of tax legislation prepared by the Joint [U.S. Senate and U.S. House of Representatives] Committee on Taxation (the "Blue Book").
- Private letter rulings and technical advice memoranda issued after October 31, 1976.
- Actions on decisions and general counsel memoranda issued after March 12, 1981 (as well as general counsel memoranda published in pre-1955 volumes of the Cumulative Bulletin).
- Internal Revenue Service information or press releases and notices, announcements, and other administrative pronouncements published by the Service in the Internal Revenue Bulletin.

2.1.2 Disregard

The verb "disregard" includes any careless, reckless, or intentional disregard of rules or regulations.

2.1.3 Person

Person means and includes an individual, a trust, an estate, a partnership, an association, a company, or a corporation.

2.1.4 Listed Transaction

The term *listed transaction* means a reportable transaction (defined below) which is the same as, or substantially similar to, a transaction specifically identified by the Secretary of the U.S. Treasury Department as a tax avoidance transaction.

2.1.5 Reportable Transaction

The term *reportable transaction* means any transaction with respect to which information is required to be included with a return or statement because such transaction is of a type that the Secretary of the U.S. Treasury Department has determined as having a potential for either tax avoidance (the legal use and application of the tax laws and cases in order to reduce the amount of tax due) or tax evasion (efforts, by illegal means and methods, to not pay taxes).

2.1.6 Negligence

The term *negligence* includes any failure to make a reasonable attempt to comply with the provisions of the internal revenue laws or to exercise ordinary and reasonable care in the preparation of a tax return. *Negligence* also includes any failure by the taxpayer to keep adequate books and records or to substantiate items properly.

2.1.7 Reasonable Basis Standard

- Reasonable basis is a relatively high standard of tax reporting; this standard is significantly higher than not frivolous or not patently improper. The reasonable basis standard is not satisfied by a return position that is merely arguable or that is merely a colorable claim.
- If a return position is reasonably based on one or more of the authorities set forth above, the return position will generally satisfy the reasonable basis standard even though the position may not satisfy the substantial authority standard (defined below).

2.1.8 Substantial Authority Standard

- The *substantial authority standard* is an objective standard involving an analysis of the law and application of the law to relevant facts. The substantial authority standard is less stringent than the more-likely-than-not standard (defined below).
- There is substantial authority for the tax treatment of an item only if the weight of the authorities supporting the treatment is substantial in relation to the weight of authorities supporting the contrary treatment.

- There is substantial authority for the tax treatment of an item if the treatment is supported by controlling precedent of a U.S. Court of Appeals to which the taxpayer has a right of appeal with respect to the item.
- Because this standard is an objective standard, the taxpayer's belief that there is substantial authority for the tax treatment of an item is not relevant.

2.1.9 More-Likely-Than-Not Standard

The *more-likely-than-not standard* is met when there is a greater than 50 percent likelihood of a tax position being upheld by the courts. This standard is more stringent than the *substantial authority standard*.

2.2 Understatement Due to an Unreasonable Position [IRC Section 6694(a)]

This penalty can be assessed because of the understatement of a taxpayer's liability due to an unreasonable position taken by the taxpayer.

2.2.1 Unreasonable Position

A position is deemed unreasonable unless:

- reasonable basis for a disclosed position exists; or
- substantial authority for the position, regardless of disclosure, exists; or
- it is reasonable to believe that a tax shelter or reportable transaction position would meet the more-likely-than-not standard.

Note: IRS Form 8275 is used to disclose items and positions that are not contrary to U.S. Treasury regulations, but are not otherwise adequately disclosed on a tax return. IRS Form 8275-R is used to disclose items and positions that are contrary to U.S. Treasury regulations.

2.2.2 Penalty for Understatement Due to Unreasonable Position

Equal to the greater of $1,000 or 50 percent of the income the preparer received for tax return preparation services.

The penalty may be imposed on the preparer if:

1. a position is taken on the tax return and understates the tax liability if there is no reasonable belief that the position would be sustainable based on its merit;
2. the preparer had knowledge or should have known about the unreasonable position;
3. disclosure of the position was not made; and
4. the position lacks reasonable basis.

2.3 Understatement Due to Willful or Reckless Conduct [IRC Section 6694(b)]

A compensated preparer is liable for a penalty if the preparer's understatement of taxpayer liability on a return or claim for refund is due to the preparer's negligent or intentional disregard of rules and regulations.

2.3.1 "Willful or Reckless" Conduct

Conduct that is either:

- a willful attempt to understate the tax liability; or
- a reckless or intentional disregard of tax rules and regulations in spite of his signed declaration on the return.

2.3.2 Supporting Documentation

A preparer is not required to obtain supporting documentation unless the preparer has reason to suspect the accuracy of the information provided by the taxpayer (client). The preparer must make reasonable inquiries if the information provided by the taxpayer appears incorrect or incomplete.

2.3.3 Penalty for "Willful or Reckless" Conduct

The penalty is equal to the greater of $5,000 or 75 percent of the income the preparer derived with respect to the tax return or refund claim. The penalty is reduced by any penalty assessed because of an understatement of a taxpayer's liability as the result of an unreasonable tax position by a tax return preparer.

3 Tax Return Preparer Penalties for Unethical Behavior

Penalties assessed under IRC Section 6695 are intended to protect the taxpayer from unethical behavior.

3.1 Failure to Provide Copy to Taxpayer (IRC Sections 6695, 6107)

A preparer is required to provide to the taxpayer (client) a copy of the tax return or a copy of the refund claim no later than the time the preparer gives the taxpayer the completed return or claim. The penalty does not apply to the extent the failure is due to reasonable cause and not due to willful neglect, and is $60 for each such failure (maximum penalty of $30,000 per calendar year).

3.2 Failure to Sign Return (IRC Section 6695)

The penalty is $60 for each such failure (maximum penalty of $30,000 per calendar year).

3.3 Failure to Furnish Identification Number of Preparer (IRC Section 6695)

The penalty is $60 for each such failure (maximum penalty of $30,000 per calendar year).

3.4 Failure to Properly Retain Records (IRC Sections 6695, 6107, 6060)

The tax return preparer is required to keep, for the three years following the last day of the return period, either: a copy of the return or claim or a listing of the name and ID of each taxpayer for whom the preparer prepared a return or claim. The penalty is $60 for each such failure (maximum penalty of $30,000 per return period).

3.5 Failure to File Correct Information Returns (IRC Sections 6695, 6060)

Any person who employed a tax return preparer at any time during that return period must file an information return with the IRS by July 31 immediately following the end of the return period, containing: the name, taxpayer identification number, and place of work of each tax return preparer so employed by that person. The penalty is $60 for each failure (maximum penalty of $30,000 per return period).

3.6 Negotiation of IRS Refund Check (IRC Section 6695)

Generally, any tax return preparer who endorses or otherwise negotiates an IRS refund check issued to a taxpayer other than the tax return preparer shall pay a penalty of $600 with respect to each such check. This rule does not apply to banks if the bank deposits into the taxpayer's account at such bank the full amount of the IRS refund check.

3.7 Failure to Be Diligent in Determining a Client's Eligibility for the Earned Income Credit [IRC Section 6695(g)]

3.7.1 Penalty

The penalty for failure to comply with the IRS' "due diligence" requirements with respect to determining eligibility for, or the amount of, the earned income credit is $600 for each failure.

3.7.2 Due Diligence Requirements

The due diligence requirements address (i) eligibility checklists; (ii) computation worksheets; (iii) reasonable inquires to the taxpayer; and (iv) record retention. The penalty will not apply with respect to a particular return or claim if the tax return preparer can demonstrate that the preparer's normal office procedures are reasonably designed and routinely followed to ensure due diligence compliance and the failure to meet the due diligence requirements was insolated and inadvertent.

4 Other Tax Return Preparer Penalties

4.1 Aiding and Abetting Understatement of Tax Liability (IRC Section 6701)

The penalty for aiding and abetting understatement of tax liability applies to any person, not just to tax return preparers. The IRS has the burden of proof to establish that any person is liable for this civil penalty. The penalty applies whether or not the understatement is with the knowledge or consent of the persons authorized or required to file the return, affidavit, claim, or other document.

The IRC imposes a civil penalty ($1,000 for all taxpayers except corporations and $10,000 for corporations) on any person/entity who:

- aids, assists in, procures, or advises with respect to, the preparation or presentation of any portion of a return, affidavit, claim, or other document;
- knows (or has reason to know) that such portion will be used in connection with any material matter arising under the IRC; and
- knows that such portion (if so used) would result in an understatement of the liability for tax of another person.

Note: Unless the law expressly states otherwise (as it does with this penalty), in any civil action (court hearing) the taxpayer has the burden of proof to establish by a preponderance of the evidence (more than 50 percent) that the law and the evidence do not support the position of the IRS concerning the matter in dispute. With respect to any criminal action (court proceedings regarding fines and/or imprisonment), the government has the burden of proof to establish by evidence beyond a reasonable doubt that the taxpayer is guilty of the charge(s).

4.2 Wrongful Disclosure and/or Use of Tax Return Information (IRC Sections 6713, 7216)

4.2.1 Penalty

A tax return preparer who discloses or uses information for any purpose other than to prepare a tax return shall pay a civil penalty of $250 for each such disclosure or use (maximum annual penalty shall not exceed $10,000) and be guilty of a misdemeanor and fined not more than $1,000 and/or be imprisoned for not more than one year, together with the costs of prosecution. (Note that a client may also bring civil suit against the tax preparer.)

4.2.2 Exceptions

Exceptions to the penalty and/or fine for wrongful disclosure and/or use of tax return information include:

- Disclosures allowed by any provision of the IRC and disclosures pursuant to a court order.
- Allowable uses (preparation of state and local tax returns and preparation of declaration of estimated tax).
- Disclosures and uses permitted by U.S. Treasury regulations for quality and peer reviews and administrative orders.

4.2.3 Consent of Client

Confidential client information may be disclosed to any party if the client specifically consents to the release of information.

Pass Key

Historically, the most commonly tested issues regarding the tax liability rules include:

- Endorsing and cashing refund checks. (Key: Endorsing and negotiating a client's refund check—regardless of amount—is forbidden.)
- Preparing returns that understate tax liability. (Key: Although a tax preparer cannot willfully aid in understating tax liability, the preparer has no affirmative duty to check the veracity of the facts presented by the client, with a possible exception for facts that appear implausible.)
- Disclosure of tax return information. (Key: Memorize the situations in which the tax preparer is able to disclose information without the taxpayer's consent—disclosure in all other situations without taxpayer consent is disallowed.)

5 Role of State Boards of Accountancy

The National Association of State Boards of Accountancy (NASBA) was created to enhance the effectiveness and advance the common interests of the Boards of Accountancy. NASBA coordinates and assists the state boards of accountancy in the licensing and regulation of CPAs. NASBA makes recommendations to the state boards, but it is up to the state boards to vote on and enact their own rules and regulations.

5.1 Sole Power to License

- Statutes in all 50 states grant to state boards of accountancy the sole power to license certified public accountants.
- Requirements for licensure vary from state to state. They require successful completion of the CPA examination and all or some of the following:
  - A residency requirement;
  - Educational requirements; and
  - Experience requirements.
- Because a state board is the only entity that can license a CPA, the state board is also the only entity with the power to suspend or revoke a CPA's license.

5.2 Disciplinary Power of State Boards

- Although each state determines what constitutes professional misconduct by a CPA sufficient to subject the CPA to disciplinary action, there are three broad categories of misconduct.
  - Misconduct while performing accounting services (e.g., negligence, fraud, dishonesty, etc.).
  - Misconduct outside the scope of accounting services (e.g., intoxication from alcohol or drugs that significantly impairs the accountant's ability to perform accounting services, insanity, etc.).
  - Criminal conviction (e.g., commission of a felony, failure to file tax returns, crimes relating to the practice of accounting, etc.).
- After investigation of professional misconduct, the state board can conduct a formal hearing for possible disciplinary action.
  - The board must find it was more likely than not that the accountant's actions constituted professional misconduct. Proof beyond a reasonable doubt (i.e., the standard in criminal cases) is not required.
  - The accountant is entitled to due process of law.
  - All adverse state board decisions are subject to judicial review.
- There are five penalties that a state board of accountancy may impose for professional misconduct:
  - Suspension or revocation of license
  - A monetary fine
  - A reprimand or censure
  - Probation
  - Requirement for continuing professional education (CPE) courses

6 Requirements of Regulatory Agencies

6.1 The American Institute of Certified Public Accountants (AICPA) and State CPA Societies

6.1.1 The Professional Code of Conduct

The Code of Professional Conduct applies to all members of the AICPA. Many state CPA societies and state boards have incorporated all, or parts of the code.

6.1.2 Joint Ethics Enforcement Program (JEEP)

- The AICPA and 49 state societies have created the Joint Ethics Enforcement Program (JEEP) for enforcement of their codes of conduct by means of a single investigation and action.
- Investigative information is shared between the AICPA and the state societies.
- JEEP objectives also include the promotion of uniformity in the codes of conduct of the AICPA and state CPA societies and uniformity in enforcement and implementation of the codes of conduct.

6.1.3 Disciplinary Action by the AICPA and State CPA Societies

- The AICPA and state CPA societies can sanction their members, but they cannot suspend or revoke a CPA's license.
- The AICPA may suspend or terminate membership for failure to pay dues or failure to comply with membership retention requirements (e.g., practice-monitoring or continuing professional education requirements).
- Membership can be suspended or terminated without a hearing for:
  - proof of conviction of a crime punishable by imprisonment for more than one year.
  - proof of conviction for willful failure to file any income tax return.
  - proof of conviction for filing a false or fraudulent income tax return or aiding in the preparation of a false or fraudulent income tax return of a client.
  - suspension or revocation of a member's license to practice public accounting as a disciplinary measure by a government authority.
- The Professional Ethics Division of the AICPA investigates potential disciplinary matters and refers appropriate cases to the Joint Trial Board.
  - The Joint Trial Board may expel a member by a two-thirds vote.
  - The Joint Trial Board may suspend a member for up to two years or impose lesser sanctions by majority vote.
- The following are grounds for Joint Trial Board sanctions:
  - Violation of the bylaws or any rule of the Code of Conduct.
  - Declaration by a court of having committed fraud.
  - Determination by the Joint Trial Board of guilt for any act discreditable to the profession, or conviction of a criminal offense that tends to discredit the profession.
  - Declaration by a court that the CPA is insane or incompetent.

- Suspension or revocation of a member's license to practice public accounting as a disciplinary measure by a government authority.
- Failure to cooperate with any Professional Ethics Division disciplinary investigation.
- Failure to comply with educational and remedial or corrective action determined to be necessary by the Professional Ethics Executive Committee within 30 days.

- Notice of disciplinary action is published in a membership periodical (i.e., CPA newsletter).
- Possible sanctions include:
  - Expulsion from the AICPA or state CPA society.
  - Suspension of membership in the AICPA or state CPA society.
  - Requirement that CPE courses be taken as a remedial measure.

6.2 Internal Revenue Service (IRS) Disciplinary Actions

6.2.1 Criminal Penalties

- The Internal Revenue Code (IRC) provides for criminal penalties for any person, including a tax return preparer, who counsels or prepares a tax return in a fraudulent or false manner with regard to any material matter.
- A person found guilty of making a false or fraudulent statement in connection with a return is guilty of a felony and may be imprisoned for not more than three years and/or fined not more than $100,000 ($500,000 for a corporation).

6.2.2 Civil Penalties

- The IRS may prohibit an accountant from practicing before the IRS.
- The IRS may impose fines for various infractions.

Note: In addition to criminal and civil penalties, a person guilty of making false and fraudulent statements on a return may be subject to a malpractice suit by the taxpayer (client).

6.3 Securities and Exchange Commission (SEC)

6.3.1 Civil Penalties

- The SEC may censure, suspend, or permanently revoke an accountant's right to practice before the SEC, including the right to sign documents required by the Securities Act of 1933 and the Securities Exchange Act of 1934.
- Suspension or revocation of the right to practice before the SEC can occur if:
  - the accountant lacks the qualifications to represent others;
  - the accountant lacks character or integrity;
  - the accountant acted unethically or unprofessionally;
  - the accountant willfully violated federal security laws or regulations;
  - the accountant was convicted of a felony or convicted of a misdemeanor involving moral turpitude; or
  - the accountant's license to practice public accounting was suspended or revoked as a disciplinary measure by a government authority.
- The SEC may impose fines of not more than $100,000 ($500,000 for a firm). The SEC can issue cease and desist orders.

MODULE 3: Federal Tax Procedures and Taxpayer Penalties

1 Audit Process

The federal income tax system is based on the self-assessment of taxes. All "persons" with taxable incomes exceeding certain amounts are required to file annual income tax returns and to timely remit taxes that are due. The audit process helps ensure that this "voluntary" assessment and payment is actually occurring.

1.1 Examination of a Return (Audit)

A return may be examined (audited) for a variety of reasons, and the examination may take place in any one of several ways. After the audit, if there are any changes to the tax payable, the taxpayer either can agree with the changes and pay the additional tax or can disagree with the changes and appeal the decision. Interest on unpaid taxes may also be due.

1.2 Selection of Returns for Audit

1.2.1 Statistical Models

The IRS utilizes statistical models (a form of discriminant analysis called the Discriminant Inventory Function System, or DIF) to select tax returns that are the most likely to contain errors and yield significant amounts of additional tax revenue upon audit.

1.2.2 Random Selection

In addition to the statistical selection of returns to be audited, a small number of additional returns are manually selected.

1.2.3 Prior Year Audit

If the taxpayer was audited in a prior year and that prior audit led to assessment of a substantial deficiency, a subsequent year may be audited.

1.2.4 Information Return Discrepancy

If information forms such as W-2s and 1099s do not match the amounts reported on a return, or if information is received from other sources on potential noncompliance, an audit may be triggered.

1.2.5 Deductions That Exceed Established Norms

If an individual's itemized deductions are in excess of norms established for certain income levels, the return may be selected for audit.

1.3 Timing of Audits

Most individual returns are audited within two years from the date of filing of the return. However, returns may be audited at any point prior to the expiration of the statute of limitations. Even then, the taxpayer may consent to extend this statute upon IRS request. Large corporations are subject to annual audits.

1.4 Review for Mathematical Errors (Correspondence Audit)

A correspondence audit arises as a result of IRS review for the following:

- Information errors (incorrect Social Security numbers or missing signatures)
- Matching issues (income reported on tax return does not match W-2 or Form 1099)
- Mathematical errors

In the case of errors, the taxpayer is typically sent a revised computation and a brief explanation of any change made along with a bill for the additional amount due or check for a refund, as appropriate. There will be no need for a formal meeting with an IRS representative. If the payment is made timely, there is no interest on the underpayment. If the required payment is not made timely, there is interest from the date of the notice.

1.5 Formal Examination (Office or Field Audit)

If a formal examination is necessary, there may be an office audit or a field audit.

1.5.1 Office Audit

An office audit is conducted by an IRS revenue agent, either in an IRS office or by correspondence, and is used for individual returns with few or no items of business income. In most cases, the taxpayer is merely required to substantiate an item of income, a deduction, or a credit.

1.5.2 Field Audit

A field audit is conducted by an IRS representative, either at the taxpayer's office or home or at the place of business of the taxpayer's representative. The IRS makes the final determination of when, where, and how the examination will take place. The taxpayer can make an audio recording of the examination interview.

1.6 After the Audit

1.6.1 Issue Resolved

Following an audit, the revenue agent may either accept the return or recommend certain changes. If agreement is reached with the taxpayer, the taxpayer signs Form 870 (Waiver of Restrictions on Assessment and Collection of Deficiency in Tax), and interest stops accumulating on the deficiency 30 days after the form is filed. The taxpayer will receive a bill for any additional taxes and interest (generally calculated from the due date of the return to the date of payment) or a check for any refund, including interest on the refund.

By signing the Form 870, the taxpayer waives the right to receive certain statutory notices and to petition the U.S. Tax Court and waives the right to the appeal process. The signing of the Form 870 normally closes the case, but the IRS may assess additional deficiencies if necessary.

1.6.2 Unresolved Issues

If agreement cannot be reached at the revenue agent level, the taxpayer receives a copy of the Revenue Agent's report and a 30-day letter (preliminary notice) notifying the taxpayer of the right to appeal. The taxpayer has 30 days to request an administrative appeal with an appeals officer (appeals conference).

1.6.3 Fast-Track Remediation

Small business owners and self-employed individuals can resolve their tax disputes through a process called fast-track remediation. The goal for resolution within fast-track remediation is 60 days. A trained mediator from the IRS Office of Appeals is assigned to help the taxpayer and the IRS reach an agreement on the disputed issue(s). Fast-track remediation is not available for issues for which there is no legal precedent in the courts, for which the courts in different jurisdictions have rendered differing decisions, and in other specialized situations. If, at the end of the fast-track mediation process, the issue remains unresolved, the normal appeals process is still available.

2 Appeals Process

2.1 Appeals Conference

If agreement cannot be reached at the revenue agent level, the taxpayer receives a copy of the Revenue Agent's report and a 30-day letter (preliminary notice) notifying the taxpayer of the right to appeal. The taxpayer has 30 days to request an administrative appeal with an appeals officer (appeals conference).

2.2 Office of Appeals

The goal of the appeals process handled by the IRS Office of Appeals is to resolve tax controversies without litigation. If an agreement is reached with the Appeals Division, the taxpayer signs Form 870-AD. Interest stops accruing when the form is received and accepted by the IRS. This settlement is normally considered binding on both parties. If agreement is not reached, a 90-day letter will be issued.

2.3 90-Day Letter (Notice of Deficiency)

If an appeals conference was not requested after receipt of the 30-day letter, or if the taxpayer and IRS still do not agree on the proposed adjustment after the appeals conference, a 90-day letter (notice of deficiency) is issued. The taxpayer has 90 days to pay the deficiency or file a petition with the U.S. Tax Court. If the taxpayer would like to litigate the case but prefers the case to be heard in the U.S. District Court or the U.S. Court of Federal Claims, the taxpayer must first pay the tax deficiency and then sue the IRS for refund in the court if the IRS denies the claim for refund.

3 Federal Judicial Process

When a taxpayer and the Internal Revenue Service cannot reach agreement on a tax matter administratively either with a revenue agent or with the Appeals Division, the dispute must be settled in the Federal Court system. Either the IRS or the taxpayer can initiate the process. In the Federal Court system, the U.S. Tax Court, a U.S. District Court, and the U.S. Court of Federal Claims are considered trial courts. The U.S. Court of Appeals, the Federal Court of Appeals, and the Supreme Court of the United States are considered appellate courts.

Appellate courts are limited to a review of the trial record of the lower court to determine if that lower court applied the proper law in arriving at its decision. Seldom will an appellate court disturb the trial court's determination of the facts.

The taxpayer can choose the route through the court system that he or she deems most favorable. Key concepts related to the federal judicial process include the following:

- **Burden of Proof**

    In most litigation, the party bringing the case has the burden of proof. In most civil tax cases, the taxpayer has the burden of proof. In certain situations, however, the burden of proof shifts to the IRS. The IRS has the burden of proof in any court proceeding on income, gift, estate, or generation-skipping tax with respect to factual issues provided that the taxpayer has introduced credible evidence, has maintained books and records as required, and has complied with reasonable IRS requests.

- **Doctrine of Stare Decisis**

    Like English law, American law is frequently made by judicial decisions. Under the doctrine of stare decisis, judges are required to respect the precedents established by prior judicial decisions on the same set of facts.

- **Appeal Outcomes**

    An appeal can have a number of possible outcomes. The appellate court may affirm (accept) or reverse the lower court's finding or it may send the case back to the lower court for further consideration (remand).

3.1 U.S. Tax Court

The U.S. Tax Court is a specialized trial court that hears only federal tax cases (income tax, estate tax, gift tax, or certain excise taxes), generally prior to the time that formal tax assessments are made by the IRS.

3.1.1 Small Cases Division Option

Taxpayers who file petitions with the U.S. Tax Court have the option of having the case heard before the informal Small Cases Division (small tax cases) if the amount of tax in dispute does not exceed $50,000 for any one tax year. Neither party may appeal the decision and the decision is not considered precedent in other courts.

3.1.2 No Payment Required to Petition/Trial by Judge (No Jury)

The U.S. Tax Court is the only forum in which taxpayers may litigate without first having paid the disputed tax in full. Trials are conducted before one judge who will be a tax expert, and there are no jury trials. Taxpayers are permitted to represent themselves. For a case to be heard, the taxpayer must petition the Tax Court, normally within 90 days of the IRS's mailing of a notice of deficiency (90-day letter) and demand for payment of the disputed amount. Cases cannot be taken to the Tax Court before the IRS sends out the notice of deficiency.

3.1.3 Decisions

The U.S. Tax Court issues two types of decisions: regular and memorandum. Small tax case decisions are published as Summary Opinions.

- **Regular Decision:** A regular decision normally involves a new or unusual point of law.
- **Memorandum Decision:** A memorandum decision concerns only the application of existing law or an interpretation of facts.

3.2 U.S. District Courts

The U.S. District Courts are the general trial courts of the U.S. federal court system. Both civil and criminal cases (not just tax cases) are filed in district courts. There is at least one district court for each state and other district courts for territories. Typically, a taxpayer will request a hearing before the district court that has jurisdiction over the location in which the taxpayer lives or conducts business.

3.2.1 Must First Pay Disputed Tax Liability and Sue IRS for Refund

A taxpayer who disagrees with the IRS may take his or her case to a U.S. District Court only after paying the disputed tax liability and then sue the IRS for a refund. Generally, a claim for refund must be filed within three years from the date the original return was filed or two years from the date the tax was paid, whichever is later.

3.2.2 One Judge and Jury Trial Is an Option

U.S. District Court cases are heard before one judge, not a panel of judges. The taxpayer can request a jury trial.

3.3 U.S. Court of Federal Claims

The U.S. Court of Federal Claims is a nationwide court that has jurisdiction over most claims for money damages against the United States, one type of which is tax refunds. The court has concurrent jurisdiction with U.S. District Courts when the claim is for less than $10,000, and there is a statute of limitations of six years from the time the claim arose. The taxpayer must pay the disputed tax and sue the IRS/government for a refund. The Court of Federal Claims does not allow jury trials on any matter. There are 16 judges.

Summary of U.S. Trial Court System

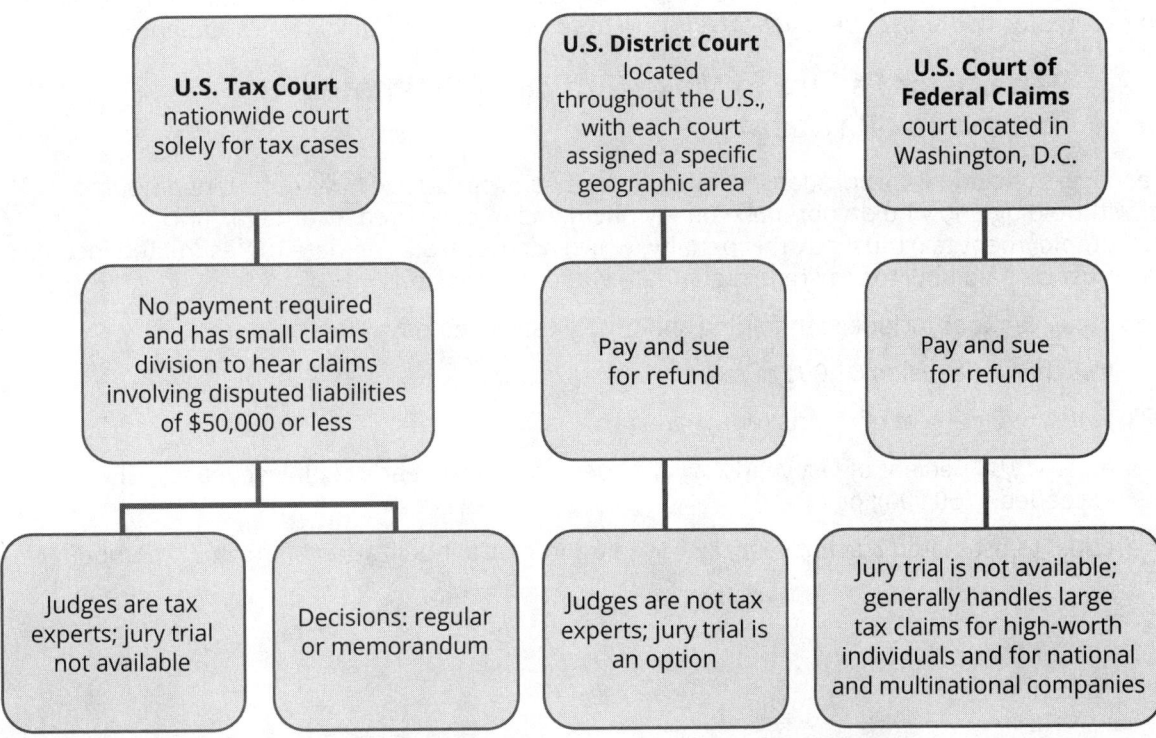

3.4 Courts of Appeals and the U.S. Court of Appeals for the Federal Circuit

The U.S. Courts of Appeals (or circuit courts) are the first level of federal appellate courts. A court of appeals hears appeals from the U.S. District Courts and the U.S. Tax Court. The U.S. Circuit Court of Appeals hears appeals from the U.S. Court of Federal Claims.

3.5 U.S. Supreme Court

The U.S. Supreme Court is the highest court in the nation and is the last level of appeal.

3.5.1 Panel of Nine Justices (No Jury)

There are nine justices (judges), who hear all cases that the Supreme Court agrees to consider (for which it grants a *writ of certiorari*) in Washington, D.C.

3.5.2 Tax Cases Are Rare

The Supreme Court seldom hears tax cases. In most cases where it does hear a tax case, it is where there is a conflict among the Courts of Appeals.

4 Taxpayer Penalties

The Internal Revenue Code contains many sections setting forth penalties, both civil and criminal, which the Internal Revenue Service can seek to impose on the taxpayer.

4.1 Earned Income Credit Penalty

The earned income credit "penalty" is more a statutory restriction on claiming the credit, rather than a penalty, per se. Taxpayers who negligently claim the earned income credit may not claim this credit for two subsequent years or for up to ten years if the claim was fraudulent.

4.2 Penalty for Failure to Make Sufficient Estimated Income Tax Payments

Taxpayers (including corporations, estates, and trusts) who do not have sufficient amounts of withholding and who do not make timely payments of estimated income tax (including self-employment tax) must pay this penalty, which accrues from the date the estimated income tax must be paid until the tax return due date without extensions.

Penalty exceptions include withholding and timely estimated payments that are:

- less than or equal to $1,000 of current year tax;
- at least 90 percent of the current year's tax;
- at least 100 percent of last year's tax (110 percent of last year's tax if last year's AGI exceeded $150,000); or
- equal to estimated current year tax based upon the "annualization of income" method.

4.3 Failure-to-File Penalty

The penalty is 5 percent of the amount of tax due for each month (or any part of) the return is late, up to a maximum of 25 percent. Other key aspects of the failure-to-file penalty are the following:

- If the return is more than 60 days late, the minimum penalty increases to the lesser of $485 or 100 percent of the tax due.
- If no tax is due, then there is no failure-to-file penalty.
- If both the failure-to-file penalty and the failure-to-pay penalty are due, the failure-to-file penalty is reduced by the amount of the failure-to-pay penalty.
- The penalty for failure to file a partnership or S corporation tax return is $235 for each month or part thereof (up to a maximum of 12 months) the return is late (or required information is missing) times the numbers of persons who are partners in the partnership at any time during the year.

4.4 Failure-to-Pay Penalty

The penalty is one-half of 1 percent per month (or any part of) up to a maximum of 25 percent of the unpaid tax.

There is no penalty if at least 90 percent of the tax is paid in by the unextended due date; and the balance is paid by the extended due date.

4.5 Negligence Penalty With Respect to an Understatement of Tax (Accuracy-Related Penalty When Understatement Is Not Substantial)

- This penalty is an accuracy-based penalty for negligence or for disregard of tax rules and regulations.
- The penalty is equal to 20 percent of the understatement of tax.
- *Negligence* means any failure to make a reasonable attempt to comply with the provisions of the IRC.
- *Disregard* means careless, reckless, or intentional disregard.
- If the IRS imposes this penalty, then the IRS cannot impose either (i) the penalty for substantial underpayment of tax; or (ii) the penalty for a substantial valuation misstatement.

4.6 Penalty for Substantial Understatement of Tax (Accuracy-Related Penalty)

- The penalty is 20 percent of the understatement of tax.
  - An understatement is *substantial* if it exceeds the greater of 10 percent of the correct tax (5 percent of the correct tax if the understatement is due to the taxpayer overstating the QBI deduction) or $5,000.
  - For C corporations other than personal holding companies, an understatement is *substantial* if the amount of the understatement exceeds the lesser of (a) $10,000,000; or (b) the greater of $10,000 or 10 percent of the correct tax.
- If the IRS imposes this penalty, then the IRS cannot impose either (i) the negligence penalty with respect to an understatement of tax which is not substantial and penalty for disregard of rules or regulations; or (ii) the penalty for a substantial valuation misstatement.

Federal Tax Procedures and Taxpayer Penalties

4.7 Penalty for a Substantial Valuation Misstatement

- The penalty is 20 percent of the understatement of tax with respect to a valuation for tax purposes to the extent the understatement exceeds $5,000 ($10,000 for corporations).
- There are two distinct substantial valuation misstatement standards: one for IRC Section 482 transactions (related parties) and one for non-Section 482 transactions (non-related parties).
- Defenses for charitable contributions must include good faith, qualified appraisals, and good faith investigation of value.
- This penalty cannot be imposed in addition to the negligence penalty or for substantial understatement.

4.8 Fraud Penalties

- Both civil penalties (at least 75 percent of the understatement of tax due to fraud) and criminal penalties (as high as $100,000; $500,000 for corporations) can apply.
- The IRS must prove that the taxpayer willfully and deliberately attempted to evade tax.
- Criminal penalty and potential imprisonment subject to an inflation adjustment, top $100,000 ($500,000 for corporations), plus the IRS must prove beyond a reasonable doubt that the taxpayer criminally, willfully, and deliberately attempted to evade tax.

5 Substantiation and Disclosure of Tax Positions

There are factors which should be considered when tax positions are taken on tax returns to avoid or reduce penalties.

5.1 Frivolous Tax Return

Frivolous positions have no basis in law or other authority. Disclosure will not protect a taxpayer or a tax preparer from penalties if a tax return position is frivolous.

5.2 Reasonable Basis Standard

- The reasonable basis standard is a tax position that has at least a 20 percent chance of succeeding, one that is arguable but fairly unlikely to prevail in court.
- This standard is not met if the taxpayer fails to make a reasonable attempt to determine the correctness of a position that seems too good to be true.
- This standard will avoid the negligence penalty with respect to an understatement of tax that is not substantial and the penalty for disregard of rules or regulations, even if the taxpayer does not disclose the tax return position for which the taxpayer has a reasonable basis.
- Reasonable basis will avoid the substantial underpayment penalty only if the taxpayer disclosed the tax return position (except for tax shelters) for which the taxpayer has a reasonable basis.

5.3 Substantial Authority Standard

- The substantial authority standard is a position that has more than a 40 percent chance of succeeding in court.

- Only analyses and reports issued by the U.S. Congress, IRS regulations, rules, and releases, and U.S. court case decisions constitute substantial authority. Tax articles and treatises do not constitute substantial authority. See discussion that follows in this module on substantial authority.

5.4 More-Likely-Than-Not Standard

The more-likely-than-not standard is met when there is a greater than 50 percent likelihood of a tax position being upheld by the courts. This standard is more stringent than the substantial authority standard.

5.5 Disclosures for Uncertain Tax Positions

Certain tax forms are used to disclose uncertain tax positions and can help taxpayer avoid understatement penalties.

- **Disclosure Statement (Form 8275)**
  - This form is used to avoid the understatement penalty.
  - It is a statement used to disclose positions taken on a tax return that are contrary to Revenue Rulings, Revenue Procedures, or other statutory provisions (except Regulations).
  - There are three parts to the form: (1) general information; (2) detailed explanation; and (3) information about pass-through entity.

- **Regulation Disclosure Statement (Form 8275-R)**

  This form is almost identical to Form 8275 but is used to disclose positions taken on a tax return that are contrary to Treasury Regulations.

- **Reportable Transaction Disclosure Statement (Form 8886)**
  - Any taxpayer that participates in a reportable transaction and is required to file a federal tax return or information return must file Form 8886 disclosing the transaction.
  - The filing requirement applies whether or not another party, related or otherwise, has filed a disclosure for that transaction.
  - The categories of reportable transactions include the following:
    — Listed transactions
    — Confidential transactions
    — Transactions with contractual protection
    — Loss transactions

5.6 General Avoidance of Penalties

In addition to the various defenses that are available, a taxpayer generally can avoid any penalty by showing that the taxpayer:

1. had reasonable cause to support the tax return position;
2. acted in good faith; and
3. did not have willful neglect.

5.7 Interest on Penalties

Interest on many penalties begins to accrue from the tax return due date (or extended due date). (Note that interest on underpaid tax begins to accrue from the date the tax was due without extension of time to file.)

6 Substantial Authority

Only the following are authority for purposes of determining whether there is substantial authority (defined below) for the tax treatment of an item (note that conclusions reached in treatises, legal periodicals, legal opinions, or opinions rendered by tax professionals are not "authority"):

- Applicable provisions of the Internal Revenue Code and other statutory provisions.
- Proposed, temporary, and final regulations construing such statutes.
- Revenue rulings and revenue procedures, tax treaties and regulations thereunder, and U.S. Treasury Department and other official explanations of such treaties.
- Court cases.
- Congressional intent as reflected in committee reports, joint explanatory statements of managers included in conference committee reports, and floor statements made prior to enactment by one of a bill's managers.
- General Explanations of tax legislation prepared by the Joint (U.S. Senate and U.S. House of Representatives) Committee on Taxation (the "Blue Book").
- Private letter rulings and technical advice memoranda issued after October 31, 1976.
- Actions on decisions and general counsel memoranda issued after March 12, 1981 (as well as general counsel memoranda published in pre-1955 volumes of the Cumulative Bulletin).
- Internal Revenue Service information or press releases and notices, announcements, and other administrative pronouncements published by the Service in the Internal Revenue Bulletin.

7 Reporting Requirements for Foreign Bank Accounts

The Bank Secrecy Act (BSA) requires U.S. persons to report certain financial accounts located outside of the United States by filing a Report of Foreign Bank and Financial Accounts (FBAR). The FBAR is used by the Financial Crimes Enforcement Network (FinCEN), a division of the Treasury Department, to help identify funds used for illegal activities or unreported income from foreign sources.

7.1 Who Must File the FBAR

A U.S. person must file an FBAR if:

- They have a financial interest in, or signature or other authority over, any financial account maintained with a financial institution located outside the United States; and
- The aggregate value of the account(s) exceeds $10,000 at any time during the calendar year.

7.1.1 U.S. Person

- A U.S. citizen or resident
- An entity created, organized, or formed in the United States (corporation, partnership, LLC, trust, estate)

7.1.2 Financial Account

- Bank accounts (checking, savings, certificates of deposit)
- Brokerage accounts and other securities accounts
- Options or commodity futures accounts
- Cash-value insurance or annuity policies
- Mutual funds

7.1.3 Maximum Aggregate Value

The maximum value of a foreign account is the highest value during the calendar year measured in the foreign currency of the account, which is then converted into U.S. dollars using the Treasury exchange rates for the last day of the calendar year. An FBAR must be filed if the maximum value of all of a U.S. person's foreign financial accounts in U.S. dollars totals more than $10,000.

7.2 Filing Requirements for the FBAR

The FBAR, FinCEN Form 114, must be filed electronically through the FinCEN's BSA E-filing System. The report is due on April 15 following the end of the calendar year being reported. There is an automatic six-month extension to file.

7.2.1 Jointly Owned Accounts

If an account is jointly owned by two or more persons, then each U.S. person with a financial interest in the account is generally required to report the entire value of the account on an FBAR. There is a limited exception available for spouses with jointly owned accounts that allows only one spouse to report the account on an FBAR.

7.2.2 Exceptions to FBAR Filing Requirements

- An entity named in a consolidated FBAR filed by a greater than 50 percent owner
- Participants and beneficiaries of IRAs and tax-qualified retirement plans
- Beneficiaries of a trust

7.3 Reporting and Record-Keeping Requirements

Records must be kept with the following information for each account reported on an FBAR for at least five years:

- Name on the account
- Account number
- Name and address of foreign bank
- Type of account
- Maximum value during the year

MODULE 4 Legal Duties and Responsibilities

REG 4

1 Legal Liabilities

Civil actions for tax malpractice are usually based on either traditional contract or traditional tort principles.

- Contract principles impose the obligation to prepare the tax return diligently and competently.
- Tort principles provide that a professional has a duty to exercise the level of skill, care, and diligence commonly exercised by other members of the profession under similar circumstances.

To prove malpractice against a tax preparer, the plaintiff must demonstrate all of the following:

1. The tax preparer owed a duty to the taxpayer.
2. There was a breach of that duty.
3. The plaintiff suffered injuries.
4. The breach of duty caused the plaintiff's injury.

1.1 Breach of Contract

If a CPA does not fulfill the terms of his engagement, the client can hold the CPA liable for breach. Contract liability generally requires *privity*, so only a party to the contract can sue under a contract theory.

> **Illustration 1   Tax Preparer Breach of Contract**
>
> Alan Sims has a signed engagement letter from his CPA, Joe Foster, stating that Mr. Foster's firm will prepare Alan's individual federal tax return and three state tax returns by April 1 if Alan provides all requested documentation by March 10. Alan wanted his tax returns completed by April 1 because he was leaving the country for a trip with his family. Alan's tax returns were not completed until April 30. This scenario could lead to a breach of contract claim as the tax preparer owed a duty to the taxpayer (to prepare the federal and state tax returns), and there appears to be a breach of that duty because the returns were not completed at the agreed upon date.

1.2 Commission of a Tort

CPA liability can also arise from commission of a tort. Three torts are relevant:

- negligence;
- constructive fraud (also called gross negligence); and
- fraud.

1.2.1 Negligence

As a general rule, a CPA owes a duty to his or her client not to perform work negligently. If the CPA performs negligently, he or she can be held liable for damages. Negligence requires a breach of the duty to exercise due care. The standard of care owed by a CPA is to perform with the same skill and care expected of ordinarily prudent CPAs under the circumstances.

1. **Elements in General**

   To make out a case for negligence, the plaintiff must show:
   - the defendant owed a duty of care to the plaintiff;
   - the defendant breached that duty by failing to act with due care;
   - the breach caused plaintiff's injury; and
   - damages.

2. **To Whom Is the Duty Owed?**
   - A CPA's duty to act with reasonable care generally runs only to clients and to any person or *limited* foreseeable class of persons whom the CPA knows will be relying on the CPA's work.
   - A minority of states follows the *Ultramares* decision, which limits CPA liability more narrowly to persons in privity of contract with the CPA (clients) and intended third-party beneficiaries.

1.3 Fraud and Constructive Fraud (Gross Negligence)

CPA liability can also arise through fraud or constructive fraud.

1.3.1 Elements of Fraud (Intentional Misrepresentation)

Actual fraud has five elements:

1. A misrepresentation of material fact;
2. Intent to deceive (knowing the statement was false);
3. Actual and justifiable reliance by plaintiff on the misrepresentation;
4. An intent to induce plaintiff's reliance on the misrepresentation; and
5. Damages.

> **Illustration 2   Tax Preparer Fraud**
>
> Mark Waters, CPA, owned Peach Tax Services Inc. and for three years intentionally misreported deductions on his clients' tax returns and electronically filed hundreds of incorrect federal income tax returns with the IRS to generate fraudulent refunds.

1.3.2 Elements of Constructive Fraud (Gross Negligence)

Constructive fraud has the same elements as actual fraud, except instead of intentionally deceiving, the defendant acts recklessly (i.e., makes a statement without knowing whether it is true or false).

1.3.3 To Whom Is the CPA Liable?

- A CPA's liability for fraud and constructive fraud is much broader than a CPA's liability for negligence. The CPA can be held liable to anyone who proves the above elements.
- Privity is not a defense to fraud. Liability is not limited to persons in privity, third-party beneficiaries or a limited class of persons who foreseeably rely.

Illustration 3   Summary of "Levels of Fault"

1. **"Reasonable care"** ("due care") is taken = No negligence = Not liable
2. **Lack of reasonable care** = Ordinary negligence

    The CPA is liable to anyone he or she knows or reasonably should expect will rely on his or her work.
3. **Lack of even slight care** = Gross negligence or constructive fraud
4. **Actual fraud** = Actual intent to deceive
5. **Criminal fraud** = Actual intent to deceive*

    Levels 1 through 4 are *civil* in nature. Only level 5 is *criminal*.

*Note the conduct that forms the basis of a level 4 civil fraud action is the same conduct that forms the basis for a criminal prosecution (level 5) by the government.

1.3.4 Damages

Damages associated with tax return preparation malpractice have multiple components including the following:

- **Taxes**: Because the filing of the tax return and payment of taxes is ultimately the responsibility of the taxpayer, the tax that a taxpayer owes is not normally a recoverable damage amount. In some situations, the tax practitioner can be held liable for the amount by which taxes were overpaid if the overpayment cannot be reclaimed through the filing of an amended return.
- **Penalties:** Courts often award damages associated with penalties imposed because of mistakes reported on tax returns.
- **Interest:** Amounts equal to the interest owed by the taxpayer may be awarded by the courts to the extent that the taxpayer has suffered actual damages related to the interest charged.
- **Costs Incurred to Correct Tax Returns:** Damages may include fees that will be incurred to file amended returns and/or challenge penalties that have been assessed.
- **Consequential Damages:** This category of potential damages includes lost investment or income opportunities for taxpayers as a result of tax preparer's mistake.

2 Privileged Communications, Confidentiality, and Privacy Acts

The rules of evidence protect information exchanged in certain confidential relationships (e.g., attorney-client, doctor-patient) by granting an evidentiary privilege—information exchanged within the scope of the relationship may not be disclosed as evidence in court without the consent of the privilege holder.

2.1 Privileged Communications

Privileges available to CPAs can include the following:

- **Attorney-Client Privilege:** This privilege is potentially available when the CPA has been engaged by the attorney prior to aid the attorney in providing legal services because the expertise of a CPA is needed.
- **Work Product Privilege:** This privilege can protect tangible materials produced in preparation for litigation as requested by an attorney but not to the communication between the attorney and accountant about the product.
- **Tax Practitioner-Taxpayer Privilege:** This privilege applies to tax advice from a tax practitioner that would qualify under the attorney-client privilege. The Tax Practitioner Privilege applies only to federally authorized tax practitioners under the IRC Section 7525. State law may vary.

2.2 Tax Practitioner Privilege

IRC Section 7525 provides that some communication between taxpayers and federal authorized tax practitioners is regarded as privileged. IRC Section 7525 provides that the same common law protections of confidentiality that apply to a communication between a taxpayer and an attorney also apply to a communication between a taxpayer and any federally authorized tax practitioner (to the extent the communication would be considered a privileged communication if it were between a taxpayer and an attorney). The tax practitioner privilege may only be asserted in any noncriminal tax matter before the Internal Revenue Service and any noncriminal tax proceeding in federal court brought by or against the United States.

2.2.1 Federally Authorized Tax Practitioner

The phrase *federally authorized tax practitioner* means any individual who is authorized under federal law to practice before the Internal Revenue Service. It is a category that includes certified public accountants, enrolled agents, and enrolled actuaries.

2.2.2 Not Applicable to Communications Regarding Tax Shelters

The tax practitioner privilege shall not apply to any written communication between a federally authorized tax practitioner and:

- any person;
- any director, officer, employee, agent, or representative of the person; or
- any other person holding a capital or profits interest in the person; and

…in connection with the promotion of the direct or indirect participation of the person in any tax shelter.

2.3 Workpapers

Workpapers belong to the accountant (or accountant's firm) that prepares them, not the client. The accountant is prohibited from showing the workpapers to anyone without the client's permission, except in the following situations:

- In response to a subpoena relevant to a court case.
- To a prospective purchaser of the CPA's practice, as long as the prospective purchaser does not disclose the confidential information.
- To a state CPA society voluntary quality-control review panel, when requested.
- In defense of a lawsuit brought by a client.
- To be used in defense of an official investigation by the AICPA/state trial board.
- When GAAP requires disclosure of such information in the financial statements.

Pass Key

Note that, although a CPA may allow a prospective purchaser to review confidential workpapers, the CPA may not turn over the workpapers to a purchaser without the client's permission.

NOTES

Business Law: Part 1

Module

1	Contracts: Part 1	3
2	Contracts: Part 2	13
3	Contracts: Part 3	25
4	Agency	41
5	Suretyship	53
6	Secured Transactions	63

NOTES

MODULE 1
Contracts: Part 1

REG 5

1 Methods of Formation

Broadly speaking, a contract is a promise that the law will enforce. Methods of contract formation include:

Pass Key

While the examiners rarely ask you to describe a contract using the descriptive terms below, it is important for you to understand them, because the examiners sometimes use them in their questions.

- **Express Contract:** A contract formed by *language*, oral or written, is an express contract.

Illustration 1   Express Contract

If Ann promises to give Barb $10 if Barb will wash Ann's car, the contract is express.

- **Implied-in-Fact Contract:** A contract formed by *conduct* is an implied-in-fact contract.

Illustration 2   Implied-in-Fact Contract

Alex goes to Doctor and tells Doctor that he is sick. Doctor examines Alex and gives him an antibiotic. Alex and Doctor have entered into a contract for Doctor's services even though no oral or written promises were exchanged. Their conduct implies their intent to enter into a contract.

- **Implied-in-Law Contract or Quasi-Contract:** A quasi-contract is not a contract at all. It is a remedy that allows a plaintiff to recover a benefit unjustly conferred upon the defendant—a remedy to *prevent unjust enrichment*.

> **Illustration 3 Quasi-Contract**
>
> Joanne gives Keith $10,000 as a down payment to purchase Keith's house. The contract is oral and, as will be discussed later, is unenforceable. Keith decides to back out. Joanne can recover the down payment in quasi-contract.

- **Unilateral Contract:** In a unilateral contract, there is *one promise*, which is given in exchange for performance (e.g., Ann promises to give Barb $10 if Barb will wash Ann's car). A contract is not formed until performance is completed.
- **Bilateral Contract:** In a bilateral contract, there are *two promises*—a promise is exchanged for a promise (e.g., Ann promises to give Barb $10 if Barb promises to wash Ann's car). Here, a contract is formed as soon as the promises are exchanged.

2 Sources of Contract Law

1. **Common Law**

   The common law is generally derived from courts. Contracts involving real estate, insurance, services, and employment (**RISE**) are governed by the common law.

2. **Uniform Commercial Code (UCC) Sales Article**

   The UCC is statutory law that has been widely adopted throughout the United States. Its Sales Article (Article 2) governs contracts for the sale of goods (moveable things). There are a number of special rules that apply to contracts for the sale of goods, which are reviewed in a later module.

3 Elements of a Legally Enforceable Contract

Generally, there are three requirements of a legally enforceable contract:

1. an agreement made up of an offer and an acceptance;
2. an exchange of consideration (something of legal value); and
3. a lack of defenses.

If these three requirements are met, there is an enforceable contract and remedies are available if one party breaches (i.e., does not perform as promised).

> **Pass Key**
>
> Notice that "a writing" is *not* a general element of a contract. Certain contracts must be evidenced by a writing (they will be discussed in this module under the Statute of Frauds portion of the Defenses section), but the general rule is that a writing is not required. Thus, if you see an answer choice on the exam saying an offer or acceptance must be in writing, scrutinize the facts carefully. If the contract is not within the Statute of Frauds, the choice probably is wrong.

3.1 Agreement (Mutual Assent) (Offer and Acceptance)

Mutual assent is often said to be agreeing to the "same bargain at the same time"—a meeting of the minds. Generally, one party will make a proposal (an offer) and the other party will agree to it (an acceptance).

3.1.1 The Offer

An offer is a statement by an offeror that gives the recipient (i.e., the offeree) the power to form a contract by accepting *before the offer is terminated*.

- **Intent to Make a Contract:** To be valid, the offer must be sufficient for a *reasonable person* to assume that the offer was a serious offer to enter into a contract. The offeror's subjective intent (i.e., whether the offeror thought he was making an offer) is irrelevant. Contract law generally follows an objective theory (would a reasonable person believe the offer was serious). Statements made in jest or frustration and understood as such by a reasonable person are not offers.
    - **Advertisements:** Widely distributed statements such as advertisements are *not* offers because they are not addressed to anyone in particular. They are usually considered only to be *invitations* seeking offers.
    - An advertisement that limits the scope of the persons who can accept (e.g., "the first five customers can buy this coffee maker for only $1") will be considered to be an offer.

> **Illustration 4   Advertisements**
>
> Steve places an ad in a local paper announcing the grand opening of his store and quoting the price of certain items. Such an ad is not an offer but is only an invitation seeking offers.

- **Terms Must Be Definite and Certain:** An offer must be definite and certain in its terms. What is essential depends on the type of contract involved. An offer for the sale of goods generally need only include the quantity term (e.g., "I offer to sell 100 widgets"). An offer to create a contract under common law (e.g., a contract involving services or real property) must include:
    - the *identity* of the *offeree* and the subject matter;
    - the *price* to be paid;
    - the *time* of performance;
    - the *quantity* involved; and
    - the *nature* of the work to be performed.

> **Illustration 5   Definite Terms**
>
> Alex asks Bob to repair a broken window at Alex's store within three days, at a price to be agreed upon later. The offer here will fail for indefiniteness of the price term.

3.1.2 Termination of Offer

To create a contract, an offer must be accepted before it is terminated. An offer can be terminated in a number of ways—through the act of either party (offeror: *revocation*; offeree: *rejection*) or by operation of law (e.g., by death of a party).

- **Revocation by Offeror:** The general rule is that the offeror can revoke an offer any time before acceptance by communicating the revocation to the offeree. Except as discussed below, this is true even where the offeror promises to keep the offer open.

> **Illustration 6 Revocation**
>
> Maurice sent Schmit an email offering to sell him a one-acre tract of commercial property for $8,000. Maurice stated that Schmit had three days to consider the offer and in the meantime the offer would be irrevocable. The next day, Maurice received a better offer from another party, and he telephoned Schmit, informing him that he was revoking the offer. This was an effective revocation.

- The revocation can be direct (e.g., a phone call to the offeree withdrawing the offer) or *indirect*, where the offeree receives correct information that the offeror no longer wants to make the offer.

> **Illustration 7 Indirect Revocation**
>
> Alex offers to sell his car to Bob for $500. Bob tells Alex that he wants to think about it. The next day, Carol, a friend of Bob, drives over to Bob's house to show Bob the car she just purchased from Alex. The offer to Bob is revoked.

- The revocation is generally effective when received by the offeree. Where revocation is by publication, it is effective when published.
- Although the general rule is that all offers can be revoked, there is an exception to the general rule which appears with some frequency on the CPA Exam where consideration is paid to keep the offer open (called an *option contract*). An option is a distinct contract in which the promisor promises to keep an offer open in exchange for consideration from the promisee.

Pass Key

The examiners frequently use irrevocability as a wrong answer choice. They will tell you about the parties' negotiations and ask you to pick a true statement. One answer choice frequently is that the offer is "irrevocable" or "it could not be revoked because it is an option." Scrutinize the facts carefully. The key point to remember is that if consideration was not given to keep the offer open, it is not an option.

- **Rejection by Offeree:** The offeree can terminate the offer by rejecting it. Once the offer is effectively rejected, it cannot be accepted.
  - The offeree can reject expressly (e.g., by saying "no"). But more interestingly, a *counteroffer* is also considered to be both a *rejection* (which terminates the original offer) *and an offer* (of which the original offeror is now the offeree who may accept or reject).

Illustration 8 Rejection by Offeree

1. Barb offers to sell Alex her car for $450. Alex says, "No." The offer is terminated. If Alex later has a change of heart and tells Barb, "I accept," Alex has at most made a new offer. No contract is created.
2. Alex offers to sell Barb his car for $450. Barb says, "No, but I'll give you $425." Barb has rejected and made a new offer through a counteroffer.

  - A rejection is effective when *received*.

Illustration 9 Rejection

On January 3, Sam sent Ben a signed letter offering to sell his warehouse for $95,000. On January 5, Ben wrote Sam a letter saying that he would not pay $95,000 because that price was too high. On January 6, Ben was advised that similar property had recently been sold for $99,000. Ben immediately emailed Sam an acceptance of Sam's January 3 offer. Ben's letter arrived the next day. There is a contract because a rejection is not effective until received. The rejection here arrived after the offer was accepted by email.

- **Termination by Operation of Law**
  - If either of the parties dies or becomes incompetent prior to acceptance, the offer is terminated by operation of law. It is *not* necessary that the death or incompetency be communicated to the other party.

  Exception: An option contract is not terminated by the death of a party.

Illustration 10 Termination

Dee offered to sell Sue a parcel of land for $300,000. If either Dee or Sue dies before the offer is accepted, the offer will terminate by operation of law. However, if Sue paid consideration for the offer (thus creating an option contract), the offer will remain open for the period of the option (i.e., Sue or Sue's estate could accept during the option period and a contract would be formed with Dee or Dee's estate).

  - If the subject matter of the offer is destroyed before the offer is accepted, the offeree's power of acceptance is terminated by operation of law.
  - If the subject matter of the proposed contract becomes illegal, the offer will terminate.

> **Illustration 11 Termination Due to Illegality**
>
> Lucky Lou offers Vegas Vernon a share in his casino business. Prior to acceptance, a law is passed banning casinos. The offer is automatically terminated.

3.1.3 The Acceptance

The acceptance is the offeree's assent to enter into a contract. Like offers, acceptances need not be in writing. An acceptance does not even require words—a simple nod of the head or fall of a gavel (in an auction) can constitute an acceptance.

- **Who May Accept:** The general rule is that only the person to whom the offer was made may accept. Thus, offers are not assignable; however, option contracts are assignable.

- **Method of Acceptance:** Generally, acceptance may be made in any manner reasonable under the circumstances (e.g., a mailed offer can usually be accepted by letter, email, etc.). However, if the offeror specifies a method of communication, that method must be used. A purported acceptance utilizing another method is a counteroffer.

- **Acceptance Generally Must Be Unequivocal:** Common law contracts follow the *mirror image rule*, which requires an acceptance to mirror the offer to be effective. An attempted acceptance that changes some of the terms or adds new terms is not a valid acceptance, but rather is a counteroffer, which serves as a rejection.

- **Generally Effective Upon Dispatch—the Mailbox Rule:** Unlike revocations, acceptances are generally effective when they are *dispatched* (i.e., mailed, emailed, faxed, etc.) if properly addressed. This is known as the mailbox rule. It is irrelevant if a properly addressed acceptance is lost or delayed.

> **Illustration 12 Mailbox Rule**
>
> On February 1, Taylor sends Jordan a letter offering to employ Jordan at Taylor's auto dealership. On February 5, Jordan sends Taylor a letter accepting the offer. On February 6, Taylor has a change of heart and calls Jordan to revoke the offer. On February 7, Taylor receives Jordan's acceptance. A contract was formed in this case on February 5, when the acceptance was sent. Taylor's attempted revocation is ineffective because it came too late (after the acceptance was sent). The date Taylor received the acceptance is irrelevant. Indeed, under the mailbox rule, a contract is formed on dispatch even if the acceptance letter is never received by the offeror.

- **Method of Communication Specified:** If the offeror required that acceptances be sent by a specific method, an acceptance sent by that method is effective when it is sent.

- **No Method of Communication Specified:** If the offer did not state how acceptances were to be sent, an acceptance sent *by any reasonable means* is effective upon dispatch (e.g., letter, email, fax, etc.).

- **Offeror May Opt Out:** The offeror can opt out of the mailbox rule by stating in the offer that acceptances must be received to be effective. In such cases, the acceptance must be received before the offer terminates.

Illustration 13 Mailbox Rule Violated

On November 1, Dee sent Steve an email offering to sell Steve a vase. The offer provided that an acceptance must be received by 5 p.m. on November 2. At 3 p.m. on November 1, Steve sent Dee an acceptance by overnight mail, but the acceptance did not reach Dee until November 3. There is no enforceable contract because the acceptance came too late. The offer provided that the acceptance had to be received by 5 p.m. on November 2, so the mailbox rule does not apply.

Pass Key

You probably will see a mailbox rule question on your exam. Often it is coupled with a revocability issue. The key is to approach such questions in three steps:

1. Was the offer revocable? Chances are it was, unless the offeree paid consideration to keep the offer open (an option).

2. Determine whether the mailbox rule applies (i.e., acceptance is effective on dispatch rather than receipt, unless the offer stated that an acceptance had to be received to be effective).

3. Compare any effective revocation date with the effective acceptance date. If a revocation was effective first, the offer was terminated and there is no contract. If the acceptance was effective first, there is a contract and the revocation was ineffective.

Be sure to remember, the mailbox rule only makes *acceptances* effective on dispatch; revocations, rejections, and counteroffers are effective only upon receipt.

3.2 Consideration

Consideration is the price of contracting. Both sides of the contract must be supported by legally sufficient consideration. The law will not enforce gratuitous promises. Something must be given in exchange for a promise for it to be enforceable. There are two elements of consideration: There must be *something of legal* value given by each party, and there must be a *bargained-for exchange*.

3.2.1 Element of Legal Value

Something is of legal value if it constitutes either a *detriment to the promisee* or a *benefit to the promisor*. That is, the promisor's promise is supported by consideration only if the promisee agrees to do something he or she is not already obligated to do (a detriment) or the promisor will obtain some benefit. Possible items of consideration include promises to perform acts or to refrain from performing; promises to pay money; and promises to give land, goods, stock, etc.

Illustration 14 Consideration

Phil (promisor) agrees to sell Lori (promisee) his television set for $200. Phil's promise (to sell) is supported by Lori's detriment (the giving of $200). Note that consideration must be present on both sides. Thus, Lori's promise (to give $200) is supported by Phil's detriment (giving the TV).

- **Need Not Have Monetary Value:** Consideration need not have monetary value. As long as the promisee is promising to do something that he is not already obligated to do or promising to refrain from doing something that he legally could do, there is consideration.

Illustration 15 Nonmonetary Consideration

1. Casey promises Pat that he will give Pat $500 if she names her first-born son after Casey. Pat does so. Naming the son after Casey is valid consideration.

2. Joanne promises Keith that she will refrain from suing Keith for 60 days on a valid claim if Keith promises to give Joanne an option to purchase Keith's property for a specified price during the 60-day period. Both promises constitute consideration. (Joanne's promise is known as a *forbearance to sue*.)

- **Need Not Flow to Party:** Note that the consideration need not flow to one of the parties; it is sufficient to promise to do something for or give something to a third party.

Illustration 16 Consideration Flowing to a Third Party

Alex promises Becky that he will pay her $10 if she promises to wash Cindy's car. Alex's promise is sufficient consideration to support Becky's promise, even though Cindy will receive the benefit.

- **Courts Will Not Inquire Into Adequacy:** As long as the consideration is not a sham, courts will not inquire into the *adequacy* of consideration (i.e., they will not compare the relative values of the consideration exchanged). There is no requirement that the consideration exchanged be of nearly equal value. The only requirement is that the consideration be *legally sufficient*, which means of legal value, as discussed above.

- **Preexisting Legal Duties Generally Not Sufficient:** A promise to perform, or performance of, an existing duty is not sufficient consideration. Note that this means in common law contracts the price term cannot be modified unless consideration is given for the modification.

Illustration 17   Preexisting Legal Duty

1. Carol is under a contract to sing at a concert for Mike. Carol decides she does not want to sing. Mike offers to pay Carol $5,000 more if she will sing. Carol agrees and sings. Mike does not have to pay Carol the additional $5,000. There was no consideration for the promise because of the preexisting legal duty rule—Carol was already obligated to sing.
2. Smith offers a $10,000 reward for recovery of his stolen car. Jones, a police officer assigned to this case, recovers the car. Jones' performance of his official duty is not sufficient consideration.

- **Exception:** If each party offers to give something different from what was originally promised—no matter how trivial—the courts will usually enforce the promise despite the preexisting legal duty rule.

Illustration 18   Modification by Both Parties

The same facts apply as in part 1 of Illustration 17, except Carol offers to sing five minutes longer than she was originally obligated to. The modification is binding.

- **Honest Dispute as to Duty:** If the scope of the legal duty owed is the subject of honest dispute, then a modifying agreement relating to it will ordinarily be given effect. This is because the parties are giving up their right to sue to have the dispute settled, and forbearance to sue is valid consideration.

3.2.2 Bargained-for Exchange

Something is not consideration unless it was given in exchange for other consideration—there must be a bargained-for exchange of consideration.

- **Gift:** Promises to make a gift are unenforceable because of lack of consideration. There is no bargained-for exchange with a gift.
- **"Past" or "Moral" Consideration:** If something had already been given or performed before the promise was made, it will not satisfy the "bargain" requirement.

Illustration 19   Moral Consideration

A loose piece of molding fell from a building and was about to hit Sam. Sherry, seeing this, pushed Sam out of the molding's path and was herself struck by it and seriously injured. Sam promised Sherry that he would pay her $100 per month for life. There is no consideration.

NOTES

MODULE 2 Contracts: Part 2

REG 5

1 Defenses

Defenses can make a contract unenforceable. Two defenses have already been discussed—lack of an agreement and lack of consideration. There are a number of other defenses that the examiners often test.

Pass Key

Defenses are the most tested area in contracts. Pay close attention to the detail below. One key to choosing the correct choice is to remember that very few defenses make a contract void (unenforceable by either party). Most defenses make a contract only *voidable* (it may be avoided at the option of the party adversely affected). Thus, if you see a choice that says a contract is void because of a certain defense, be careful—chances are good that the choice is incorrect.

1.1 Fraud

A contracting party can establish the defense of fraud if she can prove:

- **Misrepresentation of Material Fact by Defrauding Party**

  The misrepresentation must be of a *material fact*. Opinions or statements of value do not constitute facts unless made by experts.

- **Scienter (Intent to Deceive)**

  Fraud is an intentional tort. The misrepresentation must be made with scienter, an intent to deceive. This means the defrauder must make it *knowingly or intentionally*. The intent to deceive element can also be fulfilled by making the misrepresentation with a *reckless disregard for the truth*. This is called constructive fraud or gross negligence.

- **Intent to Induce Reliance**

  The purpose of the defrauding party in making the misrepresentation was to induce the victim to rely on the misrepresentation.

- **Reasonable Reliance**

  The victim did actually and reasonably rely on the misrepresentation.

- **Damages**

  The defrauder is liable to anyone who suffered a loss. The defrauded party may rescind the contract or sue for money damages, but not both.

1.2 Fraud in the Execution and Fraud in the Inducement

Fraud can also be categorized by whether or not the defrauded party knew a contract was being made.

1.2.1 Fraud in the Execution

Fraud in the execution occurs when a party is deceived into signing something that does not look like a contract (e.g., where a ball player signs a fan's autograph book that is actually a contract). Fraud in the execution makes a contract void, not voidable because there is no "meeting of the minds."

1.2.2 Fraud in the Inducement

With fraud in the inducement the defrauded party is aware she is making a contract, but terms are materially misrepresented. Most fraud is fraud in the inducement and it makes a contract voidable.

1.3 Innocent Misrepresentation

An innocent misrepresentation has all the elements of fraud *except scienter*. The misrepresentation is made innocently, not intentionally. Innocent misrepresentation makes the contract voidable by the party who relied on the misrepresentation.

1.4 Duress

Duress arises when a party's free will to contract is overcome by an *unlawful* use of a threat of harm. If the harm threatened is physical force (e.g., "sign the contract or I'll break your arm"), the contract is *void*. If the harm threatened is economic or social (e.g., "I'll fire you if you don't sign the contract" or "I'll divorce you if you don't sign the contract"), then the contract is *voidable*. However, merely taking advantage of the other person's economic condition to negotiate a favorable contract (if no threat is involved) does not constitute duress.

1.5 Undue Influence

In the case of undue influence, a party's free will to contract is overcome by the defendant's abuse of a position of trust or confidence. The person in the position of trust or confidence (e.g., a spouse, trustee, guardian, attorney, etc.) uses the position to take advantage of the other's weakness, infirmity, or distress. Undue influence makes a contract voidable.

> **Illustration 1 Undue Influence**
>
> Lawyer convinces Client, a person with intellectual disability, to sell Lawyer Client's personal property. An undue influence defense will likely succeed.

1.6 Mutual Mistake

If *both* parties to a contract are mistaken as to a material fact regarding the contract, the adversely affected party can avoid the contract. Note, however, that this rule generally does not apply to mistakes as to value, because value generally is considered to be a matter of opinion.

> **Illustration 2 Mutual Mistake as to Quality**
>
> Alex and Bob enter into a contract for Alex to buy and Bob to sell Bob's designer watch for $200. Before the sale is complete, the parties discover that the watch is a fake. Alex may avoid the contract.

If the subject matter of the contract is not in existence when the contract is made and neither party knows this, the contract is void.

> **Illustration 3 Mutual Mistake as to Existence**
>
> Ann enters into a contract with Barb to purchase Barb's car for $1,000. Unbeknown to either party, the car was destroyed by a fire earlier in the day. There is no contract—the contract is void.

1.7 Unilateral Mistake: Voidable in Some Cases

Generally, a unilateral mistake (i.e., a mistake by one party) is *not* a defense to a contract. There is one major exception that the examiners like to test—a unilateral mistake as to a *material fact* is a defense if the other party *knew or should have known* of the mistake.

> **Illustration 4 Unilateral Mistake**
>
> 1. Sue enters into a contract with Tyler to sell Tyler a parcel of land. Sue knows that the land cannot support a building taller than five stories, but most of the buildings in the area are only three stories. Unbeknownst to Sue, Tyler intends to build a 20-story building on the land. Tyler's unilateral mistake (as to suitability of the land) is not a defense. However, if Tyler showed Sue the plans to the building before the sale and Sue remained silent, the defense of unilateral mistake is available.
>
> 2. Phil is selecting bids from contractors for construction of a garage. One bid is substantially lower than the others (e.g., bid 1—$6,000; bid 2—$5,600; bid 3—$3,200) so that it is obvious that there is a mistake in the bid. The mistake will be a defense. Note that the bidder's negligence is irrelevant.

1.8 Illegality: Contract Generally Void

If the consideration or the subject matter of a contract is illegal, the contract generally is *void*. Examples of illegality include agreements to commit a crime or tort (e.g., to steal and sell an employer's trade secrets); agreements in restraint of trade; gambling contracts; usurious contracts; etc.

> **Illustration 5 Illegality**
>
> Joe enters into a contract with Jim to murder Jason in exchange for 10 kilos of cocaine. The contract is void both because the subject matter (to murder) is illegal and the consideration on the other side (cocaine) is illegal.

1.8.1 Licensing: Revenue Raising vs. Protection

If a contract is illegal because a party does not have a required license, enforceability of the contract depends on the reason for the license.

- Failure to have a license required to *protect the public* (e.g., CPAs, attorneys, doctors, realtors, etc.) makes a contract void. Even if the unlicensed party performs the contract, the party *cannot collect*.
- If the license is required merely to *raise revenue* (e.g., all vendors at a fair pay a $25 license fee), the contract is enforceable.

1.9 Minors May Generally Disaffirm Contracts

A minor (usually a person under the age of 18) may disaffirm a contract anytime while a minor, or even within a reasonable time after becoming an adult. The minor must generally return whatever she possesses when she disaffirms. Note that minority is a defense *for the minor*—the other party cannot raise the minor's minority as a defense to avoid performance.

> **Illustration 6 Contract With Minor**
>
> Bob, a 16-year-old, purchased a used car from Paul. Ten months later, the car was stolen and never recovered. Bob may disaffirm the contract and get his money back.

A person can become bound on the contracts he or she enters into as a minor upon reaching the age of majority by *ratifying* the contract. A contract may be ratified by:

- *failing to disaffirm* within a reasonable time after reaching majority;
- *expressly ratifying* the entire contract orally or in writing; or
- *retaining or accepting the benefits*.

Pass Key

Ratification is all or nothing; a person cannot ratify part and reject part. Also, ratification does not require consideration. Finally, note that it is the minor who has the right to disaffirm; the adult does not have a right to rescind merely because the minor may disaffirm.

1.10 Intoxication

Intoxication is a defense to a contract only if the intoxication prevents the promisor from knowing the *nature and significance* of his or her promise *and* the other party *knew of the impairment.*

Illustration 7 — Intoxication

Rick and Steve have a drink at lunch and then enter into a contract. Neither party is impaired. The contract is enforceable.

1.11 Adjudicated Mental Incompetency

A contract made by a party after he is adjudicated mentally incompetent is void.

Formation Defenses: Void vs. Voidable Distinction		
The defenses below go to formation. The examiners often ask whether a particular formation defense will make a contract void or voidable. This chart summarizes the rules.		
Defense	*Void*	*Voidable*
Fraud in the execution	✓	
Fraud in the inducement		✓
Innocent misrepresentation		✓
Duress (physical)	✓	
Duress (economic)		✓
Undue influence		✓
Mutual mistake		✓
Unilateral mistake		✓
Illegality	✓	
Minority		✓
Intoxication		✓
Adjudicated incompetency	✓	

Contracts: Part 2

1.12 Statute of Limitations

A statute of limitations provides that a legal action must be commenced within a certain period of time. Generally, if the statute of limitations period has expired on a contract, it is unenforceable. It does not make a contract void, but merely bars access to judicial remedies. Although contracts statutes of limitations vary, four to six years is typical. Actions for breach usually are measured from the time the cause of action accrued (i.e., the date of the breach).

1.13 Statute of Frauds: Six Contracts Requiring a Writing

Although the general rule is that contracts need not be in writing, six contracts require some type of writing to be enforceable. Both parties need not sign the writing. Only the party to be charged (i.e., the party trying to avoid the contract) must have signed.

1. Contracts in which the consideration is **marriage** (e.g., "If you get married, I'll buy you a house").
2. Contracts which by their terms cannot be performed within a **year** (e.g., "I will coach your football team for the next five years").
3. Contracts involving interests in **land** (this includes all contracts for the sale of an interest in real property—such as a contract for the sale of a house or a warehouse—and leases of real property of more than a year).
4. Contracts by **executors** or similar representatives to pay estate debts out of personal funds.
5. Contracts for the sale of **goods** *for $500 or more*.
6. Contracts to act as **surety** (i.e., to pay the debt of another).

It is very important to memorize these six types of contracts, because the examiners frequently test which contracts require a writing.

Pass Key

One key to memorizing the six categories is the mnemonic device **MYLEGS** (marriage, year, land, executors, goods, and suretyship). Contracts for services can be oral regardless of price so long as they can be completed within one year.

1.13.1 Year Contracts

Contracts that cannot be performed in one year must be evidenced by a writing. In determining if a writing is required, the one-year period runs from the date of the contract, not from when performance begins. Thus, a contract to wash a car two years hence requires a writing. Only contracts impossible to perform within one year from their making require a writing. For example, a contract to work for an employer for life need not be in writing because the employee could die the next day.

1.13.2 Land Contracts

Land contracts must be evidenced by a writing, but leases of land for less than a year do not require a writing.

1.13.3 Goods for $500 or More

Contracts for the sale of goods for $500 or more must be evidenced by a writing. If a sales contract has been modified, it is the contract as it *has been modified* that determines whether a writing is required.

> **Illustration 8 Sale of Goods for $500 or More**
>
> Ann offers to buy 200 books from Ben at $3 each to sell in her store. This contract must be in writing. Subsequently, Ann discovers that she has room for only 150 books and so calls Ben and asks if her order can be reduced. Ben agrees. The contract need not be in writing. Conversely, if the contract was for 150 books and then was modified to 200 books, a writing would be required.

> **Pass Key**
>
> The examiners often try to trick you with the $500 threshold. It applies only to goods contracts. A $200 land contract must be evidenced by a writing, and so must a $400 three-year service contract, etc. If you see $500 in an answer choice, be careful. If the contract does not involve the sale of goods, the choice is probably wrong.

1.13.4 What Writing Will Suffice

The "contract" itself need not be in writing; all that is required is some writing that provides *evidence of the material terms* of the contract that is signed by the person being sued. Thus, a letter about the contract could suffice, even a letter seeking to revoke the contract. Contracts for the sale of goods generally need only have a *quantity term* and a signature. The terms may be stated in more than one document. There is no requirement that all terms be stated in a single writing.

> **Pass Key**
>
> Remember that the signature you are looking for is the signature of the person being sued. The other party's signature is not needed and will not do.

1.13.5 Effect of Noncompliance

Failure to satisfy the Statute of Frauds does not prevent the formation of a contract; rather, it makes the contract unenforceable by one or both of the parties.

1.14 Impossibility

If after the parties enter into a contract an event occurs that will make performance of the contract *objectively impossible* (i.e., impossible for *anyone* to perform), impossibility is available as a defense. The defense discharges the adversely affected party from any further duty to perform. Note that a mere increase in the cost of performance does not make performance impossible.

> **Illustration 9　Impossibility (Situation 1)**
>
> Alex contracts with Phil to have Phil manufacture *at his factory* 1,500 wrenches. Fire then destroys the factory. Phil has the defense of impossibility because no one can make wrenches at Phil's factory because it is now destroyed.

> **Illustration 10　Impossibility (Situation 2)**
>
> Alex contracts to buy 1,500 wrenches from Phil, a tool wholesaler. Phil's warehouse, full of tools, is then destroyed by fire. Phil must still supply Alex because performance is not objectively impossible; Phil can purchase more wrenches to sell to Alex.

If the subject matter or the specified source of the subject matter of the contract has been destroyed, the contract may be avoided due to impossibility.

> **Illustration 11　Impossibility (Situation 3)**
>
> Tyler enters into a contract to repair Steve's boat. Before the boat can be repaired, it is destroyed by fire. The parties can avoid the contract on impossibility grounds.

Death or incapacity of a person to perform a personal service contract will discharge the contract due to *objective impossibility*.

> **Illustration 12　Impossibility (Situation 4)**
>
> Dee contracts to have Bob, a famous ball player, sign autographs at Dee's store. Bob then dies. Bob (or his estate) has the defense of impossibility. Note that this is objective, not subjective, impossibility because the contract called for Bob to sign, and there no longer is a Bob.

1.15 Accord and Satisfaction and Substituted Contract

An accord is an agreement to substitute one performance for another, and satisfaction is the execution of the accord. Accord and satisfaction discharge the original duty. Until the accord is satisfied a party may sue under the original contract or the accord. A substituted contract is very similar to an accord and satisfaction case, but the duties under the original contract are discharged immediately. Whether an agreement is an accord or a substituted contract depends on the intent of the parties.

> **Illustration 13 Accord and Satisfaction**
>
> Alex agrees to sell his car to Steve for $450. The parties agree to substitute a contract for the sale of Alex's bike to Steve for $100. The new agreement is the accord; when it is performed is the satisfaction.

1.16 Novation

Novation is available as a defense to a party who has been released from a contract. It occurs when a new contract substitutes a new party for an old party in an existing contract. All parties must agree to the release.

> **Illustration 14 Novation**
>
> Sam agrees to build a garage for Barb, but then gets a more lucrative construction job. Sam asks Barb if it's OK to substitute Dee to build the garage. The parties agree to substitute Dee and release Sam. There has been a novation.

A release or agreement to discharge one of the parties without replacing that party is not a novation but rather a simple release. Such an agreement usually requires new consideration or detrimental reliance to be enforceable.

1.17 Conditions Can Affect a Party's Duty to Perform

A condition is an event, the occurrence or nonoccurrence of which will end a party's duty to perform. Conditions have different names depending on when they occur. Conditions are often preceded by "if," "subject to," or similar language.

> **Illustration 15 Condition**
>
> "I will pay you $10 *if* you mow my lawn." Mowing the lawn is an express condition to payment of the $10.

A condition precedent is a condition that must occur *before* the other party must perform. Conditions concurrent are conditions that must occur *simultaneously*. For example, the payment of money and exchange of goods in most face-to-face sales contracts are conditions concurrent. The parties make the exchange simultaneously. A condition subsequent is a condition that will occur after a party's duty to perform has arisen and will cut off that duty.

Illustration 16 Condition Subsequent

"If you promise to host a weekly football party, I will pay you $1,000 per year until the Bears win their third Super Bowl." Upon the Bears winning their third Super Bowl, the duty of payment is cut off.

1.18 Prevention of Performance Is a Breach

If one party prevents the other from performing contract duties, a material breach has occurred. The non-breaching party is excused from performance.

1.19 Parol Evidence Rule

- The parol (oral) evidence rule prohibits a party in a lawsuit involving a *fully integrated* written contract (i.e., a written contract that appears to be intended to reflect the entire agreement between the parties) from introducing evidence at trial of:

  - oral or written statements made prior to the written contract or oral statements made contemporaneously with the written contract; and
  - that seek to vary the terms of the written contract.

- Oral or written modifications made after the contract has been entered into (subsequent modifications) are admissible under the parol evidence rule.

Illustration 17 Parol Evidence Rule

Bob, a 16-year-old, is looking at cars on Lori's used car lot. Lori tells Bob that if Bob buys a car today, Lori will wash the car once a week at no charge for a year. Bob selects a car and the parties sign a fully integrated agreement setting out the parties, the price, the warranty, etc., but failing to mention anything about the washing agreement. Assuming Lori's statement was not fraudulent (e.g., she actually intended to provide the washings when she made the statement but later changed her mind), Bob will not be able to introduce evidence of the statement in court. However, the parol evidence rule would not prohibit Bob from introducing evidence of his age, since that is not seeking to vary the contract's terms.

Pass Key

The examiners often ask parol evidence questions. There are two key areas to examine:

1. Examiners love to test the time element in parol evidence rule questions. Remember that prior or contemporaneous statements that contradict the writing are inadmissible. Subsequent statements that contradict (or change a term) are admissible.

2. Examiners sometimes combine the parol evidence issue with a Statute of Frauds issue, usually in an oral modification fact pattern. The key is to address each issue separately. First determine whether the modification is enforceable (is the contract *as modified* within the Statute of Frauds). Then determine whether it is admissible in evidence (subsequent modifications are admissible) under the parol evidence rule.

2 Remedies

The last contracts issue remaining is what to do when a party fails to perform something he or she is contractually obligated to do (i.e., what to do when there is a *breach*). This is the province of remedies. At common law, if there has been a material or substantial breach, the non-breaching party can be discharged from the contract. If the breach is only minor, the non-breaching party is not discharged, but is entitled to damages.

2.1 Damages

Once there is a breach, the next step is to determine the damages to which the non-breaching party is entitled. Numerous damage measures are set out below, but the key to all of them is that they are intended to *put the non-breaching party in as good a position as he would have been had there been no breach*.

> **Pass Key**
>
> Even if you cannot remember a specific remedy measure, remember the goal of contract remedies and you should be able to pick the correct choice in most damages questions.

2.1.1 Compensatory Damages (Benefit of the Bargain)

The standard measure of damages for personal service contracts awards the non-breaching party enough *money* to obtain substitute performance (i.e., the difference between the cost of substitute performance and the contract price).

> **Illustration 18 Compensatory Damages**
>
> Bob contracts to build a garage for Barb for $5,000. Bob gets a more lucrative construction job and refuses to build Barb's garage. Barb hires Jim to build a garage for $6,000. Barb can collect $1,000 from Bob.

2.1.2 Consequential Damages if Foreseeable

In addition to the standard measure of damages, a party may also collect all damages that are *reasonably foreseeable* as a result of the breach (e.g., extra weathering of Barb's car resulting from no garage or extra storage fees).

2.1.3 Specific Performance (Used With Land or Unique Items)

Specific performance is essentially a court order that the breaching party perform or face contempt charges. It is available if interests in land or unique personal property (e.g., one-of-a-kind items, such as a patent) are involved. In such cases, money would be an inadequate remedy (a specific piece of property or unique item of personal property cannot necessarily be purchased with money).

Specific performance cannot be used to force a party to perform personal service contracts (courts consider this a form of involuntary servitude, which is prohibited by the 13th Amendment). If specific performance is available, a party can receive either specific performance or compensatory damages, but not both.

2.1.4 Liquidated Damages (Damages Agreed to in the Contract)

A liquidated damage clause is a clause in a contract that specifies what damages will be if there is a breach (e.g., forfeiture of a down payment for breach). A liquidated damage clause is enforceable if the amount is (i) *reasonable in relation to the actual harm done*, and (ii) *not a penalty*.

2.1.5 Punitive Damages

Punitive damages generally are not available for breach of contract. They are available for fraud, which is a tort cause of action.

Pass Key

Punitive damages often appear as a choice in contracts questions. It is an incorrect choice unless the question asks which remedy is not available or the cause of action is for fraud (a tort) rather than breach of contract.

2.1.6 Rescission or Cancellation

Rescission or cancellation cancels the contract and restores the parties to their former position. Rescission or cancellation is available for mutual or unilateral mistakes, fraud, and most material contract breaches. Under the common law, a party cannot rescind or cancel if a contract has been substantially performed (the doctrine of substantial performance). The non-breaching party's only remedy is monetary damages for the minor breach.

2.1.7 Limitations on Monetary Damages

In order to fairly compensate parties for harm done, the law imposes the limitations of foreseeability and mitigation on monetary damages.

- **Foreseeability**

    Consequential damages are awardable only for those damages that at the time the contract was formed a party could reasonably foresee would result from a breach.

- **Mitigation (Reasonable Efforts to Avoid Damages)**

    Under contract law, a non-breaching party cannot recover for damages that could have been reasonably avoided. The party must mitigate damages.

MODULE 3 Contracts: Part 3

REG 5

1 Introduction

The Sales Article of the UCC (Article 2) applies only to sales of goods. You already know a substantial part of the Sales Article because it generally follows common law contracts discussed earlier in this unit. This module will highlight the differences between the two. If an issue is not covered, assume that the Sales Article follows the contract rule.

1.1 Goods—Moveable Personal Property

The UCC Sales Article applies to the sale of goods, which is defined as all things moveable. This includes most tangible personal property (e.g., cars, cows, and groceries). The following are *excluded from the Sales Article* and are covered by common law contracts:

- Contracts for personal services and real estate.
- Contracts for intangible personal property, such as stock or patent rights.
- Contracts for fixtures—things attached to the land.

1.2 Merchants—Deal in Goods of the Kind Sold

A number of UCC rules depend on whether one or more of the parties are merchants. You must be careful to note the status of the parties. A merchant is one who deals in goods of the kind sold or who has special knowledge regarding the goods being sold.

The UCC is not limited to merchants. It applies to all contracts for sale of goods.

1.3 Obligation of Good Faith

The UCC imposes an obligation of good faith on both parties to a sales contract. Merchant sellers must also observe reasonable standards of fair dealing in the trade.

2 Creation of a Contract

2.1 Agreement (Mutual Assent)—Offer and Acceptance

2.1.1 Offer—Merchant's Firm Offer

Under the common law, consideration is needed to make an offer irrevocable. There is a limited exception to this rule that only arises under the UCC—merchant's firm offers. Certain offers by merchants are irrevocable without consideration. Merchant's firm offers are irrevocable for the time stated, or if no time is stated, for a reasonable time, but in *no event longer than three months*. To qualify as a merchant's firm offer:

- The seller must be a *merchant* (regularly deals in goods of the kind sold);
- The offer must be in *writing* and *signed* by the merchant; and
- The offer must give *assurances that it will be kept open* for a certain time.

Pass Key

It is important to remember that the firm offer rule applies only to offers for the sale of goods by merchants and only if the offer is in writing. The examiners often try to fool you. They may say that a merchant phones a buyer offering to sell goods and promises to keep the offer open. The firm offer rule does not apply because the offer is oral. They might say that a person writes a friend offering to sell a car and promises to keep the offer open. The firm offer rule does not apply because the seller is not a merchant. Finally, they might say that a realtor offers in writing to sell a parcel of land and promises to keep the offer open. The firm offer rule does not apply because the contract is for land, not for the sale of goods.

2.1.2 Acceptance

Under the Sales Article, an offer that does not specify the means of acceptance may be accepted by any means reasonable under the circumstances. But an offer specifying the means of acceptance must be accepted by the specified means—the offer is the master of the offer. The Sales Article modifies the common law of acceptance in the following ways.

- **Mirror Image Rule Does Not Apply Under UCC**

    Under common law contracts, the terms of an acceptance must mirror the terms of the offer or there is no contract—just a counteroffer. This is not so under the UCC. Under the Sales Article an acceptance will be effective even if it states new or different terms. Generally, under the UCC the new or different terms will be ignored unless the contract is between merchants. In a contract between merchants, the terms of the acceptance control unless the offeror objects or the changes are material.

Pass Key

Examiners like to test new or different terms in an acceptance. Remember that under the common law, the acceptance must mirror the offer. Under the Sales Article, new or different terms are ignored unless the contract is *between merchants*. Between merchants, minor changes can generally be made in the acceptance.

- **Promise to Ship or Prompt Shipment**
    - Under the Sales Article, an offer to buy goods for current or prompt shipment can be accepted by either a promise to ship or by prompt shipment, unless the offer indicates otherwise.

Illustration 1   Valid Acceptance

Bob sends Steve an order for 400 widgets at $1 per widget. Steve can accept by either promising to ship the widgets or by promptly shipping the widgets.

- If prompt shipment of goods is an acceptance, what happens if the seller ships goods that do not conform to the contract? Under the UCC, a shipment of nonconforming goods is *both an acceptance and a breach* of contract.

Illustration 2 — Acceptance and Breach of Contract

Barb orders 100 black widgets from Sam. Sam is out of black widgets, so sends 100 blue widgets. The shipment is both an acceptance and a breach of contract, and Barb may sue Sam for damages.

- If the seller reasonably notifies the buyer that nonconforming goods are shipped only as an accommodation to the buyer, the shipment is not an acceptance. It is a counteroffer.

Illustration 3 — Counteroffer

The same facts as the example above, but Sam sends a note before shipment that the blue widgets are intended only as an accommodation. Barb may accept or reject the widgets, but Sam has not breached any contract.

Pass Key

You must remember that the accommodation shipment rule applies only when shipment is used as the means of acceptance. The examiners often try to trick you by stating that a party accepts an order by promising to ship. Then the party discovers he lacks the goods and ships nonconforming goods as "an accommodation." This is a breach, not an accommodation.

2.1.3 Auctions

The UCC contains special rules regarding auctions, which are rarely tested on the exam. Just to be safe, the key points to remember are as follows:

- Generally, the bid is the offer and the fall of the hammer is the acceptance.
- Unless otherwise stated, all auctions are "with reserve," which means that the seller does not have to sell unless an adequate bid is made.
- In an auction "without reserve" the goods must be sold to the highest bidder. The goods only can be withdrawn if no bid is made within a reasonable time.

2.2 Consideration

- **Modifications Enforceable Without Consideration**

    At common law, a modification of a contract is not enforceable unless consideration is given. The UCC abandoned this rule. Under the UCC, a modification of a contract for the sale of goods is enforceable, even without consideration, as long as the modification is sought in good faith.

- **Payment by Check**

    A sales contract may be paid by check, unless the seller demands cash, in which case the seller must give the buyer a reasonable time to obtain the cash.

> **Illustration 4 Modification**
>
> Rick, a book distributor, offers to sell Steve, a bookstore owner, 100 books for $1 each. Steve accepts. Rick subsequently discovers that he will lose money on the deal, and so asks Steve if he would be willing to pay $1.05 for each book. Steve agrees. The modification is binding.

> **Pass Key**
>
> *Be careful.* This exception applies *only in the sale of goods*. If the example above were to bind books (a common law service contract), the modification would not be binding because of the preexisting duty rule.

2.3 Defenses

- As at common law, fraud is a defense to a contract under the UCC. The defrauded party either may sue for damages or seek rescission. Under the Sales Article, a party may rescind and sue for money damages.
- The UCC statute of limitations is four years. An action must be brought within four years of the time the cause of action accrued (from the time the contract was breached).

2.3.1 Statute of Frauds

Contracts for the sale of goods for $500 or more must be evidenced by a writing signed by the party being sued. There are four exceptions, provided below:

1. Contracts for **specially manufactured goods** (i.e., goods not generally suitable for sale to others, such as bowling shirts with a team name embroidered on them).

2. Where a merchant sends another merchant a **written confirmation** of a contract that is sufficient to bind the sender, it will also bind the recipient if she does not object within 10 days (e.g., Randy Retailer calls Wendy Wholesaler and orders $600 worth of goods, and then sends Wendy a written and signed confirmation of the order. If Wendy does not object, the confirmation is sufficient to bind Wendy even though she did not sign it). This is known as the merchant's confirmatory memo rule.

3. Contracts that parties have **admitted** in court.

4. Contracts that have been **performed**, to the extent that the performance has been accepted (e.g., an oral contract for 200 widgets at $5 each cannot be enforced, but if 150 widgets are delivered and accepted, it is enforceable to the extent of the 150 accepted widgets).

Pass Key

The exceptions to the Statute of Frauds for goods can be remembered with the mnemonic **SWAP**—**S**pecially manufactured goods, **W**ritten merchant's confirmatory memo, **A**dmission in court, and **P**erformance.

Illustration 5 — Specially Manufactured Goods

Sam and Ben orally agree that Sam will specially manufacture a machine for Ben for $40,000. After Sam spends $30,000 to build the machine, Ben tells Sam that he no longer needs it. Even though the contract is oral, Ben is bound because the goods were specially manufactured.

- **Price Measured as Modified**

    If a sales contract has been modified, it is the contract as it *has been modified* that determines whether a writing is required.

Illustration 6 — Modification Effective Without Writing

Able signs a contract to purchase 600 books from Baker for 90 cents each. Subsequently, Able in good faith asks that the price be reduced to 80 cents, and Baker agrees. The modification is effective without a writing because the contract as modified is for only $480.

- **What Writing Will Suffice—Quantity Only Essential Terms**

    Under the common law, the writing must include *all essential terms*. Under the UCC, terms may be omitted (e.g., if the memorandum is silent, a sale will be at a reasonable price and delivery at the seller's place of business). The only terms that cannot be omitted are the quantity term (unless the contract is an output or requirement contract) and the signature term.

- **Impossibility and Impracticability**

    Under contract law, if an event occurs that makes the contract objectively impossible to perform (i.e., no one could perform), the contract is discharged. The UCC is more lenient. Under the Sales Article, a contract will be discharged for mere impracticability. The contract need not be impossible to perform. It need only be impracticable—extremely more burdensome than anticipated because of the occurrence of an unforeseen event.

- **Failure of Agreed-Upon Method of Transportation (No Defense)**

    If the method of transportation called for in the contract is unavailable or commercially unreasonable, the seller may use a different means of transportation and the buyer must accept (e.g., if goods are to be delivered by one shipping company and that shipping company is on strike, then the seller can use a different shipping company).

3 Delivery, Risk of Loss, and Title

This section deals with the code's rules for delivery, risk of loss, and passage of title in sales contracts. These issues are commonly tested.

3.1 Delivery and Risk of Loss

As a general rule, the seller's basic duty is to hold conforming goods for the buyer and give the buyer reasonable notice to enable the buyer to take delivery. Many contracts stray from this rule. The UCC has specific rules for when and where delivery of goods is to be made, and these rules apply if the contract is silent. Risk of loss (who will bear the loss if the goods are destroyed) generally depends on the time delivery is made. Note that if goods are damaged or destroyed after risk of loss has passed to the buyer, the buyer is not discharged from the contract; rather, the buyer must still pay the contract price.

3.1.1 For Risk of Loss to Pass, Goods Must Be Identified

Title and risk of loss cannot pass until the goods are first *identified*. Goods are identified when they are marked, segregated, or in some manner identified as goods for a specific buyer.

3.1.2 As Parties Agree

The most important rule to remember is that if the parties designate when and where delivery will occur or risk of loss will pass, their agreement governs.

3.1.3 Where No Specific Agreement

The code divides cases where there is no agreement on delivery or risk of loss into two broad categories: noncarrier cases and carrier cases.

- In *noncarrier cases* the buyer will usually pick up the goods at the seller's place of business (e.g., buying goods at the grocery store).
- In *carrier cases* the parties contemplate a common carrier will be used to ship the goods (e.g., shipping goods by UPS).

1. Noncarrier Cases
- If the seller is not a merchant, risk of loss passes to the buyer upon the seller's *tender of delivery* of the goods to the buyer.

> **Illustration 7 Risk of Loss When Seller Is Not a Merchant**
>
> Steve is not in the business of selling computers, but agrees to sell a computer to his neighbor, Bill, for $400. Bill gave Steve the $400. When Steve tendered delivery of the computer, Bill said he would come back later to pick it up. Before Bill returns, the computer is destroyed by fire through no fault of Steve's. Steve may keep the $400 because Bill had the risk of loss when the computer was destroyed.

- With merchant sellers, risk of loss passes only upon actual delivery to the buyer (i.e., when the buyer takes physical possession).

Illustration 8 — Risk of Loss When Seller Is a Merchant

The same facts as the example above, but Steve is a computer merchant. Steve must get a computer for Bill or pay damages because Steve still had the risk of loss when the computer was destroyed.

2. Carrier Cases

If a common carrier is involved, the contract is either a *shipment* contract or a *destination* contract.

- With shipment contracts, risk of loss passes to the buyer when the goods are delivered to the carrier.
- With destination contracts, risk of loss passes to the buyer when the goods reach the destination and seller tenders delivery.

Illustration 9 — Shipment Contract

Brenda Corp. entered into a shipment contract with Sally Co. to purchase a used computer from Sally Co. It was understood that Sally Co. would ship the computer to Brenda Corp.'s main office. Even though Sally Co. must arrange for the shipment, Brenda Corp. bears the risk of loss during shipment, and if the computer is damaged while in transit, Brenda Corp. must still pay for the computer.

- **FOB (Free on Board)**

    FOB is a delivery term. FOB means "free on board" and is always followed by a location. On the exam, it is usually FOB the seller's place of business or FOB the buyer's place of business. FOB the seller's place is a shipment contract. The seller must get the goods to the carrier for risk of loss to pass. FOB buyer's place is a destination contract. The seller must get the goods to the destination and tender delivery for risk of loss to pass.

Illustration 10 — Free on Board

Ann, an appliance retailer, agreed to purchase 100 microwaves from Stan, an appliance wholesaler. The contract provided that the goods were to be shipped to Ann by common carrier *FOB Stan's loading dock*. If the microwaves are destroyed during shipment, Ann must still pay because she had the risk of loss. If the contract were *FOB Ann's store* and the microwaves were destroyed in transit, Stan would bear the loss.

- **Effect of Breach on Risk of Loss**

    If the seller sends nonconforming goods (goods that do not meet the contract description), the risk of loss remains on the seller, regardless of the shipping terms, unless the buyer accepts the defective goods.

> **Illustration 11   Nonconforming Goods**
>
> Betsy orders 100 microwaves from Stan with the shipping terms *FOB Stan's loading dock*. Stan sends 100 toaster ovens. If the toaster ovens are destroyed in transit or shortly after the goods reach Betsy (before acceptance), Stan bears the risk of loss despite the *FOB Stan's loading dock* term.

3.1.4   Risk in Sale on Approval and Sale or Return Contracts

Under the code, *all sales are final*, unless otherwise agreed. The UCC provides for two types of nonfinal sales: sale on approval and sale or return.

1. **Sale on Approval—Risk on Seller Until Approval**

    In a sale on approval, the sale is not final until the buyer gives approval (i.e., a sale with a trial period). Title and risk of loss remain with the seller until the buyer approves.

> **Illustration 12   Sale on Approval**
>
> Stacy sells a television to Ben. The agreement provides that Ben may return the television within 30 days if he is not happy with it. During the 30-day period, Stacy bears the risk of loss until Ben indicates his acceptance. If the television is destroyed on the 15th day, and Ben has done nothing to accept, Stacy bears the loss.

2. **Sale or Return—Risk on Buyer Until Returned**

    A sale or return is a completed sale on delivery, but the buyer has the right to return the goods (this is sometimes called a *sale on consignment*). Risk of loss passes to the buyer when the seller completes the delivery requirements. Risk remains with the buyer until the goods are completely returned.

> **Illustration 13   Sale or Return Contract**
>
> Dan is a distributor of magazines. Each month, Dan sells 1,000 magazines to Richard, a retailer. The contract provides that Richard may return whatever magazines are left at the end of the month to Dan. This is a *sale or return* contract. If any magazines are stolen from Richard's store, he bears the loss.

> **Pass Key**
>
> The most frequently tested Article 2 issue is risk of loss. The key things to remember are:
>
> - Risk of loss is *not* determined by who has title.
>
> - *Noncarrier cases*: If the seller is not a merchant, risk of loss passes to buyer upon seller's tender of *delivery*. If the seller is a merchant, risk of loss only passes when the buyer gets physical *possession*.
>
> - *Common carrier cases*: With *shipment contracts* (i.e., FOB seller's place), risk of loss passes when the seller gets the goods *to the carrier*. With *destination contracts* (i.e., FOB buyer's place), risk of loss passes when the goods *reach the destination* and seller *tenders delivery*.
>
> - If the goods are nonconforming, risk of loss is always on the seller regardless of the shipping terms.

3.2 Title

- Title can pass at the time and place the parties agree, but before title can pass, the goods must be identified to the contract.

- If there is no agreement as to when title will pass, title passes when the seller completes her delivery requirements. The time of delivery can vary depending on the delivery term used.

- If the buyer rejects the goods, whether the rejection was rightful or wrongful, title revests in the seller. (Recall that if nonconforming goods are shipped, risk of loss remains with the seller despite the buyer's title.)

Illustration 14   Passing of Title

Bea agreed to purchase 100 blenders from Steve *FOB Steve's warehouse*. Title passes to Bea at the time the blenders are given to the carrier, because that is when delivery occurs. If the delivery term were *FOB Bea's store*, title would pass when the blenders are delivered to Bea's store.

4 Warranties

4.1 General

In sales, a seller must make a *perfect tender* (i.e., the goods and delivery must conform exactly to the contract without any defects). If the goods do not conform to the contract, the buyer may reject them. To fulfill the requirement of perfect tender, the goods must conform to all warranties. In this regard, there are four warranties that you must know:

1. Express warranties
2. The implied warranty of title
3. The implied warranty of merchantability
4. The implied warranty of fitness for a particular purpose

In reviewing the material on warranties, it is important to note how the warranty is made, who makes the warranty, and how the warranty can be disclaimed.

4.2 Express Warranties

- An express warranty will arise from any statement of fact or promise made by the seller, any description of the goods made by the seller, or any sample or model shown by the seller. The express warranty is that the goods will conform to the statement of fact, to the description, or to the sample or model.

- An express warranty can be made by any seller (not limited to merchants) and may be oral or written. Statements of value or opinions do not generally create an express warranty. The statement must involve facts. Additionally, the UCC requires that the express warranty be a *part of the basis of the bargain* (i.e., made at a time when it could have played some part in the buyer's decision to buy).

> **Illustration 15 Express Warranty**
>
> A statement that a car is a "1967 Ford and a beauty" creates a warranty that the car is a 1967 Ford, because this is a fact. It does not create the warranty that the car is a "beauty," because this is an opinion, not a fact.

> **Pass Key**
>
> When examiners test express warranties, they frequently ask about the requirement that the express warranty be a part of the basis of the bargain. Look for this in express warranty questions. For example, if a used-car retailer tells a customer that the engine in a car was rebuilt, the statement creates a warranty that the engine was in fact rebuilt, if the statement was made any time before the contract is signed. If the statement was made after the contract was signed, however, no warranty is made.

4.3 Implied Warranty of Title

- Implied in every sales contract is the warranty that the seller has *good title and the right to transfer* that title. The seller also impliedly warrants that there are no unstated *encumbrances* (i.e., no unstated liens or attachments on the goods). If the seller is a merchant, he also impliedly promises that the goods do not *infringe* on any patent or trademark.

- The implied warranty of title can only be disclaimed by specific language or by circumstances that indicate the seller is not guaranteeing he has title (e.g., judicial sale). A general disclaimer cannot disclaim title (e.g., "merchandise is sold as is," "with all faults," "seller makes no warranties beyond the face of this instrument," or "I disclaim any and all warranties").

Pass Key

The examiners love the warranty of title. The key point to remember is that it cannot be disclaimed by a general disclaimer such as "as is" or "with all faults." It can be disclaimed only specifically (e.g., "I do not warrant title") or by circumstance (e.g., judicial sale).

4.4 Implied Warranty of Merchantability

- In every sale by a merchant who deals in goods of the kind being sold, there is an implied warranty that the goods are fit for *ordinary purposes*. The warranty is implied—no writing or oral promise is required.

- The implied warranty of merchantability is made only in sales by merchants. Note, however, that the buyer need not be a merchant.

- Merchantability can be disclaimed by a statement that the goods are sold "as is" or "with all faults." Absent a general disclaimer, such as "as is," merchantability can only be disclaimed by using the word "merchantability" (i.e., a purported disclaimer stating "we hereby disclaim any and all warranties" is ineffective). A disclaimer may be oral. If the disclaimer is in writing, it must be conspicuous.

4.5 Implied Warranty of Fitness for Particular Purpose

- The implied warranty of fitness for particular purpose arises when the buyer relies on any seller (does not need to be a merchant) to select goods suitable for the buyer's particular purpose. The seller must know of the particular purpose and that the buyer is relying on him or her to select the goods.

- Merchantability requires the goods to be fit for ordinary purposes. Fitness requires the goods to be fit for the buyer's specified purpose. Fitness can be made by any seller. It is not limited to merchants.

Illustration 16 Implied Warranty of Fitness

Ben goes to *Sam the used car man* and tells Sam that he wants to buy a car suitable for towing his two-ton boat. Sam selects a pickup truck for Ben. There is an implied warranty of merchantability that the truck will be fit for ordinary purposes, such as driving around town, and an implied warranty of fitness for particular purpose that the truck can tow a two-ton boat.

Fitness, like merchantability, can be disclaimed by selling the goods "as is" or "with all faults." If not disclaimed by an "as is" sale, fitness must be disclaimed by a conspicuous disclaimer. The writing need not mention fitness (e.g., "I make no warranties beyond the face of this contract" is sufficient).

Pass Key

Examiners often test on implied warranties. The following are the key things to remember:

- Any implied warranty can be disclaimed, if the correct words are used (even by merchants).
- Implied warranties arise without a writing. They are automatically implied in a sales contract.
- Differences between merchantability and fitness: The warranty of merchantability can only be made by merchants and is a warranty only that the goods will be fit for ordinary purposes. The warranty of fitness can be made by any seller, but only if the buyer is relying on the seller to pick goods suitable for a particular purpose and is a warranty that they will be fit for that purpose.

Warranties

Type	How Arise	By Whom	Disclaimer
Express	By affirmation of fact, promise, description, model or sample	Any seller	Cannot disclaim
Implied			
Warranty of Title (title is good, transfer rightful, no liens or encumbrances)	By sale of goods	Any seller	By specific language or circumstances showing seller does not claim title
Warranty of Merchantability (fit for ordinary purpose)	By sale of goods of the kind regularly sold by the merchant	Merchant only	By disclaimer mentioning "merchantability" (if written disclaimer, it must be conspicuous)*
Warranty of Fitness for Particular Purpose (fit for buyer's particular purpose)	By sale of goods where seller has reason to know of particular purpose and of buyer's reliance on seller to choose suitable goods	Any seller	By conspicuous *written* disclaimer*

*These may also be disclaimed by language such as "as is"; by inspection (or refusal to inspect); or by course of dealing, course of performance, or usage of trade.

5 Remedies

5.1 Remedies of Buyer or Seller

1. **Anticipatory Repudiation—Sue or Wait**

   Anticipatory repudiation occurs when either the buyer or seller indicates in advance of performance that he will not perform. The nonbreaching party may sue immediately, cancel the contract, demand assurances (see below), or wait until the time for performance and sue then if the other party fails to perform. The repudiating party has the right to withdraw the repudiation until the other party relies (e.g., by bringing suit).

2. **Right to Demand Assurances if Reasonable Grounds Exist**

   Under the UCC Sales Article, if one party has reasonable grounds to believe that the other party will not perform when required, she may make a written demand for an assurance of performance from the other. Failure to give this assurance within a reasonable time is an anticipatory repudiation.

3. **Punitive Damages—Not Available in Sales**

   Punitive damages are not available under the Sales Article.

4. **Duty to Mitigate—Avoid Damages**

   Both buyer and seller have a duty to mitigate damages. They cannot recover for damages that could have been avoided.

5.2 Seller's Remedies

1. **Seller's Right to Cancel and Sue for Damages**

   If the buyer breaches the contract, the seller can cancel or rescind and/or sue for damages.

2. **Seller's Right to Withhold Delivery and Stop Goods in Transit**

   The seller may withhold delivery if the buyer has failed to make a required payment or has repudiated the contract. The seller may also stop delivery of goods in transit for the same breaches.

3. **Seller's Right to Resell and Sue for Damages**

   If the buyer breaches, the seller has the right to resell the goods. The seller may also sue the buyer for any losses the seller may have. This is usually the *difference between the contract price and the resale price* plus any additional or incidental damages (e.g., storage fees and the cost of resale).

4. **Seller's Right to Full Contract Price**

   The seller can collect the full contract price plus incidental damages if the goods cannot be resold for any price (often the case when the goods are specially manufactured) or if the goods are destroyed after risk of loss has passed to the buyer.

5. **Liquidated Damages—Must Be Reasonable**

   A liquidated damages clause in a sales contract is valid if the amount is reasonable with respect to the harm done and is not a penalty. Even if there is no liquidated damage clause, if the buyer has made a down payment and breaches, the seller may keep the lesser of $500 or 20 percent of the price.

Contracts: Part 3

5.3 Buyer's Remedies

5.3.1 Buyer's Right to Reject for Any Nonconformity

Under the UCC, the seller must make a "perfect tender"—a delivery free from any defects. If the goods do not conform to the contract, the buyer may reject all of the goods, reject some of the goods, or accept all of the goods. The buyer may also sue for damages.

The buyer usually has the right to inspect goods prior to payment. However, the buyer may not inspect prior to payment in a COD (cash on delivery) sale.

5.3.2 Buyer's Right to Cancel or Rescind

If the goods are nonconforming, the buyer can cancel the contract and sue for damages.

5.3.3 Buyer's Right to Sue for Damages

- **For Accepted Nonconforming Goods**

    The buyer may accept nonconforming goods and sue for damages. Damages are usually the difference between the value of conforming goods and the value of the goods as delivered plus incidental and consequential damages.

- **For Rejected or Undelivered Goods**

    If the goods are undelivered or buyer rightfully rejects, the buyer may:

    - Cover (i.e., the buyer can purchase comparable goods (cover) and sue the seller for the difference between the contract price and the cost of cover).
    - Sue for the difference between the market price and the contract price plus any incidental and consequential damages.

5.3.4 Buyer's Right to Specific Performance or Replevin

Specific performance may be used in a sales contract if the goods are unique or if the buyer cannot reasonably cover. Replevin (the right to recover goods wrongfully in the hands of the seller) may be used if the goods are identified and the buyer cannot reasonably cover.

> **Illustration 17   Specific Performance**
>
> Bob, an engine assembler, contracts with Steve, a parts manufacturer, for 1,000 engine parts to be picked up by Bob on June 1. Steve has several similar contracts with other engine assemblers. By June 1, Steve has completed a run of 2,000 parts of the type Bob wants, but Steve has not identified any as the ones for Bob. When Bob arrives, Steve refuses to deliver any parts to Bob. If Bob cannot get replacement goods in time, he has a right to specific performance. If the goods had been identified to the contract, Bob could have replevied them.

5.3.5 Buyer's Rights on Seller's Insolvency

If the buyer has paid part or all of the price and the seller is insolvent, the buyer may recover the goods from the seller if the goods are identified.

6 Entrusting

If the owner of goods entrusts them to a merchant who deals in goods of the kind sold, and the merchant sells them in the ordinary course of business to a bona fide purchaser for value, the purchaser gets good title even though the merchant did not have good title. But be careful. This rule applies only if the goods were entrusted to a merchant (not, for example, a bank), and the goods were sold in the ordinary course of business (not at a bulk sale of the merchant's business).

NOTES

MODULE 4 Agency

REG 5

1 Creation of the Agency Relationship

Agency is a legal relationship in which one person or entity (the principal) assents to have another person or entity (the agent) act on the principal's behalf and the agent consents to so act.

1.1 Requisites for Creation

1.1.1 Principal With Capacity and Consent

As a general rule, all that is required to create an agency relationship is a principal with contractual capacity (i.e., not a minor and not incompetent) and consent of the parties (i.e., the parties agree to act as principal and agent).

1. **Writing**
   - A writing generally is not required to create an agency relationship, even if the contract that the agent is to enter on the principal's behalf must be evidenced by a writing under the Statute of Frauds.
   - However, many states require a written agency agreement if the agent is to buy or sell an interest in land for the principal.
   - Note that a contract to find a buyer or seller (normal real estate broker's agreement) and a contract to build a house are contracts for services. An oral agency involving such transactions is valid.
   - Agency agreements that cannot be performed in one year must be evidenced by a writing.

2. **Capacity**
   Only the principal must be competent. The agent need not have capacity. Thus, a minor or mentally incompetent person can be appointed as an agent.

3. **Consideration**
   Consideration is not required to form an agency relationship.

Pass Key

The examiners often ask what is necessary to create an agency. Generally, all you need is consent and a principal with capacity. A writing is necessary only if the agent will enter into land sale contracts. Thus, an answer that says a writing is required or the agent's authority must be signed by the principal usually is wrong.

Agency

1.1.2 Power of Attorney

- A power of attorney is a written authorization of agency.

- The agent under a power of attorney is referred to as an "attorney in fact." But the agent need not be a lawyer. It just means that the agent has the power to act on behalf of the principal.

- Generally only the principal is required to sign the power of attorney. There is no requirement that the *agent* sign the instrument.

- The agent's authority is normally limited to specific transactions.

1.2 Rights and Duties Between Principal and Agent

Certain duties are implied in every agency relationship.

1.2.1 Duties of Agent to Principal

The agent has whatever duties are expressly stated in the contract. The agent also owes the following four duties:

1. Duty of Loyalty

An agent owes the principal a duty of loyalty; the agent must act solely in the principal's interest in connection with the agency. An agent breaches this duty when she has interests adverse to the principal (e.g., the agent obtains kickbacks from a third party).

> **Illustration 1   Duty of Loyalty**
>
> Petshop hired Andy as its store manager and gave Andy authority to purchase pets for the store. Andy occasionally purchased dogs from Tremendous Dogs. When Andy bought dogs from Tremendous, it paid Andy 5 percent of the purchase price as incentive to do more business. Petshop was unaware of the payments, which Andy kept. Andy has breached his duty of loyalty and can be forced to turn over his profit to Petshop.

2. Duty of Obedience

An agent must obey all reasonable directions of the principal.

> **Illustration 2   Duty of Obedience**
>
> Paul hires Audrey as his purchasing agent for televisions, but instructs Audrey not to disclose to sellers that she is working for Paul. If Audrey discloses to a seller that she is working for Paul, she breaches her duty of obedience and will be liable to Paul for any damages the disclosure caused.

3. Duty of Reasonable Care

An agent owes the principal a duty to carry out the agency with reasonable care (i.e., the duty not to be negligent).

4. **Duty to Account**

   Unless otherwise agreed, the agent has a duty to account to the principal for all property and money received and paid out when acting on behalf of the principal. The agent cannot commingle the principal's property with the agent's property.

5. **Subagent**

   If an agent is authorized to hire a subagent, the subagent owes a duty of care to both the agent and the principal.

1.2.2 Principal's Remedies

If an agent breaches the duties she owes to the principal, the principal can recover damages from the agent:

1. **Tort Damages**

   The principal can recover tort damages from the agent if the agent negligently or intentionally breached a duty owed to the principal.

2. **Contract Damages**

   If the agent was compensated, the principal can collect contract damages. If the agent did not receive consideration, a contract was not formed and so contract damages are not available.

3. **Recovery of Secret Profits**

   If the agent obtained a secret profit, as in Illustration 1, the principal can recover the secret profit, usually by imposing a constructive trust on the profit.

4. **Withhold Compensation**

   If the agent committed an intentional tort or intentionally breached her duty to her principal, the principal may refuse to pay the agent.

1.2.3 Duties of Principal to Agent

In addition to any duties expressed in the agency agreement, the principal owes the agent the following duties:

1. **Compensation**

   Unless the agent has agreed to act gratuitously, the principal has an implied duty to give the agent reasonable compensation.

2. **Reimbursement/Indemnification**

   The principal also has an implied duty to reimburse (i.e., indemnify) the agent for all expenses incurred in carrying out the agency.

3. **Remedies of the Agent**

   If the principal breaches her duties to the agent, the agent can bring an action against the principal for any damages caused. If the relationship is not contractual, however, the agent may not seek the contract remedy of specific performance. The agent has a *duty to mitigate* damages (e.g., a wrongfully fired agent must seek comparable work to replace lost income).

1.2.4 Power to Terminate Relationship

Because an agency relationship is consensual, either party generally has the power to terminate the relationship at any time. However, the parties don't necessarily have the *right* to terminate at any time.

> **Illustration 3   Termination at Will**
>
> Porthos hires Athos as his purchasing agent for nine months, at a salary of $2,000 per month. Either party can terminate the agency the next day, but a wrongful termination will be a breach of contract.

1.2.5 Agency Coupled With an Interest

Only the agent (not the principal) can terminate an agency coupled with an interest. This arises where the agent has an interest in the subject matter of the agency, such as where the agency power is given as security. In effect, the agent has paid for the right to be appointed as the agent, usually by giving credit. Death, incapacity, or bankruptcy of the principal will not end an agency coupled with an interest.

> **Illustration 4   Agency Coupled With Interest**
>
> Paul borrows $20,000 from Alex, promising to pay Alex within a year and appointing Alex as his agent to sell Blackacre if Paul fails to pay. Alex's agency is coupled with an interest. However, if Paul hires Alex to sell Blackacre in exchange for a 5 percent commission, Paul has the power to terminate the agency at any time because Alex has not acquired an interest in Blackacre.

2 Agent's Power to Contractually Bind Principal

An agent's power to bind a principal can arise through:

- a grant of actual authority;
- apparent authority or estoppel; or
- ratification.

2.1 Actual Authority

Actual authority (sometimes called "real authority" or simply "authority") is the authority the *agent reasonably believes* he possesses because of the principal's communications to the agent. An agent with actual authority has the power and the right to bind the principal to contracts with third parties. Actual authority can be either *express* or *implied*.

2.1.1 Express Actual Authority

Actual authority includes all powers that the principal expressly grants within the "four corners" of the agency agreement.

2.1.2 Implied Actual Authority

Authority that the agent could reasonably believe is implied along with the express grant is called implied actual authority. This includes the authority to do things *reasonably necessary* to carry out the agency (e.g., a person hired to manage a business will usually have authority to hire employees, buy merchandise, etc.).

Pass Key

The examiners have tested on the implied authority of a business manager a number of times. The key is to remember that the manager is there to run the business, not destroy it. Thus, she has authority to hire and fire employees, purchase inventory, and pay business debts. She has no implied authority to sell or mortgage business fixtures or other property of the principal (other than inventory). Also remember that generally an agent does not have implied authority to borrow money on the principal's behalf—such authority must be expressed.

2.1.3 Termination of Actual Authority

Termination of actual authority can occur by:

1. **Act of the Parties**

    Termination of an agency can occur through the acts of either the principal (a revocation) or the agent (a renunciation). If the termination violates the parties' contract, damages could be available. If the agency is coupled with an interest, only the agent has the power to terminate the agency relationship.

2. **Accomplishment of Objective or Expiration of Stated Period**
    - If the agency is for a limited purpose (e.g., Phil appoints Andrea to purchase Blackacre for him), actual authority is terminated when the objective is accomplished (i.e., Andrea purchases Blackacre).
    - If the agency is for a stated period (e.g., six months), actual authority is terminated upon expiration of the period. If no time is stated, the actual authority terminates after a reasonable time.

3. **Automatic Termination of Actual Authority**

    Actual authority is terminated automatically, by operation of law upon any of the following events:
    - *death* of either the principal or the agent (however, the death of the principal does not terminate the agency until the agent has notice of the principal's death);
    - *incapacity* of the principal;
    - *discharge* in bankruptcy of the principal;
    - *failure* to acquire a necessary license;
    - *destruction of the subject matter* of the agency (e.g., Paula hires Alex to purchase an antique car, which is destroyed before it can be purchased); or
    - *subsequent illegality* (e.g., Hister, a U.S. corporation, hires Alex to sell certain raw materials to a company in Asia. Subsequently, the Asian company is nationalized by the government where it is located. The government then makes it illegal for the company to purchase materials from companies outside of Asia).

Pass Key

Termination of agency by operation of law is a heavily tested issue. Be sure to memorize the above list.

2.2 Apparent Authority

Even though an agent might not have actual authority, there are situations in which the agent will nevertheless have the *power* (but not the right) to bind the principal, because the principal's conduct has caused *third parties to reasonably believe* that the agent had authority.

2.2.1 Principal's Conduct

Note that apparent authority requires a holding out *by the principal* or negligent inaction *by the principal*. The purported agent's mere representation that she is an agent is not sufficient to establish apparent authority.

2.2.2 Distinguish From Actual Authority

Apparent authority is based on the third party's reasonable belief that the agent has the power to bind the principal. Actual authority arises from the *agent's* reasonable belief that the agent has the power to bind the principal, not from the third party's belief. In either case, the principal is bound. However, if the agent lacked actual authority, the principal can hold the agent liable for acting without authority.

- **From Position:** A principal who holds another out as his agent vests the agent with the power to enter into all transactions that a reasonable third party would believe a person in the agent's position would have.

> **Illustration 5   Apparent Authority From Position**
>
> Pam hires Alex to manage her pet store. Alex has the apparent authority to hire and fire employees, make deposits, etc.

- **Not Affected by Secret Limiting Instructions:** A principal who issues secret instructions to the agent will limit the agent's *actual* authority but not the agent's *apparent* authority. Apparent authority is based on the third party's reasonable beliefs, and secret instructions are unknown to the third party.

> **Illustration 6   Apparent Authority Not Affected by Secret Limiting Instructions**
>
> Pam hires Alex to manage her pet store. It is customary in the area for pet store managers to have actual authority to purchase inventory (pets). Pam tells Alex that he may purchase pets for the store, but may not purchase a pet for more than $200. Tom, a dog breeder, offers to sell Pomeranian puppies to the pet store for $250 each, and Alex accepts. Alex has apparent authority to purchase the puppies, but not actual authority. Thus, Pam will have to pay Tom for the puppies, but can hold Alex liable for any loss that results.

- **General vs. Special Agent:** A general agent will perform a series of transactions involving a continuity of service. A special agent will perform one or more transactions *not* involving continuity of service. Therefore, the general agent has broader apparent authority than a special agent.

Illustration 7 — Apparent Authority of General vs. Special Agent

Pam hires Alex to manage her pet store. Pam also hires Jordan to distribute advertising brochures at the city park on the day of the annual Art in the Park festival. Alex is a general agent, and Jordan is a special agent. Alex has broader apparent authority than Jordan.

- **Termination of Apparent Authority:** When a principal terminates an agent's *actual* authority, the agent will continue to have *apparent* authority until the principal notifies third parties who might have known of the agency. *Actual notice* must be given to terminate apparent authority to old customers. *Constructive notice* (e.g., an ad in a newspaper) must be given to terminate apparent authority as to potential customers who may have known of the agency but who had not done business with the agent. If an agent's authority is terminated by operation of law, apparent authority also is terminated by operation of law and no notice is needed.

Illustration 8 — Termination of Apparent Authority

Allen has been Patty's office manager for 10 years and has regularly purchased office supplies from Terri. Patty fires Allen, but does not notify Terri. If Allen purchases more office supplies from Terri purportedly on Patty's behalf, Terri can make Patty pay for the supplies because of Allen's apparent authority.

2.3 Estoppel to Deny Existence of Agency

If a person has not made any communications that indicate another is the person's agent, but the person intentionally or carelessly caused a third party to believe another is the person's agent and the third party detrimentally and justifiably relies on this belief, the person will be estopped from denying the other person acted as his or her authorized agent and so will be bound. This is sometimes called agency by estoppel.

2.4 Ratification

Ratification allows a principal to choose to become bound by a previously unauthorized act of his or her agent.

2.4.1 Requirements

1. The agent must have indicated that she was acting on behalf of the principal (if the third party did not believe that the agent was acting for a principal, there can be no ratification).
2. All material facts must be disclosed to the principal.
3. The principal must ratify the entire transaction—there can be no partial ratification.
4. Ratification does not require consideration, and the principal need not notify the third party of the ratification (because the third party already thinks he has a contract with the principal).

2.4.2 May Ratify Expressly or Impliedly

The principal may ratify expressly, or may ratify impliedly by accepting the benefits of the contract when there is an opportunity to reject them.

2.4.3 What May Be Ratified?

Generally, any act may be ratified unless performance would be illegal; the third party withdraws prior to ratification; or there has been a material change of circumstance so that it would not be fair to hold the third party liable.

2.4.4 Who May Ratify?

Only the purported principal may ratify. The agent cannot take over the contract. Only a disclosed principal may ratify. An undisclosed principal cannot ratify.

2.5 Contractual Liability

2.5.1 Principal Liable if Agent Had Authority or Principal Ratified

The principal will be bound by the agent's acts if the agent acted with actual authority or apparent authority, or if the principal ratified the transaction. The principal's liability does not depend on whether the principal's existence or identity was disclosed.

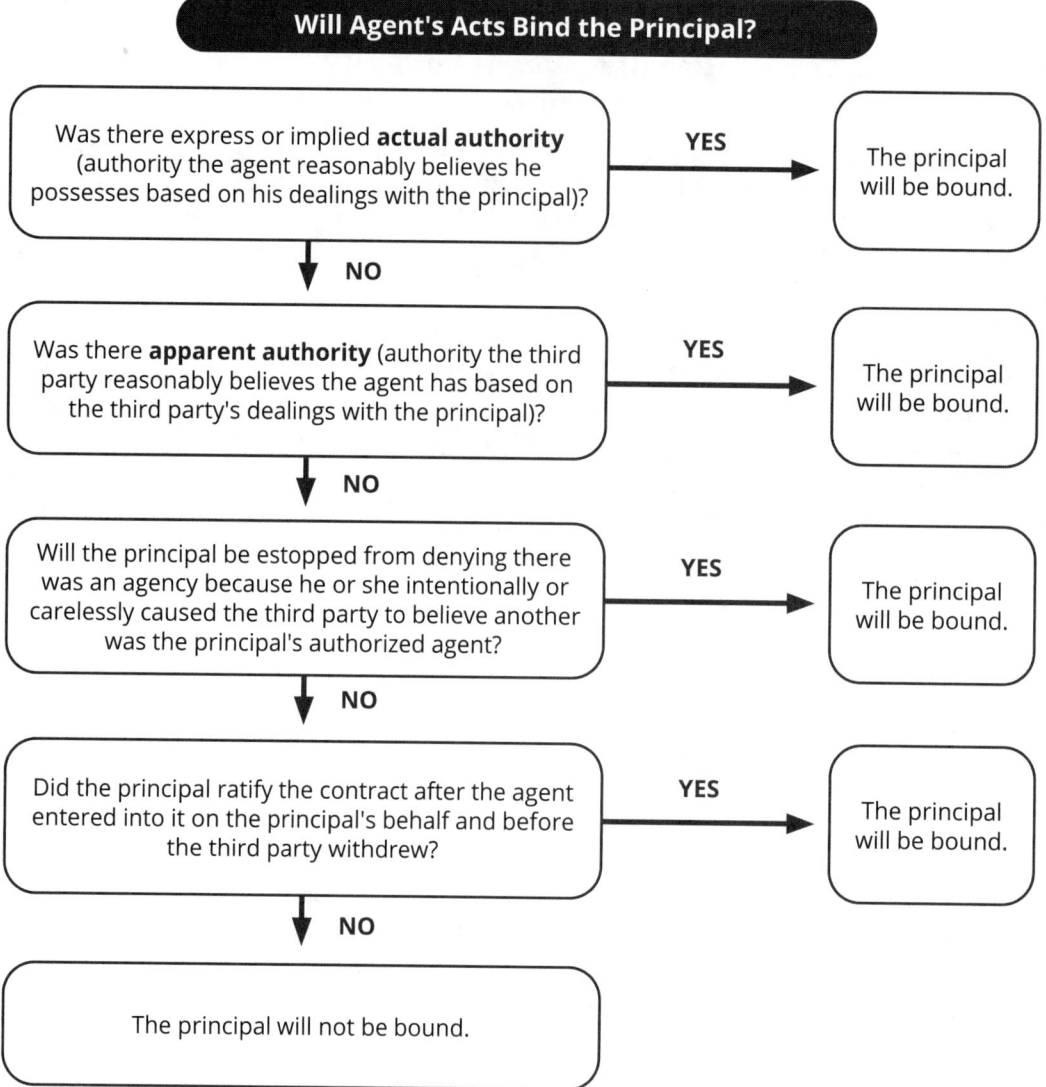

2.5.2 Agent's Liability

1. **Disclosed Principal (Agent Not Liable if Authorized)**

   If the agent discloses the existence and identity of the principal (a disclosed principal situation), the third party cannot hold an authorized agent liable on the contract. Every person representing himself as an agent impliedly warrants that he has the authority he purports to have. If, in fact, the agent has no such authority, the third party can hold the agent liable for any damages caused based on breach of this implied warranty.

2. **Unidentified and Undisclosed Principal (Agent Liable)**

   If the principal's identity is not disclosed to the third party (an unidentified or partially disclosed principal situation), or neither the existence nor the identity of the principal is disclosed to the third party (an undisclosed principal situation), the agent is liable on the contract with the third party.

   - **Third Party's Election:** The third party can hold either the principal or the agent (but not both) liable if the principal was undisclosed or unidentified. The third party must elect whom to hold liable.

   - **No Apparent Authority With an Undisclosed Principal:** If the principal is undisclosed, there can be no apparent authority because there is no holding out of the agent by the principal.

   - **No Effect on Actual Authority:** The fact that the principal is undisclosed has no effect on the agent's actual authority since actual authority arises from the communications between the principal and the agent.

Pass Key

The examiners often ask about undisclosed principal situations. There are a few key points to remember.

- The principal is bound if the agent had authority. It is irrelevant whether the principal was disclosed, unidentified, or undisclosed. If the agent did not have authority, the principal is bound only if he ratifies.

- The agent can be held personally liable if the principal is unidentified (identity is not disclosed but the fact that a person is acting as an agent is disclosed) or undisclosed (neither identity nor existence are disclosed).

2.5.3 Third Party's Liability

1. **Generally Only Principal Can Hold Third Party Liable**

   As a general rule, only the principal (not the agent) can hold the third party liable on a contract the agent entered into on the principal's behalf, even if the principal's existence or identity were not disclosed.

Illustration 9   Third Party's Liability

Ann entered into a contract with Top Corp. to purchase televisions on behalf of Paul. Paul instructed Ann to enter into the contract in her own name without disclosing that she was acting on behalf of Paul. If Top Corp. repudiates the contract, Paul may hold Top liable even though it did not know it was dealing with Paul.

2. Exceptions

The principal cannot hold the third party liable where:

- the principal's *identity was fraudulently* concealed (e.g., if the third party indicates that she will not do business with the principal, the principal cannot get around this by dealing through an agent); or
- the performance to the principal would *increase the burden* on the third party (e.g., Big Rubber Company cannot employ Small Rubber Company as an agent to enter into a rubber requirements contract without disclosing that the contract is for Big Rubber Company).

3 Tort Liability

3.1 In General: Respondeat Superior

1. As a general rule, a principal is not liable for the torts committed by his agent—only the agent is liable.

2. However, there is an exception for employers. Under the doctrine of respondeat superior, an employer can be liable for an employee's torts committed within the scope of employment.

3. This does not relieve the agent of liability. The injured person may sue both the employer under respondeat superior and the agent.

3.2 Employer-Employee Relationship

An employer (or master) is liable only for torts of an employee (or servant) and is usually not liable for torts of independent contractors.

1. Right to Control Manner of Performance Is Key

The most important factor in determining whether a person is an employee or an independent contractor is the right of the principal to *control* the manner in which the person performs. An employer has the right to control employees, but has little control over the methods used by independent contractors.

2. Additional Factors

Where right to control is not clear, the courts look to other factors, such as whether the worker has a business of his own, provides his own tools and facilities, length of the employment (short or definite vs. long or indefinite), basis of compensation, and the degree of supervision.

- A clear example of an employee is one who works full time for the employer, uses the employer's facilities or tools, is compensated on a time basis, and is subject to the supervision of the principal.
- A clear example of an independent contractor is one who has a calling of her own and who uses her own facilities or tools, is hired for a particular job, is paid a given amount for that job, and who follows her own discretion in carrying out the job. For example, a CPA who performs an audit for a corporation is an independent contractor.

3.3 Scope of Employment

An employer is not liable to an injured party merely because an employee caused the injury—the injury must also have occurred within the *scope of the employment*. That is, the injury must have occurred while the employee was working for the employer within the time and geographic area in which the employee was to work.

1. **Activities**

   The conduct causing the injury need not actually have been authorized by the employer; rather the conduct need only be (i) of the *same general type* the employee was hired to perform; and (ii) actuated, at least in part, by a desire to serve the employer.

   > **Illustration 10 Liability of Employer for Employee**
   >
   > Although a bar owner might not authorize a bouncer to beat up boisterous customers, the owner nevertheless can be held liable if this occurs because the conduct is of the same general nature as the bouncer's job.

   - **Intentional Torts**

     The employer usually is liable only for an employee's negligence and is not liable for intentional torts, since intentional torts are seldom within the scope of employment. However, where the tort is authorized or where use of force is authorized (as with a bouncer), the employer can be liable.

   - **Crimes**

     An employer generally is not liable in tort for an employee's conduct that constitutes a serious crime (e.g., carrying an illegal weapon).

   > **Pass Key**
   >
   > The examiners often ask about a principal's liability for its agent's torts. Remember, if the agent is an employee and committed a tort while trying to serve the principal/employer, the principal/employer generally will be liable unless the tort was unexpected (e.g., illegal conduct).

2. **Time and Geographic Area**

   It is not enough simply that the conduct that caused the injury was of the same general type the employee was hired to perform. The conduct must also have occurred within usual employment time and space limits. Small detours from an employer's directions (e.g., driving a few blocks out of the way, stopping for lunch, etc.) fall within the scope of the employment. Major deviations (frolic) from an employer's directions (e.g., driving 15 miles out of the way to attend a party) fall outside the scope of employment.

3. **Cannot Limit Liability by Agreement With Employee**

   An agreement between the employer and employee that the employer will not be liable for employee torts does not prevent a third party from holding the employer liable. The employer can seek reimbursement from the employee.

3.4 Employer Liability for Independent Contractors

Although the general rule is that an employer is not liable for torts committed by independent contractors, an employer can be liable for the torts of an independent contractor if the employer authorized the tortious act or if the work involved an ultra-hazardous (or inherently dangerous) activity.

Illustration 11 Liability of Principal for Agent's Torts

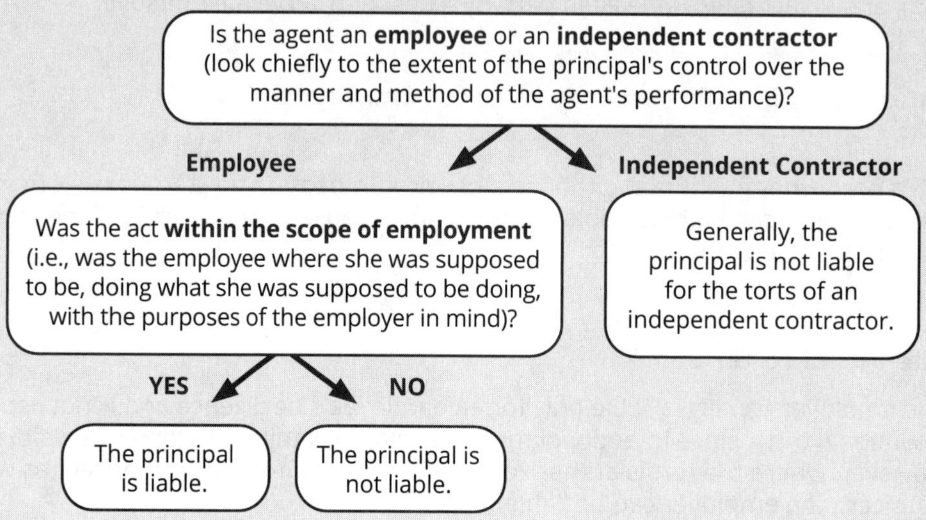

Is the agent an **employee** or an **independent contractor** (look chiefly to the extent of the principal's control over the manner and method of the agent's performance)?

Employee

Was the act **within the scope of employment** (i.e., was the employee where she was supposed to be, doing what she was supposed to be doing, with the purposes of the employer in mind)?

- YES → The principal is liable.
- NO → The principal is not liable.

Independent Contractor

Generally, the principal is not liable for the torts of an independent contractor.

MODULE 5
Suretyship

REG 5

1 Introduction

Broadly speaking, a surety is one who agrees to be liable for the debt or obligation of another. A suretyship transaction involves three parties: the creditor (i.e., the obligee), the principal debtor (i.e., obligor), and the surety.

1.1 Surety vs. Guarantor

A surety in the narrow sense of the term is directly liable on the contract and is distinguished from a guarantor, who is liable to the creditor only if the debtor does not perform his or her duty to the creditor.

> **Illustration 1 Surety vs. Guarantor**
>
> 1. Alex loans Becky $10,000 with a June 1 due date. Cindy is surety on the note evidencing the indebtedness. On June 1, Alex, the creditor-obligee, may demand performance directly from Cindy. Cindy is liable even though Alex has not made demand upon Becky or placed Becky in default.
>
> 2. Alex loans Becky $10,000 with a June 1 due date. Cindy guarantees Becky's performance on the note evidencing the indebtedness. On June 1, Alex, the creditor-obligee, may demand performance from Cindy if and only if Becky defaults on the obligation (which usually means fails to pay).

A guarantor of collectibility is liable only if the creditor is unable to collect from the debtor after exhausting all legal remedies, including demand, suit, judgment, and exhaustion of all supplementary proceedings.

1.2 Statute of Frauds

The Statute of Frauds requires written evidence of the promise to answer for the debt of another signed by the surety. A suretyship undertaking not evidenced by a written memorandum is unenforceable.

2 The Surety's Rights

2.1 Against Creditor

After a default, a surety generally has no right to a notice of default or to have the creditor try to collect from the principal debtor or to have the creditor apply to the debt any security that the creditor has.

Pass Key

When a debtor defaults in a suretyship situation, the creditor may do any of the following in any order:

- Immediately demand payment from the surety
- Immediately demand payment from the debtor
- Immediately go after collateral, if there is any

The surety does not have the right to require the creditor to take any of the above-mentioned actions. A guarantor of collectibility would have the right to require a creditor to first proceed against the debtor or against available collateral.

Illustration 2 Surety's Rights and Obligations

Principal is in bankruptcy. Creditor holds a mortgage on Principal's factory as security on an obligation. Surety has also agreed to serve as a surety on the obligation. There will be considerable delay before Creditor can realize on the security due to the bankruptcy. Surety has no right to force Creditor to go against the collateral. Surety must pay in full. Surety is then subrogated to Creditors' rights against Principal on the mortgage (see below).

2.2 Against Principal Debtor

2.2.1 Exoneration (Suit to Compel Payment)

The principal debtor owes the surety a duty to perform. If the principal fails to pay the creditor, the surety may bring a suit for exoneration in equity to compel the principal to pay.

2.2.2 Subrogation (Enforcement of Creditor's Right Against Principal)

After paying the principal debtor's obligation, the surety may enforce (i.e., is subrogated to) any rights that the creditor had against the principal debtor. This includes the right to enforcement of any security interest and any priority in bankruptcy that the creditor had.

2.2.3 Reimbursement (Suit Against Principal After Payment)

The surety is entitled to reimbursement from his principal debtor for any amount the surety paid on behalf of the debtor. This is also called a right to "indemnification." Reimbursement should be distinguished from exoneration. In the latter, the surety compels the principal debtor to pay the creditor and the surety does not pay.

2.3 Against Cosureties

2.3.1 Defined: Two or More Sureties of the Same Obligation

Cosureties are two or more sureties of the same obligation. Cosureties are jointly and severally liable (i.e., any one or more may be liable for the entire obligation).

2.3.2 Exoneration (Suit to Compel Payment)

If it becomes necessary for the sureties to pay the creditor, one surety may compel the cosureties, by a suit in equity for exoneration, to pay their pro rata shares of the debt.

2.3.3 Contribution

On payment, a surety is entitled to contribution from the cosureties for their share of the payment. Contribution should be distinguished from exoneration in that the right of contribution arises only after the surety has already paid more than her share.

- If the contract does not specify the liability of each surety, each surety is liable for a pro rata share determined by the number of solvent sureties.

> **Illustration 3   Cosureties (Solvent vs. Insolvent)**
>
> There are three solvent and two insolvent sureties. Each solvent surety is liable for one-third of the debt.

- Where cosureties are obligated for varying amounts by their agreements and the debt is reduced by part payment by the principal, each cosurety remains liable for the original amount stated in the agreement. But payment of more than the pro rata share of the reduced debt entitles a cosurety to contribution from the cosureties for the excess in the proportion of the amounts of their original liability.

> **Illustration 4   Amounts Owed by Cosureties**
>
> C loans D $9,000, and X, Y, and Z agree to be cosureties. The maximum liability of each is: X, $6,000; Y, $3,000; and Z, $9,000. After making payments, D defaults and Z pays the entire balance of $6,000.
>
> Z can collect a pro rata share from X and Y. X would have to contribute 6,000/18,000 of $6,000, or $2,000. Y would have to contribute 3,000/18,000 of $6,000, or $1,000.

- If a cosurety's obligation is discharged in bankruptcy, her agreed share should not be considered in determining the pro rata share of the remaining cosureties. The cosurety is eliminated from the calculation because nothing can be collected from the cosurety.

> **Illustration 5 Cosurety Is Bankrupt**
>
> C loans D $9,000 and X, Y, and Z agree to be cosureties. The maximum liability for each is: X, $6,000, Y, $3,000 and Z, $9,000. After making payments, D defaults and Z pays the entire balance of $6,000.
>
> X's debts, including his surety obligation, were previously discharged in bankruptcy. Z cannot collect anything from X. Z can collect 3,000/12,000 of $6,000 from Y, or $1,500. X was eliminated from the calculation because X was discharged in bankruptcy.

Pass Key

The examiners often ask about sureties' pro rata liability. Be sure you understand this concept.

3 Defenses of Surety

1. **Defrauded Principal**

   The surety may use as a defense that the principal debtor was induced to enter into the contract by the creditor's fraud. However, fraud by the principal debtor is not a good defense for the surety against the creditor unless the creditor was aware of the fraud.

2. **Duress Upon Principal**

   The surety is not liable if the principal debtor's promise was obtained by duress and the surety did not know of the duress.

3. **Illegality of the Principal's Obligation**

   The surety is not liable if the underlying obligation between the creditor and principal debtor is illegal.

4. **Discharge of Principal's Obligation**

   If the underlying obligation is paid or the principal debtor tenders performance and the creditor refuses to accept it, the surety is no longer liable. If the creditor releases the principal, the surety is discharged unless the creditor reserved her rights against the surety.

5. **Surety's Incapacity or Bankruptcy**

   The surety's own contractual incapacity (e.g., minority, adjudicated insanity, etc.) or bankruptcy is a defense for the surety.

6. Lack of Consideration

Like all contracts, the promise to serve as a surety must be supported by consideration to be enforceable. But that does not mean that the surety must be paid. An unpaid surety (called a "*gratuitous surety*") will be bound if he or she makes the promise to act as surety before consideration flows from the creditor to the principal debtor.

> **Illustration 6   Gratuitous Surety**
>
> A mother's gratuitous promise to serve as surety on her son's car loan is supported by consideration if the mother's promise is made before or contemporaneous with the time the seller becomes obligated to deliver the car. But if the gratuitous promise is made after the son receives the car, there is no consideration to support the promise.

7. Variations of the Surety's Risk

Any variation of the contract that changes a gratuitous surety's risk will discharge the gratuitous surety. A variation of a contract that changes a compensated surety's risk will discharge the surety only if the change is material and increases the surety's risk of loss.

> **Illustration 7   Compensated vs. Gratuitous Surety**
>
> The principal is originally obligated to build a parking lot 148 feet by 90 feet. If the principal and creditor agree to change the contract to a lot 138 feet by 90 feet, a gratuitous surety is discharged. The risk has been varied. But a compensated surety would not be discharged, both because the change does not appear to be material and because it makes performance easier (a smaller parking lot).

8. Extension of Time vs. Delay in Collection

If the principal debtor and creditor agree to extend time, the above rules apply (gratuitous surety discharged; compensated surety discharged if the change is material and increases risk). However, if the creditor does not agree to extend time, but rather merely delays in collection, the surety is not discharged.

9. Loss of Security

The release of security held by the creditor discharges the surety in the amount of the value of the security released. If the security is lost due to the creditor's inaction (e.g., failure to take the steps necessary to perfect it), the surety is discharged in the amount of the value of the security unless substantial and burdensome acts were required for protection of the security.

10. Release of Cosurety

A release of a cosurety without the other cosurety's consent results in the remaining cosurety losing the right of contribution against the released cosurety. Thus, the remaining surety is discharged to the extent that the surety could have recovered from the released surety.

> **Illustration 8 Release of Cosurety**
>
> Ingot loans Flange $50,000. Quill and West agree to act as compensated cosureties in the amount of $50,000 each. Ingot releases West without Quill's consent and Flange defaults on the entire obligation. Ingot demands payment from Quill. Quill is discharged for 50 percent of the loan, or $25,000, because this is the amount Quill could have collected from West by reason of the right of contribution.

11. No Defense Situations

The principal's fraud against the surety (e.g., the principal debtor lies to get the surety to agree) is not a defense against the creditor unless the creditor knows of the lie. The fact that the principal debtor is or has become bankrupt or incapacitated is not a defense for the surety.

4 Creditors' Rights Outside of Suretyship

When a debtor owes a creditor money and does not have sufficient funds to pay, the debtor has a few options to alleviate the debt. Besides filing a petition in bankruptcy (discussed in the bankruptcy modules), the debtor can enter into a creditors' composition or make an assignment for the benefit of creditors.

4.1 Creditors' Composition

A creditor's composition is an agreement between the debtor and at least two creditors that the debtor pays the creditors less than their full claims in full satisfaction of their claims. Contract consideration arises from the agreement by each creditor with each other to take less than his or her full claim. This procedure results in the debtor being discharged in full for the debts owed the participating creditors after the debtor has paid the agreed amount.

4.2 Assignment for the Benefit of Creditors

In an assignment for the benefit of creditors, the debtor transfers some or all of his or her property to a trustee, who disposes of the property and uses the proceeds to satisfy the debtor's debts. The debtor is not discharged from unpaid debts by this procedure since creditors do not agree to any discharge.

5 Judicial Liens and Garnishment

5.1 In General

Creditors without a security interest or mortgage in the debtor's property can gain rights in the debtor's property through imposition of a judicial lien on property in the debtor's hands or garnishment of property in the hands of a third party.

5.2 Prejudgment Attachment

Before final judgment in a suit on a debt is rendered, if the creditor has reason to believe that the debtor will not pay, the creditor can ask the court to provisionally attach a piece of the debtor's property.

1. The court then issues a writ of attachment (to the local sheriff) and the property is seized so a creditor who prevails will be assured of recovering on the judgment through sale of the property.

2. Generally, a hearing must be held before property can be attached by the court, and most courts require that a creditor post a bond for any damages that result if the creditor does not ultimately prevail in the suit.

5.3 Judicial Lien

1. If a debtor is adjudged to owe a creditor money and the judgment has gone unsatisfied, the creditor can request the court to impose a lien on specific property owned and possessed by the debtor.

2. After the court imposes the lien, it will issue a writ (e.g., a writ of attachment), usually to the local sheriff, to seize property belonging to the debtor, sell it, and turn over the proceeds to the creditor.

3. Most states protect certain property of the debtor to ensure that the debtor does not become destitute.

    - Many states provide a "homestead" exemption that excludes items of a person's household, up to a certain amount, from the liens of most creditors (the exclusion does not apply to persons with purchase money security interests ("PMSIs") in personal property or purchase money mortgages against real property).

    - When a taxpayer fails to pay federal taxes, the IRS can file a lien on all of the taxpayer's property, including property exempt from levy under state law.

5.4 Garnishment

Where a debtor is adjudged to owe a creditor money and the debtor has property in the hands of a third party (e.g., money the debtor is owed by an employer, money in a bank account, debts owed to the debtor), a writ of garnishment may be sought.

1. The writ orders the person holding the property to turn it over to the creditor or be held personally liable for the value of the property not turned over.

2. Federal law provides that Social Security payments are not subject to garnishment, execution, levy, or attachment.

3. States often limit the amount of an employee's wages that may be garnished (e.g., no more than one-fourth of an employee's weekly salary) to prevent the debtor from becoming destitute.

6 Mechanic's and Materialman's Liens

6.1 Mechanic's Liens and Artisan's Liens

Under common law, a mechanic or artisan who works on property and either improves it or repairs it automatically has a lien on the property—for the price of the repairs—for as long as the property is in the lienor's possession. These liens are possessory—they dissolve as soon as the lienor lets the owner have the property back. If a mechanic, artisan, innkeeper, etc., goes unpaid, he or she may give the owner notice of the intention to sell the retained property to pay the owner's bill. Alternatively, the lienor may foreclose on the property by filing suit.

6.2 Materialman's Lien

Materialman's liens often are imposed in favor of contractors who perform work on, or provide supplies for, real property improvements. The unpaid materialman must file a notice with the local recorder of deeds in order to preserve his or her lien.

7 Fraudulent Conveyances

A fraudulent conveyance occurs when a debtor transfers property with the intent to hinder, delay, or defraud any of her creditors. A fraudulent conveyance is void or voidable and will be set aside in a proper proceeding.

In determining if a fraudulent conveyance occurred, a court will consider whether:

1. the transfer was to an insider (e.g., relative, partner, and co-employee);
2. the debtor retained possession or control of the property transferred;
3. the transfer was not disclosed or was concealed (i.e., done secretly);
4. the transfer was of substantially all the debtor's assets;
5. the value received by the debtor for the asset was not reasonable; and
6. the debtor was insolvent or became insolvent shortly after the transfer.

8 Fair Debt Collection Practices Act (FDCPA)

The Federal Fair Debt Collection Practices Act (FDCPA) curbs abuses by collection agencies in collecting consumer debts. The act does not apply to a creditor attempting to collect its own debts; just to services that collect consumer debts for others.

8.1 Prohibited Acts

The act severely restricts collection agencies' ability to call third parties, such as relatives of the debtor, to indirectly pressure the debtor. A collection agency can contact third persons to discover a debtor's whereabouts, but may not disclose that it is a collection agency or that the debtor owes a debt. The FDCPA also prohibits:

- Contacting the debtor at inconvenient or unusual times; in most cases "convenient" times are between 8 a.m. and 9 p.m.
- Contacting the debtor directly if the debtor is represented by an attorney.
- Using harassing or abusive language in talking to the debtor (e.g., "pay or we'll break your knee caps").
- Making false or misleading claims (e.g., "we can have you thrown in jail for not paying").
- Contacting the debtor at her place of employment if the employer objects.

8.2 Remedies Under the Act

8.2.1 Debtor's Power to Terminate Contacts

A debtor has the power to terminate the collection agency's contacts by notifying the agency in writing that the debtor will not pay the debt and to stop further communication. The agency must stop communications except to inform the debtor that it is bringing a lawsuit or seeking other remedies.

8.2.2 Damages

The FDCPA gives debtors the right to sue for actual damages caused by the collection agency's misconduct. The FDCPA also provides a statutory $1,000 damage award.

8.2.3 Federal Trade Commission

The Federal Trade Commission can bring administrative enforcement actions under the act to force a collection agency to comply with the act's provisions.

NOTES

MODULE 6 Secured Transactions

REG 5

1 Introduction

1.1 Secured Transactions and Security Interest

Secured transactions questions generally involve credit transactions. A *debtor buys* something from a *creditor or secured party* on credit. The creditor wants to be able to rely on something other than the debtor's promise to ensure payment. A *security interest* on *collateral* is that something. A security interest is a limited right in specific personal property (the *collateral*) of the debtor that allows the creditor to take the property (commonly referred to as repossessing) if the debtor fails to fulfill the credit obligation.

1.2 Attachment and Perfection

A security interest is effective between the parties as soon as certain steps are taken to *attach* the interest. Once the interest attaches, if the debtor defaults, the creditor has some right to take the collateral from the debtor to satisfy the debt. Attachment does not provide the creditor with rights against third parties who might also have an interest in the collateral. To gain rights over third parties, a creditor must take added steps to *perfect* the security interest. Perfection basically serves as a form of notice that the creditor has a security interest in the collateral, and because of this notice, gives the creditor rights in the collateral superior to certain third parties.

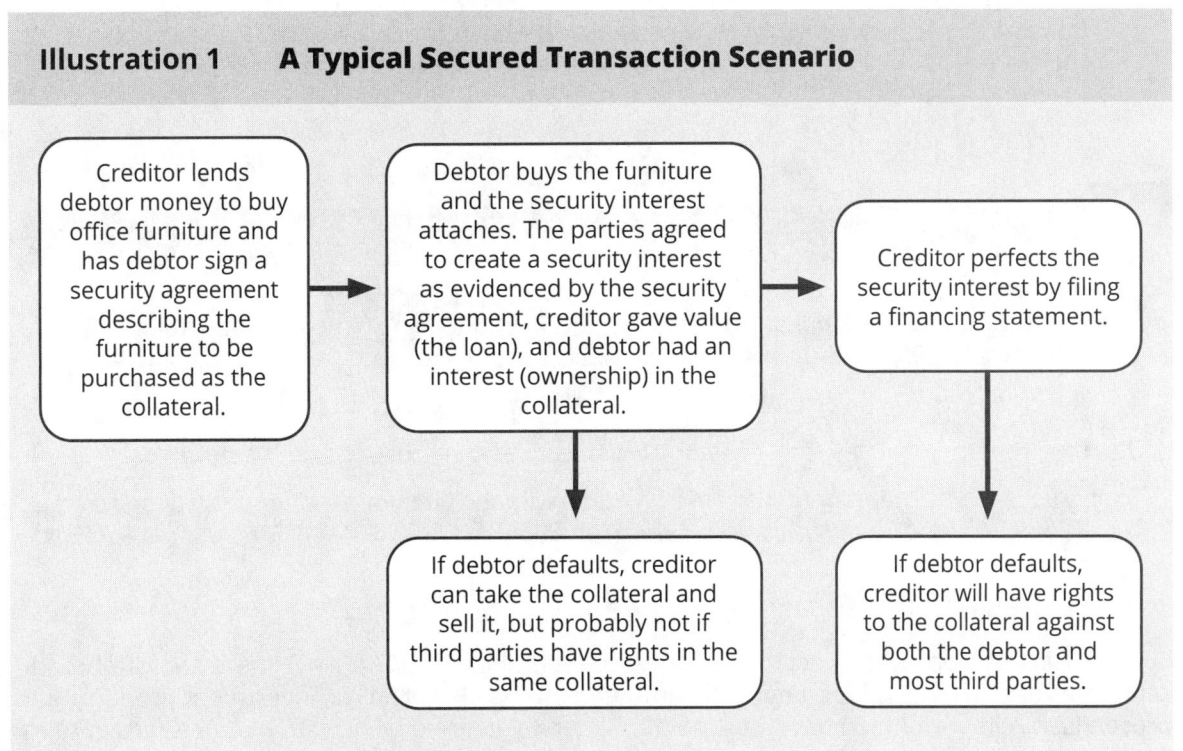

Illustration 1 — A Typical Secured Transaction Scenario

1.3 Scope of Article 9, Secured Transactions

Article 9 of the Uniform Commercial Code (UCC), with certain exceptions, applies to most contractual security interests in personal property or fixtures (personal property so attached to real property as to become part of the real property) and outright sales of accounts receivable. Article 9 does not apply to security interests in land (i.e., mortgages), wage claims, and statutory liens, such as mechanic's liens.

There is a special type of security interest—a purchase money security interest (PMSI)—that has priority over all other types of security interests in the same collateral, if the PMSI is properly perfected. A PMSI arises when:

1. a creditor sells the collateral to the debtor on credit, retaining a security interest for the purchase price; or
2. the creditor advances funds used by the debtor to purchase the collateral.

Notice that the creditor may, but need not, be the seller of the collateral.

> **Illustration 2 PMSI**
>
> 1. Becky purchases a $1,000 stereo on credit from Radio Hut and signs a security agreement giving Radio Hut a security interest in the stereo. Radio Hut has a PMSI in the stereo because it supplied the credit that enabled Becky to purchase the collateral.
> 2. Becky goes to Bank and asks Bank for $1,000 to purchase a stereo. Bank gives Becky the money, Becky signs a security agreement giving Bank a security interest in the stereo, and Becky buys the stereo from Radio Hut. Bank has a PMSI in the stereo because it advanced the money that was used to purchase the collateral.
> 3. Becky wants to borrow $1,000 from Bank. Bank agrees to give Becky the money if Becky will give Bank a security interest in a stereo that Becky already owns. Although Bank has a security interest, it will not have a PMSI in the stereo. Becky already owned the stereo (Bank did not advance funds used to purchase the collateral).

Pass Key

Examiners frequently ask questions involving PMSI creditors. You must be able to spot PMSI creditors on the CPA Exam. Remember, a PMSI creditor exists if:

1. the creditor sells the collateral on credit, retaining a security interest; or
2. the creditor advances funds used by the debtor to purchase the collateral.

Simply ask—did the debtor purchase the collateral with the creditor's money or creditor's credit?

1.4 Types of Collateral

Collateral is the property subject to a security interest. Under UCC Article 9, there are four broad categories of collateral: goods, intangible and semi-intangible collateral, investment property, and proceeds. It is important to know the type of collateral you are dealing with because certain rules (e.g., how to perfect, where to perfect, and priority) depend on the type of collateral involved.

1.4.1 Goods

Goods include consumer goods, inventory, and equipment. The category into which a particular good falls is determined by how the debtor uses the item, not by the nature of the item.

> **Illustration 3　Classifying Goods**
>
> If a debtor uses a car as a delivery vehicle for his business, it is equipment. If he uses a car for household purposes, it is consumer goods. If he buys a car to sell at his auto dealership, it is inventory.

1.4.2 Intangible Collateral Accounts

An account is any right to payment for goods, services, real property, or use of a credit card *not* evidenced by an instrument or chattel paper (e.g., the money you owe your doctor after a checkup).

1.4.3 Investment Property

Investment property includes stocks, bonds, mutual funds, etc.

1.4.4 Proceeds

Proceeds include whatever is received upon the sale, exchange, collection, or other disposition of collateral.

2　Creation (Attachment) of the Security Interest

Recall that attachment establishes the right of a creditor in collateral vis-a-vis the debtor. Generally, a security interest will attach to an item of collateral if the parties agree that the security interest will attach. The agreement can be in writing (including electronic documents) or it can be oral if the secured party takes possession of the collateral (which is called a pledge). If the security agreement is in writing, it must be signed by the debtor. Additionally, the debtor must have rights in the collateral, and the creditor must have given value for the security interest.

2.1　Property in Which Debtor Acquires Interest in Future (After-Acquired Property)

A secured party will sometimes want to obtain a security interest not only in a debtor's present property, but also in property that the debtor will obtain in the future. This is permissible and is facilitated by including an "after-acquired property clause" in the security agreement. The security interest attaches to the after-acquired property *as soon as the debtor acquires an interest in the property*.

2.2　Duties of Secured Party After Attachment

A secured party has a duty to file or send the debtor a termination statement when the debt is paid, confirm for the debtor the unpaid amount left on the secured debt, and to use reasonable care to preserve any collateral in the secured party's possession.

3 Perfection of the Security Interest

3.1 Introduction

Attachment merely establishes rights between the debtor and the creditor. If the creditor attaches a security interest to an item of collateral, the creditor gains the right to take that collateral if the debtor defaults on the secured obligation. To acquire the maximum priority in the collateral over other parties who may have an interest in the collateral (e.g., subsequent purchasers of the collateral, unsecured creditors, and other priority creditors), the secured party must "perfect." There are five methods of perfection:

1. Filing
2. Taking possession of the collateral
3. Control
4. Automatic perfection
5. Temporary perfection

Pass Key

The examiners like to ask about the relationship between perfection and attachment. A key point to remember is that a security interest cannot be perfected before it attaches to the collateral, but attachment and perfection can occur at the same time (e.g., by taking possession of the collateral).

3.2 Perfection by Filing

A security interest may be perfected as to all kinds of collateral except deposit accounts and money by filing a financing statement.

3.2.1 Documents to Be Filed (the Financing Statement)

The law simply requires "notice" filing—it does not require a filing of a copy of the security agreement. "Notice" is given by the filing of a "*financing statement*." The financing statement must give the names and addresses of the debtor and creditor and an indication of the type of collateral covered by the financing statement (such as "the debtor's inventory and equipment").

3.2.2 Timing

A creditor can file a financing statement before all of the steps for attachment are complete. In that case, the security interest is not perfected until it attaches to the collateral.

3.3 Perfection by Taking Possession (Pledge)

A secured party may perfect a security interest in most types of collateral simply by taking possession of the collateral. This is similar to when a pawn shop takes an item in exchange for a loan of money. The property owner can redeem the pledged item by paying back the amount borrowed.

3.4 Perfection by Control

Security interests in investment property may be perfected by "control." Basically, a secured party (or other purchaser) has control of an item of investment property when the secured party has taken whatever steps are necessary to be able to have the investment property sold without further action from the owner.

If the collateral is a securities account (few people actually physically possess the stocks or bonds they own) the creditor will have control if the owner instructs the brokers or mutual fund company that the secured party now has whatever right in the account the owner has or that the broker or mutual fund company is to comply with the secured party's orders without further consent of the owner.

> **Illustration 4   Control**
>
> Alex borrows $100,000 from Bank. As security, Bank requires Alex to give it a security interest in his Squabb brokerage account, which has a current market value of $200,000. Bank can perfect this interest through control by having Alex instruct Squabb to follow Bank's orders regarding the account.

3.5 Automatic Perfection

Article 9 provides that a security interest can be perfected simply by the attachment of the security interest without any added requirements. This is called an *automatic perfection*. Historically, only two types of automatic perfection have appeared on the exam:

1. **PMSI in Consumer Goods**

    Recall that a PMSI arises where the creditor either sells the collateral to the debtor on credit and reserves a security interest or advances the funds that are used to purchase the collateral and reserves a security interest. The only type of PMSI that is automatically perfected is a PMSI in consumer goods. A PMSI in inventory or equipment collateral must be filed to be valid.

2. **Small-Scale Assignment of Accounts**

    A small-scale assignment of accounts (e.g., assignment of a few accounts receivable) is automatically perfected.

3.6 Temporary Perfection

3.6.1 Twenty-Day Period for Proceeds

If a creditor has a perfected security interest in collateral and that collateral is sold, the creditor has a temporary, perfected security interest in the proceeds of the collateral that was sold. The temporary perfection lasts for 20 days.

> **Illustration 5   Temporary Perfection**
>
> Sally trades in her old stereo, which is collateral for Bank's loan, for a new stereo. Bank's security interest in the new stereo is continuously perfected for 20 days from Sally's receipt of the new stereo.

3.6.2 Movement of Debtor (Four-Month Grace Period)

If the debtor moves from one state to another, perfection in the first state generally is valid for *four months* after the debtor moves to the second state. To maintain its priority, the creditor must perfect in the new state within this four-month period.

4 Rights on Default

4.1 Right to Take Possession of and Sell Collateral

The right to take possession of and sell the collateral on default is the most important and most used of the rights on default.

4.1.1 Taking Possession

The secured party may take possession by self-help without judicial process if she can do so *without a breach of the peace*.

The secured party may always take possession of the collateral by replevy action, a judicial action seeking the transfer of personal property.

4.1.2 Sale

After default and repossession, the secured party may sell or lease the collateral, either in its condition when taken or after reasonable preparation or processing. Disposition may be by either *public* (auction) or *private* sale.

- The sale or lease must be commercially reasonable in all respects: method, manner, time, place, and terms.
- The debtor and others parties must generally be given notice of the sale.
- The sale wipes out all subordinate interests, such as the interest of secured parties with lower priority, lien creditors, and the debtor's interest. A good faith purchaser of the collateral at the sale takes free of all subordinate interests, but is subject to superior interests.
- The debtor has the right to redeem by paying off the indebtedness and costs before the sale, but this right is cut off by the sale.

Pass Key

The examiners often ask about the effect of a sale of the collateral. Remember that all subordinate claims are wiped out and there is no right of redemption by subordinate security interest holders or the debtor.

4.1.3 Proceeds

Proceeds of a default sale are distributed in the following order:

1. First, to pay the expenses of repossession and sale.
2. Second, to pay creditors with a security interest in the collateral in order of priority; the creditor with the highest priority must be paid in full before any proceeds can go to the secured creditor with the next highest priority.
3. Finally, any surplus is paid to the debtor.

If sale of the collateral does not bring in enough money to pay the expenses of the sale and the debt, the secured party may bring a court action to recover the deficiency from the debtor.

4.2 Retention of Collateral in Satisfaction of Debt

- **Transactions Not Involving Consumers:** After default, a secured party may keep the collateral in full or partial satisfaction of the debt (i.e., the secured party may keep the collateral, offset its value against the debt, and seek to recover the difference from the debtor).
- **Transactions Involving Consumers:** With consumers, the secured party may keep the collateral only in full satisfaction of the debt (i.e., no deficiency may be recovered).
- **Notice Must Be Given in Full or Partial Satisfaction Cases:** In either case, the secured party must give notice of its intent to keep the collateral to the debtor and other secured parties.
- **Compulsory Disposition of Consumer Goods (60 Percent Rule):** In *consumer goods* cases in which the debtor has paid at least 60 percent of the loan, the secured party must sell the collateral *within 90 days* after repossession, unless the debtor waives this right.

4.3 Debtor's Right of Redemption (Pay All Creditors in Full)

Until the sale or discharge of the debt through retention of the collateral, the debtor may redeem the collateral by paying all of the obligations secured by the collateral plus all reasonable expenses incurred relating to the repossession.

4.4 Judicial Action (Reduce Claim to Judgment)

Instead of using self-help, on default, the secured party may bring an ordinary judicial action for the amounts due and levy on the collateral after judgment. The secured party may have the collateral seized at the same time that he or she begins the judicial action.

NOTES

Business Law: Part 2

Module

1	Bankruptcy: Part 1	3
2	Bankruptcy: Part 2	11
3	Federal Laws and Regulations	17
4	Business Structures: Part 1	27
5	Business Structures: Part 2	41

MODULE 1

Bankruptcy: Part 1

REG 6

1 Introduction

There are six basic types of bankruptcy cases under federal law: Chapter 7, liquidation; Chapter 9, municipal debt adjustment; Chapter 11, reorganization; Chapter 12, family farmers with regular income; Chapter 13, adjustment of debts of individuals with regular income; and Chapter 15, ancillary and other cross-border cases.

1.1 Chapter 7 Liquidation: Trustee Appointed

- In a Chapter 7 liquidation case, a trustee is appointed. The trustee collects the debtor's assets, liquidates them, and uses the proceeds to pay off creditors to the extent possible.
- If the debtor is an individual (or a married couple), the debtor's debts are then discharged (i.e., the debtor is relieved from personal liability for most debts), with certain exceptions.
- If the debtor is an artificial entity (e.g., a corporation), it is dissolved. No discharge is given but the effect is the same—the debts are wiped out.

1.2 Chapter 13: Adjustment of Debts of Individuals With Regular Income

- In a Chapter 13 case, the debtor repays all or a portion of his debts over a three-year period to a maximum of a five-year period.
- Although there is not a liquidation, a Chapter 13 trustee oversees the handling of a Chapter 13 proceeding.
- At the conclusion of a Chapter 13 proceeding, the remaining debts of the debtor are discharged.

1.3 Chapter 11 Reorganization: No Liquidation, Trustee Not Required

- In a Chapter 11 reorganization case (usually used by businesses but also available to individuals), a trustee usually is not appointed.
- The debtor remains in possession of his or her assets and a plan of reorganization (i.e., a plan to pay off debts at a different time and/or amount from what was originally due) is adopted.
- Creditors are paid to the extent possible and the business continues.

Pass Key

The examiners often ask if a trustee is required for a particular type of bankruptcy. There are a few key points to remember:

- A trustee is required for Chapter 7 and Chapter 13.
- A trustee is *not required* for Chapter 11, although the court may appoint one if one is needed.

1.4 Chapter 15: Ancillary and Cross-Border Cases

Chapter 15 is the U.S. adoption of the Model Law on Cross-Border Insolvency promulgated by the United Nations. It was adopted to promote a uniform and coordinated legal regime for cross-border insolvency cases.

2 Dismissal or Conversion of a Chapter 7 Case

A Chapter 7 case by an *individual consumer* debtor may be dismissed (or with the debtor's consent converted to a case under Chapter 13) upon a finding that granting relief under Chapter 7 would constitute abuse or because the debtor has sufficient income to pay debts.

2.1 Determine Whether Income Is Lower Than the State Median

If an individual filing for Chapter 7 liquidation and his or her spouse have monthly income greater than the state median income for a family of the same size, the state, any interested creditor, or the court may file a motion to dismiss the case, either under the means test or for general abuse because the debtor has sufficient income to pay debts.

2.2 Means Test

The means test is used to determine whether creditors would be better off under a Chapter 13, five-year reorganization. Sixty times the debtor's average monthly income, less allowable expenses, is compared with a high and low threshold ($9,075 and $15,150).

- If 60 times the debtor's average monthly income less allowable expenses is less than $9,075, the debtor may continue under Chapter 7.
- If 60 times the debtor's average monthly income less allowable expenses is $15,150 or more, there is a presumption of abuse and the debtor usually will have to convert the case to Chapter 13.

3 Who May Be a Debtor

Only a person who resides, or has a place of business, in the United States is eligible to be a debtor under the Bankruptcy Code. "Person" generally includes individuals, partnerships, corporations, and the like.

3.1 Limitation in Chapter 7 Liquidations

Railroads, savings institutions, insurance companies, banks, and small business investment companies may not file for bankruptcy under Chapter 7.

3.2 Compare Chapter 11 Reorganizations

Anyone who may be a debtor (except a stockbroker or commodity broker) under Chapter 7 may also be a debtor under Chapter 11. Additionally, a railroad may be a debtor under Chapter 11.

Although Chapter 11 is intended primarily for business debtors, an individual is eligible for relief under Chapter 11.

>
> ### Pass Key
>
> As trivial as it might seem, the key to many past bankruptcy questions was knowing who may and who may not file under the various chapters. So be sure you are familiar with this information.

4 Rights and Duties of Debtors and Creditors Under Chapters 7 and 11

4.1 Automatic Stay

- When a bankruptcy petition is filed in either a voluntary case or an involuntary case, an *automatic stay* becomes effective against most creditors.
- The stay stops almost all collection efforts (e.g., filing a lawsuit or simply demanding payment).
- The automatic stay does not apply to criminal prosecutions, paternity suits, and cases brought to establish or collect spousal or child support obligations.

4.2 Duties of Debtor

After a petition is filed, a debtor must file, among other things:

- A list of creditors and their addresses
- A schedule of assets and liabilities
- A schedule of current income and expenditures
- A statement of the debtor's financial affairs
- Copies of pay stubs received within 60 days before filing
- Copies of federal tax returns from the last tax year. If the debtor has not paid taxes for the previous tax year, he or she must do so before the bankruptcy may proceed.

Note: If an individual debtor in a voluntary Chapter 7 case fails to file any of the items specified above within 45 days after filing the petition, the case is automatically dismissed on the 46th day.

4.3 Chapter 7 and Chapter 11: Voluntary Cases

4.3.1 Debtor Files for Order of Relief

A voluntary case under Chapter 7 or Chapter 11 is commenced by the debtor filing a petition for relief.

4.3.2 Debtor Need Not Be Insolvent but Must Pass Income Tests

The debtor need not be insolvent to file. However, as previously discussed, a Chapter 7 case may be dismissed if the debtor has too much income.

4.3.3 Spouses May File Jointly

Spouses may file jointly to avoid duplicate fees.

Pass Key

Although it may seem trivial, "spouses may file jointly" often appears as a correct answer on the CPA Examination.

4.3.4 Voluntary Petition Constitutes an Automatic Order for Relief

A filed voluntary petition constitutes "an order for relief," which simply means a case may proceed unless a court orders otherwise.

4.4 Chapter 7 and Chapter 11: Involuntary Case

Unsecured creditors may petition a debtor involuntarily into bankruptcy proceedings under Chapter 7 or Chapter 11.

4.4.1 Grounds: Generally Not Paying Debts When Due

For an involuntary petition, creditors must show that the debtor generally is not paying debts as they become due.

4.4.2 Ineligible Debtors: Farmers and Charities

Farmers and nonprofit charitable organizations may not be petitioned involuntarily into bankruptcy.

4.4.3 Who Must Join Petition: Owed at Least $18,600

Only creditors who are owed, individually or in aggregate, *at least $18,600 in unsecured, undisputed debt* may petition a debtor involuntarily into bankruptcy. The number of creditors who must file depends on the debtor's total number of creditors.

- **Fewer Than 12 Creditors: One or More Owed $18,600**

    If a debtor has fewer than 12 creditors, any one or more creditors who are owed at least $18,600 in unsecured debt may file.

> **Illustration 1 Who Must Join Petition**
>
> Dee has four creditors she is not paying. Alex is owed $17,000, Bob is owed $4,000, Carla is owed $4,000, and Sam is owed $18,000, a loan secured by Dee's $20,000 car. Alex must join in an involuntary petition; Bob and Carla's claims are not sufficient. Sam may not file. Sam's claim is adequately secured.

- **12 or More Creditors: Three Owed $18,600**

    If a debtor has 12 or more creditors, *at least three creditors* who are owed at least $18,600 in aggregate, in unsecured, undisputed debt must join in the involuntary petition.

Pass Key

The number of creditors and amounts owed necessary to file an involuntary petition is a favorite exam issue. Two points should be noted:

- Usually, the examiners use this information to create "distracters" (i.e., wrong answers), such as "To file a *voluntary* petition, a debtor must owe at least $18,600" or "have at least 12 creditors." You should take time to memorize the $18,600 and one or three creditor minimums. Remember, they apply only to *involuntary* petitions.

- If a problem states the number of creditors that a debtor has, the examiners frequently have asked the number needed to file an involuntary petition. For example, if the question says the debtor has 19 creditors, then three or more must file. If the question says the debtor has eight creditors, then only one need file.

Pass Key

Odd as it may seem, the Bankruptcy Code does not require a debtor to be insolvent to file for bankruptcy. A voluntary petition may be filed by *anyone who owes debts*, and an involuntary petition may be filed if the debtor is *generally not paying debts as they become due*, regardless of the debtor's ability to pay. An answer choice that suggests the debtor must be insolvent to file for, or be petitioned into, bankruptcy is wrong, but be sure to remember that an individual consumer debtor's Chapter 7 case may be dismissed or converted to Chapter 13 if his income is too high.

4.5 Section 341 Meeting: Creditors' Meeting

Ordinarily, within 20 to 40 days after the order for relief, a meeting of the creditors (called a "Section 341 meeting") is held. All interested parties, including creditors, the bankruptcy trustee, and the debtor must be given notice of the meeting.

4.6 Property of the Bankruptcy Estate

4.6.1 Property Included

- The debtor's estate (i.e., assets available to pay off creditors) generally includes all of the debtor's real and personal property at the time of filing.

- The estate also includes income generated from estate property (e.g., interest from bonds that are part of the estate) received within *180 days* after the filing of the petition for relief.

- It also includes property the debtor receives from divorce, inheritance, or insurance within *180 days* after the filing of the petition.

- Leases of property may be assumed and retained by the trustee, assumed and assigned to another, or rejected by the trustee.

Pass Key

The fact that inheritance received within 180 days after the filing of a petition for relief is included in the debtor's estate has been tested often.

4.6.2 Property Excluded From Estate

Money the debtor earns after a petition is filed ("post-petition earnings") and basic household items needed to live (such as clothing, medical devices, and the like) are excluded from the bankruptcy estate.

4.6.3 Trustee Is a Hypothetical Lien Creditor as of Filing Date

The trustee is treated as having a lien on all of the debtor's property the instant the bankruptcy petition is filed.

This means that the trustee has priority over all creditors except creditors with prior perfected security interests or prior statutory or judicial liens.

4.6.4 Power Over Fraudulent Transfer

The trustee also has power to set aside fraudulent transfers made within two years of the filing date.

A fraudulent transfer is any transfer made with *intent* to hinder, delay, or defraud creditors or any transfer in which the debtor received *less than equivalent value* while the debtor was insolvent.

Illustration 2 Fraudulent Transfer

A few days before filing a voluntary petition in bankruptcy and while Debtor was insolvent, Debtor gave Friend a $5,000 cash gift. The gift can be set aside (recovered from Friend) as a fraudulent transfer.

4.6.5 Trustee Can Disaffirm Preferences

The trustee has the power to set aside preferences. When the payment is "set aside," the payment is taken back from the creditor who received it and becomes part of the bankruptcy estate.

- **A Preferential Payment Is:**
    - a *transfer* made to or for the benefit of a creditor;
    - on account of an *antecedent debt* (i.e., already existing) of the debtor;
    - made within *90 days* prior to the filing of the petition (one year if the creditor is an insider, such as an officer of the debtor organization or a close relative of the debtor);
    - made while the debtor was *insolvent*; and
    - results in the creditor *receiving more than the creditor would have received* under the Bankruptcy Code.

Pass Key

Preferential payment is one of the most heavily tested issues when it comes to bankruptcy questions on the CPA Exam. Be sure to memorize the definition above and the explanations above. Understanding this material is one of the keys to your success.

- **Transfer**

    A transfer includes not only the payment of money or the giving of property, but also the giving of a security interest.

Illustration 3   Preferences

Deanna, a retailer, owes Carla money. A few days before Deanna filed her bankruptcy petition, Deanna gave Carla a security interest in all of Deanna's inventory, which Carla perfects. Carla's interest can be set aside as a preference.

- **Antecedent (Preexisting) Debt (Rather Than a Contemporaneous Exchange)**

    A payment is a preference only if it is for an antecedent (preexisting) debt. *A contemporaneous exchange for new value is not a preference*.

Illustration 4   Contemporaneous Exchange for Value

A few days before Deanna, a retailer, filed for bankruptcy, she received from Alex, a supplier, six cases of goods to be put into Deanna's inventory. Deanna paid for the goods in full on their arrival. There is no preference here; this is a contemporaneous exchange for value.

Pass Key

The exception for contemporaneous exchanges for new value has often been tested on past exams.

- **Insolvency: Presumed During 90 Days Preceding Bankruptcy**

    The debtor is presumed to be insolvent during the 90 days immediately preceding the date the bankruptcy petition is filed.

- **Receipt of Greater Share: Creditor Received More**

    A preference exists only if the creditor receives more than she would receive in a bankruptcy distribution. Therefore, payment to a *fully secured* creditor is not a preference, because the creditor would have received the collateral and been paid in full anyway.

- **Exceptions: Transfers That Cannot Be Set Aside by Trustee**
    - **Transfers in the Ordinary Course of Business**

        A transfer made to repay a debt that the debtor incurred in the ordinary course of business is *not* a voidable preference.

> **Illustration 5 Transfers in the Ordinary Course of Business**
>
> A regular monthly installment payment will not be set aside as a preference. Similarly, payment of a current utility bill or a current lease payment does not constitute a preference.

4.7 Claims Against the Estate

Claims include all rights to payment from the debtor's estate.

- To have a claim allowed (i.e., a right of payment against the debtor's estate), unsecured creditors must file a proof of claim, and shareholders must file a proof of interest with the bankruptcy court.
- Unless someone objects, a filed claim or interest will automatically be allowed by the court. An unsecured creditor who fails to timely file a claim may not take part in the distribution of the debtor's estate.
- The general rule is that a perfected security interest passes through and survives bankruptcy even if the creditor does not file a proof of claim.

4.8 Miscellaneous

The trustee can also serve as a professional (e.g., tax preparer, accountant or lawyer) for the estate if the court approves.

A trustee serving as tax preparer for the estate may receive compensation as a professional in addition to the trustee's compensation, if a court approves.

MODULE 2: Bankruptcy: Part 2

REG 6

1 Features of a Chapter 7 Liquidation

The goal of federal bankruptcy law is to give an honest debtor a "fresh start" financially by discharging most debts owed by the debtor. In a liquidation, a bankruptcy trustee is appointed. The trustee collects all of the debtor's nonexempt property, liquidates it, and pays off all of the debtor's creditors. Most debts of an individual are discharged (that is, the debtor is relieved from personal liability for most debts) but certain debts survive bankruptcy.

1.1 Objections to Discharge

Creditors often want to prevent debtors from receiving a Chapter 7 discharge. The code provides two kinds of ammunition for such claims: objections to discharge and nondischargeable debts. The first type of ammunition destroys the entire Chapter 7 case—none of the debtor's debts will be discharged. The second type of ammunition prevents the discharge of specific debts. The following will prevent the debtor from receiving any discharge:

- **Debtor Not an Individual**

    Technically, only individuals (i.e., real people as opposed to artificial entities, such as corporations) can receive a discharge under Chapter 7. Artificial entities seeking relief under Chapter 7 usually are dissolved at the conclusion of the case, and so their debts are wiped out.

- **Fraudulent Transfers or Concealment of Property**

    The debtor is not entitled to a discharge if she transferred, destroyed, or concealed property in the year before or after the petition was filed with intent to hinder, delay, or defraud creditors.

- **Unjustifiably Failed to Keep Books and Records**

    The debtor is not entitled to a discharge if he unjustifiably concealed, falsified, or failed to keep or preserve adequate books and records from which the debtor's financial condition or business transactions might be ascertained.

- **Prior Discharge Within Eight Years**

    A debtor is entitled to only one discharge within an eight-year period. Eight years must elapse before another discharge can be granted.

1.2 Exceptions to Discharge

Certain debts *of an individual* are not discharged under Chapters 7 or 11. Those debts not discharged are called the "exceptions to discharge."

Pass Key

It is important to remember that a bankruptcy case does not discharge all debts. The examiners often ask a broad question such as, "Which of the following is true under the Bankruptcy Code?" and one of the choices often is that "all debts of the debtor are discharged." This is not true.

The examiners often ask what debts will not be discharged by a bankruptcy. The key to remembering the six nondischargeable debts that most commonly appear on the exam is the word "**WAFTED**": **W**illful and malicious injury, **A**limony, **F**raud, **T**axes, **E**ducational loans, and **D**ebts undisclosed in the bankruptcy petition.

1.3 Reaffirmation of Discharged Debts

Sometimes a debtor does not want a particular debt discharged in bankruptcy (e.g., to maintain good relations with a particular creditor). The debtor may *reaffirm* such debts only if the agreement to reaffirm the debt was made *before* the granting of the discharge.

1.4 Distribution of the Debtor's Estate: Payment and Priorities

Once the debtor's assets have been collected and liquidated, and all objections at that level have been disposed of, the trustee will distribute the assets of the estate. There are three basic categories of claimants, *paid in the following order*:

1. Secured claimants
2. Priority claimants
3. General creditors who filed their claims on time

Payments are made in full to secured claimants to the extent of the value of the collateral securing their claims (claims in excess of the collateral are treated like claims of other general creditors). Whatever is left over then is used to pay first-priority claimants in full, then second-priority claimants in full, then third-priority claimants are paid, and so on. If money is left after paying all of the priority claimants, it is then split among the general creditors who filed claims on time. If there is not sufficient money to pay all creditors at a particular level, the creditors share pro rata.

Priority claimants include the following (from highest to lowest priority):

1. Support obligations owed to spouses and children
2. Expenses of the bankruptcy administration, including filing fees, court fees, trustee fees, and the like
3. Claims that accrue in the ordinary course of business after an involuntary petition is filed
4. Wage claims of employees for sums earned within 180 days of bankruptcy, up to $15,150
5. Sums owed for employee benefits up to whatever of the $15,150 above is left
6. Claims of grain farmers and fishermen up to $7,475
7. Consumer deposits up to $3,350
8. Tax claims
9. Personal injury claims arising from intoxicated driving

Pass Key

The priority rules are perhaps the most heavily tested rules on the CPA Exam when it comes to bankruptcy issues. Your memorization of the order of payment and the dollar limitations specified below is key for success on the exam. Most important, though, remember that payments are made first to secured creditors to the extent of the value of the collateral securing their claims and that claims in excess of the collateral are treated like claims of other general creditors.

Pass Key

It is important to understand the relationship between the exceptions to discharge and payment priorities. Some items are both a priority and an exception; other items are one, but not the other. Payment is made according to the priority rules (without regard to whether the debt is excepted from discharge). After all possible payments have been made, any remaining debts are discharged unless they are one of the exceptions to discharge. In some cases, a debt that is an exception to discharge will have been paid in the distribution process. For example:

- If creditors are paid in full through the eighth priority (tax claims, etc.), then the fact that a tax claim is an exception to discharge is irrelevant because it has been paid.

- If, however, payment is made only through the fourth priority, claims within the fifth through ninth priorities are discharged except unpaid eighth-priority (tax) claims, because they are an exception to discharge.

2 Features of Reorganization Cases Under Chapter 11

2.1 Creation of Creditors' Committee

In a Chapter 11 case, shortly after the order for relief is effective, a committee of *unsecured* creditors is appointed, usually consisting of willing persons holding the *seven largest unsecured claims* against the debtor.

A person engaged in business other than real estate with debts not exceeding about $2.6 million can elect to be treated as a small business. Such a debtor can request that a creditors' committee not be appointed.

2.2 Equity Security Holders' Committee

If the debtor is a corporation, an equity security holders' (i.e., stockholders) committee may be appointed consisting of the seven largest holders of the equity securities to ensure that the equity security holders receive adequate representation. The committees can consult with the debtor, investigate the debtor's finances, participate in preparing the reorganization plan, etc.

2.3 Debtor Generally Remains in Possession

In a Chapter 11 reorganization case, committees are appointed to consult with and advise the debtor, but a trustee generally is *not* appointed.

Instead, the debtor remains in possession of the debtor's assets because the debtor is presumed to be in the best position to run the business.

Pass Key

The examiners like to ask about the trustee in a Chapter 11 case. Remember the general rule that a trustee usually is not appointed in a Chapter 11 case; the debtor usually remains in possession of the estate's assets.

2.4 Chapter 11 Reorganization Plan

The debtor may file a reorganization plan under Chapter 11 any time during the bankruptcy case. Unless a trustee has been appointed, the debtor has an *exclusive right* to file a plan during the first *120 days* after the order for relief is effective. Other interested parties (e.g., creditors) may file a plan if:

- a trustee has been appointed;
- the debtor has not filed a plan within 120 days after the order for relief became effective; or
- the debtor has filed a plan but has not obtained the acceptance of every impaired class (e.g., creditors whose claims are reduced by the plan or will be paid later than contracted for) within *180 days* after entry of the order for relief.

2.4.1 Contents of the Plan

A Chapter 11 plan must, among other things:

- classify all claims (e.g., secured, first priority, second priority, impaired, unimpaired, etc.);
- describe the treatment to be accorded each impaired class;
- treat each claimant within a particular class identically; and
- establish ways to implement the plan.

2.4.2 Acceptance of the Plan by Creditors

- Any creditor or equity security holder who has filed a claim against the debtor's estate must be given an opportunity to *accept* or reject the plan.
- A class of impaired claims is deemed accepted if it is accepted by creditors holding at least *two-thirds in amount* and *more than one-half in number* of the allowed claims.
- A class of impaired interests (e.g., equity security holders) is deemed to have accepted the plan if it is accepted by equity security holders having at least two-thirds in amount of the allowed claims.

2.4.3 Confirmation of the Plan by Court

- The court will confirm the plan if it meets certain conditions, such as being accepted by all impaired classes, providing for payment in full for priority administrative expenses and gap claims, and the plan is feasible (i.e., has a reasonable chance of succeeding).

- A plan can be confirmed by the court even if it is not accepted by *all* impaired classes if at least one impaired class has accepted, and the court finds that the plan is not unfairly discriminatory and is fair and equitable with respect to any dissenting impaired classes. This is called a *cram down*.

2.5 Effects of Confirmation

- A confirmed Chapter 11 plan is binding on all creditors, equity security holders, and the debtor regardless of whether they accept the plan.
- Generally, once confirmed the debtor pays debts according to the plan.
- Unless the order provides otherwise, confirmation discharges the debtor from all pre-confirmation debts (except that debts not discharged under Chapter 7 are also not discharged under Chapter 11).
- Confirmation also terminates the automatic stay.

3 Features of a Chapter 15 Case

3.1 Commencement of Ancillary Proceeding

A Chapter 15 ancillary case is commenced by a "foreign representative" filing a petition for recognition of a "foreign proceeding." This operates as the principal door of a foreign representative to U.S. courts.

- The petition must show the existence of the foreign proceeding and the appointment and authority of the foreign representative.
- After notice and a hearing, the U.S. court is authorized to issue an order recognizing the foreign proceeding as either a "foreign main proceeding" (i.e., a country where the debtor's main interests are located) or a "foreign non-main proceeding" (i.e., a country other than one where the debtor's main interests are located).

Upon recognition of a foreign main proceeding, the automatic stay and other provisions of the Bankruptcy Code take effect in the United States.

The U.S. court is authorized to issue preliminary relief as soon as the petition for recognition is filed.

3.2 Foreign Representative's Powers

The foreign representative is authorized to operate the debtor's business. Once recognized, a foreign representative may seek additional relief from the bankruptcy court and is authorized to bring a full-blown (as opposed to ancillary) bankruptcy case under Chapters 7 or 11. The foreign representative may participate in a pending U.S. insolvency case and may intervene in any other U.S. case in which the debtor is a party.

3.3 Prohibition Against Discrimination

Chapter 15 prohibits discrimination against foreign creditors (except certain foreign government and tax claims, which may be governed by treaty).

3.4 Requirements of Notice and Cooperation

Chapter 15 requires notice to foreign creditors concerning a U.S. bankruptcy case, including notice of the right to file claims. Under Chapter 15, U.S. courts and trustees must "cooperate to the maximum extent possible" with foreign courts and foreign representatives.

NOTES

MODULE 3 Federal Laws and Regulations

REG 6

1 Worker Classification

It is important for a business to properly determine whether a person performing services for the business is an employee or an independent contractor. All of the payroll issues discussed below arise only in an employer-employee setting and do not apply when dealing with an independent contractor.

When determining whether a worker is an employee or an independent contractor, no one factor is determinative; it is a weighing process.

Businesses must consider:

- Whether the business controls (or at least has the right to control) what the worker does and how he or she performs the work (right to control the manner and method of the work indicates an employee);
- Whether the worker owns his or her own business, tools, and the like (indicative of an independent contractor);
- Whether the worker is paid by the job (indicative of an independent contractor), or hourly or by salary (indicative of an employee);
- Whether the job is of limited duration (indicative of an independent contractor) or ongoing or continuous (indicative of an employee); and
- Whether the worker receives benefits (indicative of an employee).

2 Federal Insurance Contributions Act (FICA)

The Federal Insurance Contributions Act (FICA) provides workers and their dependents with benefits in case of death, disability, or retirement.

2.1 Participation

All full-time and part-time employees must participate in the program. The self-employed must also participate if their net profit exceeds $400 in a year. Very few workers are exempt (e.g., certain government workers and ministers).

2.2 Funding

FICA is funded by taxing income earned from labor (e.g., wages, salaries, tips, bonuses, commissions, etc.). FICA is funded by *both employers and employees*, including self-employed individuals.

2.2.1 Employer Responsibility

Employers must match their employees' contributions to FICA. Employers are *responsible for paying the tax and withholding* the employee's contribution.

- An employer that fails to withhold the employee's contribution is liable to pay the employee's half, but has a right to reimbursement from the employee. If an employer voluntarily pays the employee's share, it is deductible for the employer and taxable income for the employee.
- Penalties apply to employers who fail to make timely FICA deposits or who fail to supply their federal taxpayer identification number.

2.2.2 Employee Responsibility

For 2023, employees were liable to make FICA contributions of 6.2 percent of their *net taxable wages* of up to $160,200 and Medicare contributions of 1.45 percent of their entire gross wages. Individuals with income exceeding a threshold amount ($200,000 single and $250,000 married filing jointly) are liable for an additional Medicare tax of 0.9 percent of their entire gross wages. Gross wages include *all earned income*, such as salary, bonuses, and commissions. Gifts, interest, dividends, etc., are not wages.

2.2.3 Self-Employed Person Responsibility

Self-employed individuals pay into FICA through the self-employment tax, which is equal to the employer's and the employee's contribution (15.3 percent). It is imposed only on net profits and only if the net profits exceed $400 in a year.

Pass Key

The examiners often ask what income is subject to FICA. It is key to remember that an employee's *gross wages* are subject, and that a self-employed person's *net profits* are subject.

2.3 Deductibility by Employer

The employer's contribution is deductible as an ordinary business expense. The employee's contribution is *not* deductible by the employee. Because a self-employed person pays both contributions, one-half of the self-employment tax is deductible in arriving at adjusted gross income.

2.4 Benefits

FICA provides a number of benefits, including disability pay, retirement pay, survivor's benefits, dependent's benefits, and medical benefits under Medicare (not Medicaid, which is a state-run program). Benefits are available to all covered employees regardless of whether they are receiving benefits from a private plan. Employees may not opt out of Social Security, even if they are covered by a private plan.

Pass Key

The most important things to remember about Social Security for exam purposes are:

- The employer must pay the tax and collect an employee's portion of the tax.
- All income derived from labor is taxed; unearned income is not taxed.
- All employees are subject to the tax up to a maximum dollar amount for the Social Security with no limit on the Medicare; self-employment income is subject to both employer and employee taxation for income over $400.

3 Unemployment Compensation (FUTA)

The Federal Unemployment Tax Act (FUTA) establishes a state-run system of insurance to provide income to workers who have lost their jobs. Although FUTA provides federal guidelines, the states actually administer the program, set standards, and determine payments.

3.1 Participation

All employers who have quarterly payrolls of at least $1,500 or who employ at least one person for 20 weeks in a year must participate in the system. Unlike FICA, *self-employed persons do not participate*.

Pass Key

Because most employers must participate under FUTA, the examiners often try to trick you into thinking that every employer must participate. This is not true. The $1,500 minimum or time requirements must be met.

3.2 Funding

Unemployment taxes are payroll taxes generally assessed only against the *employer*. The federal unemployment tax rate currently is 6.0 percent on the first $7,000 per year of compensation for each employee.

Employers can get a credit against the federal tax due for payments made on account of state unemployment taxes of up to 5.4 percent of the first $7,000. Moreover, the state rate can be reduced if the employer has a below-average rate of unemployment claims from prior employees.

3.3 Employer Deductibility

The employer's payment is deductible as an ordinary business expense. Because the employee generally does not pay the tax, it is not deductible by the employee.

Pass Key

When the examiners test on unemployment issues, they often test what an employer may deduct as an expense. It is key to remember that the employer may deduct the tax (because the employer pays it), but the employee may not take a deduction.

3.4 Benefits

Unemployment benefits are generally available only when an employee's job termination was not his or her fault. Benefits are distributed to employees by the state governments. The amount paid varies from state to state, but is usually determined by how long the employee has worked and his or her former rate of pay. Note that payments are not limited to the amount that has been paid by the employer on the employee's behalf.

Pass Key

The most important things to remember about FUTA for exam purposes are:

- The *employer* must pay if it employs an employee for at least 20 weeks in a year or paid $1,500 in wages in a quarter. The employee does not pay.
- Because the employer pays, the tax is deductible as a business expense. The employee cannot deduct the payment.
- If an employer's claim rate is low, the employer *may get a deduction* for state unemployment tax.
- The employee's benefits are *not limited to the contributions* made on his behalf.

4 Workers' Compensation

Workers' compensation programs are state-run programs designed to enable employees to recover for injuries incurred while on the job. In most states, coverage is compulsory.

Employers are strictly liable regardless of fault. The only requirement is that the employee's injury occurred while acting in the scope of employment.

>
> ### Pass Key
>
> Fault is the most frequently tested issue in workers' compensation. Remember that an employee can collect even if the employee was negligent, grossly negligent, or assumed the risk. An employee cannot recover for injuries resulting from intoxication, fighting, or self-inflicted wounds. Remember, the purpose of workers' compensation is to enable employees to recover for work-related injuries regardless of negligence.

4.1 Participation

Most employers must participate in workers' compensation programs. There are exceptions for agricultural workers, domestic workers, casual workers (e.g., *temporary* office workers), public employees, and independent contractors. Some states also exempt employers who have up to only three or four employees.

4.2 Funding

The employer pays for workers' compensation by purchasing insurance from the state or a private carrier. Some states also allow employers to be self-insuring if they can prove that they are financially responsible. In most states, coverage is compulsory.

In states in which coverage is not mandatory, an employer who elects not to participate in workers' compensation gives up the common-law defenses of contributory negligence, assumption of the risk, and the fellow servant doctrine. Also, damage awards are not limited to what would be recovered under workers' compensation.

4.3 Deductibility

Workers' compensation insurance premiums are ordinary business expenses deductible by the employer. Because employees do not pay, there is no deduction for the worker.

4.4 Benefits

Workers' compensation provides benefits for any injury or disease (including aggravations of existing diseases) resulting from employment. Benefits include money for loss of income, disability, loss of limbs, prosthetic devices, medical services, burial costs, and survivors' benefits. The program works like other insurance—benefits are not limited to what was paid in on the employee's behalf.

5 Affordable Care Act

The purpose of the Affordable Care Act (ACA) is to improve access to health care in the U.S. by providing workers with access to affordable health care coverage. Health care coverage may be offered through:

- A plan provided by the employer
- A plan purchased through a Health Insurance Marketplace, where employees may qualify for financial assistance
- Coverage provided under a government-sponsored program such as Medicare, most Medicaid, and health care programs for veterans
- Direct purchase by the employee from an insurance company

5.1 Participation

Both employers and employees are required to participate:

- Certain employers must offer health care coverage or pay a penalty.
- An individual must obtain health care coverage for himself, a spouse, and tax dependents.

5.2 Funding

Both the employer and the employee contribute to the purchase of affordable coverage:

- The employer may subsidize the cost of the coverage in order to ensure that it is affordable.
- The employee will pay a certain amount for coverage, whether purchased through the employer or through another source.

5.2.1 Employer Responsibility

Under the ACA, employers with 50 or more full-time employees are called applicable large employers, or ALEs. ALEs are required to provide full-time employees the opportunity to purchase affordable minimum essential health care coverage for themselves and their dependents under an eligible employer-sponsored health care plan.

- All types of employers can be ALEs, including tax-exempt organizations and government entities.
- An employee who works for an employer on average at least 30 hours a week or 130 hours of service a month is a full-time employee.
- Coverage is considered affordable if the employee's contribution to the plan does not exceed 9.5 percent of the employee's household income for the taxable year.
- A dependent is an employee's child who has not reached the age of 26.
- Employers who do not comply with the ACA will pay a penalty for failure to do so.
- Employers are required to file annual information returns with the IRS and must also provide information to employees about coverage.

5.2.2 Employee Responsibility

The ACA comes with an "individual mandate" requiring all Americans to buy health coverage. Formerly, a penalty was imposed on persons who failed to purchase health coverage, but the penalty has been eliminated. Employees who have minimum essential coverage will report this fact on their tax return each year. Unemployed persons or people working for companies not required to provide affordable health care may purchase insurance through the Health Insurance Marketplace.

5.3 Benefits

The ACA does not create a national health insurance plan. Rather, it sets national standards for how health insurance is structured and priced, and places new requirements on individuals and employers. Because purchasing coverage is mandatory, the ACA makes it illegal for an insurer to deny coverage to individuals with preexisting conditions or to charge more for their coverage.

5.4 Penalties for Failure to Comply With ACA

The employer must pay a fee for failure to comply with the Affordable Care Act. Note that an employer is not obligated to calculate its liability and should not make a payment without first being contacted by the IRS.

1. **Penalty Type 1:** An ALE will owe the first type of employer shared responsibility payment if it does not offer minimum essential coverage to at least 95 percent of its full-time employees (and their dependents) and at least one full-time employee receives the premium tax credit for purchasing coverage through the Health Insurance Marketplace.
   - On an annual basis, this payment is equal to $2,880 (2023) for each full-time employee, with the first 30 employees excluded from the calculation.

2. **Penalty Type 2:** Even if an ALE member offers minimum essential coverage to at least 95 percent of its full-time employees (and their dependents), it may owe the second type of employer shared responsibility payment for each full-time employee who receives the premium tax credit for purchasing coverage through the Marketplace.
   - In general, a full-time employee could receive the premium tax credit if:
     —the minimum essential coverage the employer offers to the employee is not affordable;
     —the minimum essential coverage the employer offers to the employee does not provide minimum value; or
     —the employee is not one of the at least 95 percent of full-time employees offered minimum essential coverage.
   - On an annual basis, this payment is equal to $4,320 (2023) for each full-time employee who receives the premium tax credit. The total payment in this instance cannot exceed the amount the employer would have owed had the employer not offered minimum essential coverage to at least 95 percent of its full-time employees (and their dependents).

5.5 Deductibility

Employers may deduct the costs of insurance premiums paid for the benefit of their employees as a business expense. None of the penalties required of the employer under the employer shared responsibility provisions are tax deductible for the employer.

6 Premium Tax Credit

The premium tax credit is a refundable credit that helps eligible lower or moderate-income taxpayers (those earning between 100 percent to 400 percent of the federal poverty level) cover the premiums for their health insurance purchased through the Health Insurance Marketplace. The Health Insurance Marketplace is a resource provided by the government where individuals, families, and small businesses can:

- Compare health insurance plans for coverage and affordability.
- Get answers to questions about health care insurance.
- Find out eligibility for tax credits for private insurance or health programs like Medicaid.
- Enroll in a health insurance plan.

Through 2025, those earning more than 400 percent of the federal poverty level are eligible for subsidies that cap marketplace health insurance premiums at no more than 8.5 percent of household income.

6.1 Eligibility

To be eligible, a taxpayer must meet all of the following requirements:

- Must have household income that falls between 100 percent and 400 percent of the federal poverty level.
- Cannot use the filing status of Married Filing Separately.
- Cannot be claimed as a dependent by another person.
- Must be enrolled in health insurance coverage through the Marketplace for at least one month and:
  - is not able to get affordable coverage through an eligible employer-sponsored plan that provides minimum value; or
  - is not eligible for government health coverage such as Medicare or Medicaid.

The taxpayer's eligibility for advance payments of the premium tax credit will be determined by the system when they apply for insurance through the Marketplace.

6.2 Benefit

The amount of the credit depends on income, the cost of the plan, the taxpayer's address, and the size of their family. The credit can be received monthly, in which case it is paid directly to the insurer to reduce premium costs, or it can be taken as a refundable credit against federal taxes.

7 Foreign Corrupt Practices Act

The Foreign Corrupt Practices Act (FCPA), enacted in 1977, generally prohibits the payment of bribes to foreign officials to assist in obtaining or retaining business.

7.1 Elements of a Violation

The act applies if the offered bribe was made through any transaction involving interstate commerce, such as an email, a phone call, or through the mail.

- Bribes include the offer of anything of value, such as money or property, in return for benefits to which the party would not be entitled.
- The Act also covers payments or promises made to someone other than a government official if the offeror knows that any part of what is being offered will be used to bribe a government official.

7.2 Penalties

Violations are punishable by civil fines of up to twice the amount of the benefit expected to be received as a result of the bribe, criminal penalties, the appointment of an independent auditor to monitor compliance, and imprisonment of up to five years.

NOTES

MODULE 4
Business Structures: Part 1

REG 6

1 Summary of Entities

Nearly half of the recent Business Structures questions on the exam simply require the examinee to differentiate the attributes of the various business structures. The major attributes are summarized in the following chart. More detail regarding each business structure follows.

Overall Summary of Entities and Their Attributes

Attributes	Sole Proprietorship	General Partnership/ Joint Venture	Limited Liability Partnership (LLP)	Limited Partnership	Limited Liability Company (LLC)	Corporation	Subchapter S Corporation
Formation	*No formalities* Owner simply operates a business	*No formalities:* Can be formed by verbal or written agreement, or mere conduct	*Formalities:* File statement of qualification with state	*Formalities:* File Certificate of Limited Partnership with state	*Formalities:* File articles of organization with state	*Formalities:* File articles of incorporation or corporate charter with state	*Formalities:* Same as regular corporation plus file "S" election
Liability of Owners	Unlimited personal liability for all business obligations	Unlimited personal liability for all partnership obligations	Partners are generally not liable for partnership obligations, unless caused by their own negligence	**General partner:** unlimited personal liability **Limited partner:** only investment is at risk	Members generally not personally liable beyond their investment	Shareholders generally not personally liable beyond their investment	Shareholders generally not personally liable beyond their investment
Management	Sole proprietor manages directly or can appoint manager	Owners manage directly or can agree to appoint managing partner	Partners manage directly or can agree to appoint a managing partner	**General partner(s)** is (are) exclusive manager(s); **Limited partners** ordinarily do not manage	Members manage directly or can agree to appoint a manager	Managed by board of directors, which appoints officers to run day-to-day operations	Managed by board of directors, which appoints officers to run day-to-day operations
Transferability	Sole proprietor can sell business at will	Partners cannot transfer ownership interest without unanimous consent	Partners cannot transfer ownership interest without unanimous consent	Partners (whether general or limited) cannot transfer ownership interest without unanimous consent	Absent agreement otherwise, members cannot transfer ownership interest without unanimous consent	Shareholders are free to transfer ownership interest unless they agree otherwise	Shareholders generally may transfer ownership unless they agree otherwise, but cannot transfer to foreign or entity shareholders

(continued)

(continued)

| Taxation* | "Flow through" taxation" | "Flow through" taxation | "Flow through" taxation (but partners not managing have passive loss restrictions) | "Flow through" taxation (but limited partners have passive loss restrictions) | "Flow through" taxation (but members not managing have passive loss restrictions) | Income taxed at corporate level and taxed again to shareholders when dividends are distributed | "Flow through" taxation (but shareholders not managing have passive loss restrictions) |

*Default treatment, but entities may elect to be taxed differently under the "check the box" rules.

2 Sole Proprietorship

2.1 Advantages, Implications, and Constraints of a Sole Proprietorship

A sole proprietorship is the simplest form of business ownership. One person owns the business and manages all of its affairs, and the sole proprietor is not considered an entity separate from the business. No formality is required to form a sole proprietorship, and nothing need be filed with the state in which the business operates (unless the state or city requires a business license).

- **Personal Liability**

  The sole proprietor is personally liable for all obligations of the business.

- **Duration**

  A sole proprietorship cannot exist beyond the life of the sole proprietor. It may be terminated at any time by its owner.

- **Tax Treatment**

  For tax purposes, profits and losses from the business flow through the business to the sole proprietor.

- **Transferability**

  A sole proprietor is free to transfer his interest in the sole proprietorship at will.

2.2 Choice as a Business Entity

The sole proprietorship may be a good choice of business entity when an individual wants to form a business that he or she will manage, wants to claim the income or losses from the business on personal taxes, and does not want to bother with a lot of formality. The individual risks all of his or her personal assets, however, when this type of business entity is formed.

3 General Partnership/Joint Venture

3.1 Formation

A general partnership is formed whenever two or more persons intend to carry on as co-owners a business for profit.

- Papers need not be drawn up to form a partnership.
- Nothing need be filed with the state.
- An express agreement is not required; an agreement can be implied from conduct.

Illustration 1 Formation of Partnership

Steve and Becky decide to operate a hot dog cart together. Steve agrees to pay for the cart, and Becky agrees to make and sell the hot dogs. The two also agree to split the profits. A partnership has been formed even though Steve and Becky never expressly agreed to form a partnership.

Pass Key

A very common business entities question on past exams asks simply: What type of business entity can be formed without filing organizational documents with the state? A partnership or a sole proprietorship are the only possibilities. Formation of all other business entities requires filing some sort of organizational document with the state.

3.1.1 Joint Venture Compared

Courts sometimes try to distinguish joint ventures from general partnerships, but the legal requirements and consequences, and advantages and disadvantages, of forming a joint venture generally are identical to those of a general partnership. For exam purposes, the key difference between a joint venture and a general partnership is that a joint venture is formed for a single transaction or project or a related series of transactions or projects.

3.1.2 When Intent Is Unclear: Sharing of Profits

If it is unclear whether the parties intended to enter into a partnership, an agreement to share profits gives rise to a presumption that the parties intended to form a partnership.

3.1.3 Generally, a Writing Is Not Necessary

As a general rule, a general partnership agreement need not be in writing. However, if the partners want to enforce an agreement to remain partners for longer than one year, a writing is required under the Statute of Frauds.

Pass Key

The examiners often ask what is necessary to form a general partnership. The key is to remember three simple elements: (i) two or more persons (ii) who agree (expressly or impliedly) (iii) to carry on as co-owners a business for profit. There is no requirement of a writing, even if the partnership is to own land, unless the partnership is to last for more than one year.

3.2 Not a Taxable Entity for Income Tax Purposes

Partnerships are treated as entities for most purposes (e.g., may hold property and sue and be sued in own name, etc.), but they are not taxable entities for income tax purposes.

3.3 Operation of a General Partnership

Absent an agreement to the contrary, all partners have *equal rights* to manage the partnership business. Management rights and voting power are not based on the amount contributed.

> **Illustration 2   Management Rights in General Partnership**
>
> Alex, Becky, Cindy, Deanna, and Elias form a general partnership—Glorious Jeans—to manufacture coffee-colored clothing. Alex contributes 40 percent of the capital, Becky contributes 30 percent of the capital, Cindy contributes 20 percent of the capital, Deanna contributes 10 percent of the capital, and Elias agrees to design all the clothes. Each partner has an equal right to participate in the management of the partnership.

3.3.1 Required Approval

Decisions regarding matters within the ordinary course of the partnership's business may be controlled by majority vote unless the partnership agreement provides otherwise. Matters outside the ordinary course of the partnership's business require consent of all the partners. Examples of areas requiring unanimous consent include:

- admitting new partners;
- confessing a judgment (admitting liability in a lawsuit) or submitting a claim to arbitration; and
- making a fundamental change in the partnership business (e.g., the sale of a partnership).

> **Illustration 3   Fundamental Change in Partnership Business**
>
> In the partnership described in the previous example, the decision whether to buy cloth from Supplier may be approved by any three partners, but a decision to shift production from the manufacture of clothing to the manufacture of small appliances would have to be approved by all the partners.

3.3.2 Agency Law Governs

Every partner is an agent of the partnership for the purpose of its business and the partnership is their principal. An act of a partner apparently carrying on in the ordinary course of business the business of the partnership will bind the partnership through apparent authority. If a partner acts without actual or apparent authority, the partnership can still become bound if it knows of the material facts of a transaction and assents (i.e., ratifies), either expressly or by accepting the benefits of the transaction.

3.4 Rights of Partners

3.4.1 Rights in Partnership Property

A partnership owns all money and property contributed to the partnership by the partners and all other property acquired by the partnership. Partners do not own partnership property. As a general rule, partners have no right to possess or use partnership property other than for partnership purposes. Thus:

- an individual partner may not assign or sell partnership property for his own benefit; and
- a partner's personal creditors cannot attach partnership property to satisfy an individual partner's debt.

> **Illustration 4　Partnership Property vs. Personal Property**
>
> Alex and Becky agree to form a partnership to sell antique cars. Alex contributes 10 antique cars from his collection and Becky contributes $200,000. The cars and the cash are partnership property. Alex may no longer use the cars for personal use—even if they are titled in his name—and Becky may no longer freely spend the $200,000. The cars and cash can be used only for partnership purposes.

3.4.2 Rights in Partnership Interest

A partner may assign her interest in the profits and surplus at any time. The assignee obtains the right to receive the partner's share of the profits. The assignee does not become a partner and so has no right to attend partnership meetings, inspect the partnership books and records, vote, etc. An assignee can obtain such rights only if admitted to the partnership as a partner, which generally requires the approval of all the partners.

> **Pass Key**
>
> The examiners like to ask about the effect of a partner transferring interest in a partnership without the consent of the other partners. The key is to remember that such a transfer does not make the assignee a partner (that can be done only with the consent of all of the partners). Thus, the transferee has no power to manage the partnership, inspect the partnership's books and records, vote, etc. Generally, the assignee's only right is to get whatever distribution the assignor would have gotten. The same rule applies to a creditor with a charging order and an heir who receives a deceased partner's interest.

- **Creditors May Attach a Partner's Interest (Called a Charging Order)**

    A creditor of an individual partner may obtain from a court a *charging order* against an individual partner's share of profits.

- **Upon Death, Heirs Are Entitled to a Deceased Partner's Share of Profits**

    When a partner dies, his or her right to profits vests in his or her heirs. The partner's right to partnership property vests in the surviving partners.

3.4.3 Right to Inspect Books and Records

Every partner has the right to inspect and copy the books and records of the partnership.

3.5 Duties and Legal Obligations of Partners

3.5.1 Fiduciary Duties Owed to Other Partners

Each partner owes a fiduciary duty to the partnership and other partners.

3.5.2 Each Partner Is Personally Liable for All Partnership Obligations

Partners are personally liable for all contracts entered into and all torts committed by other partners within the scope of partnership business or which are otherwise authorized. The partners' liability is *joint and several*. This means that each partner is personally and individually liable for the entire amount of all partnership obligations. In many states, however, a creditor cannot satisfy a judgment against an individual partner unless the partner was named in the lawsuit and the assets of the partnership are exhausted.

3.6 Profit and Loss Allocation

3.6.1 Profits

Absent an agreement to the contrary, all partners have *equal rights* to share in the profits of the partnership.

> **Illustration 5 Sharing of Profits**
>
> Alex, Becky, Cindy, Deanna, and Elias form a general partnership—Glorious Jeans—to manufacture coffee-colored clothing. Alex contributes 40 percent of the capital, Becky contributes 30 percent of the capital, Cindy contributes 20 percent of the capital, Deanna contributes 10 percent of the capital, and Elias agrees to design all the clothes. Alex, Becky, Cindy, Deanna, and Elias will share profits equally absent an agreement to the contrary.

3.6.2 Losses

Unless the partners agree otherwise, they share losses in the same manner as they share profits.

> **Illustration 6 Sharing of Losses**
>
> Assume the same facts as in the previous illustration. If there is a $100,000 loss, absent an agreement to the contrary, Alex, Becky, Cindy, Deanna, and Elias will each be responsible for $20,000 of the loss.

>
> **Pass Key**
>
> The examiners often ask how partners will share profits and/or losses. The key is to remember that, as with the partners' management powers, unless the partners provide otherwise, *profits and losses will be split equally*, regardless of the partners' contributions. If a partner cannot contribute his or her share of losses (e.g., because of bankruptcy or other refusal), the remaining partners must make up the share on a pro rata basis.

3.7 Distributions

Unless agreed otherwise, partners are not entitled to compensation for services rendered to the partnership.

> **Illustration 7 Compensation**
>
> In the previous example, if Alex, Becky, and Cindy never did any work for Glorious Jeans, and Deanna and Elias worked full time to manufacture the clothes, Deanna and Elias would have no right to be paid for their services (unless Alex, Becky, and Cindy breached an agreement to work).

3.8 Termination: Dissociation of a General Partnership

Dissociation is a change in the relationship of the partners caused by any partner ceasing to be associated in the carrying on of the business. Dissociation of a partner does not necessarily cause a dissolution and winding up of the business of the partnership. A partnership at will (i.e., one without a stated termination point) may be rightfully dissolved by a partner's notice of withdrawal or dissociation at any time.

3.8.1 Events of Dissociation

A partner is dissociated from the partnership when the partner gives notice of withdrawal, dies, becomes bankrupt, or is expelled, or if an event occurs that was set out in the partnership agreement as an event that would cause a dissociation.

3.8.2 Consequences

When a partner dissociates, his right to participate in management ceases, although the dissociated partner's apparent authority to bind the partnership will continue until third parties are given notice of the dissociation.

3.8.3 Dissociated Partner's Liability to Other Parties

Generally, a dissociated partner remains liable for the debts incurred by the partnership prior to dissociation unless there has been a release by the creditor or a novation.

A dissociated partner may be held liable for debts incurred by the partnership for up to two years after dissociation unless the partner gives notice of dissociation. If a new partner is admitted, the new partner is not personally liable for debts incurred by the partnership before becoming a partner.

3.9 Termination: Dissolution of a General Partnership

3.9.1 Events Causing Dissolution

Generally, a partnership is dissolved and its business must be wound up if the partnership is at will (i.e., has no expiration date) and a partner gives notice of withdrawal, the partners agree to dissolution, or a court orders dissolution. The death of a partner does not cause a dissolution if the remaining partners agree to continue the partnership within 90 days of the partner's death.

Pass Key

The examiners often ask about the basic characteristics of a partnership. One characteristic that has been key to several past questions is that a partnership is not of unlimited duration—because any one of the above events can trigger a dissolution.

3.9.2 Partnership Continues After Dissolution

A partnership continues to exist after dissolution until its business is wound up, at which time the partnership is terminated. For example, each partner will continue to have apparent authority to bind the partnership, and each partner will continue to be liable for the obligations of the partnership. The partnership is terminated only after the winding-up process is complete.

3.10 Distribution of Assets—Final Accounting

3.10.1 Order of Distribution

When a solvent partnership is dissolved and its assets are reduced to cash, the cash must be used to pay the partnership's liabilities in the following order:

- **Creditors**

  Creditors, including partners who are creditors, must be paid before the non-creditor partners receive any payments.

- **Partners**

  After obligations to creditors are satisfied, each partner is entitled to payment, first to return their contributions and then on account of profits.

3.10.2 Application

- **Amounts Due or Owed**

  To determine the amounts due or owed, deduct from the assets left upon dissolution any amounts owed to creditors (including partners who are creditors) and then deduct the amounts needed to return the partners' contributions (if not already repaid).

- **Divide Profit (if Any)**

  If money still remains, it is profit that must be divided among the partners. If the assets at dissolution are less than what is needed to pay the creditors and return contributions, then there is a loss that must be divided among the partners. In either case, remember that unless the partnership agreement provides otherwise, profits are divided equally among partners, and losses are divided the same as profits.

Illustration 8 — Dissolution of Partnership

Alex, Becky, and Cindy contributed $30,000, $15,000, and $5,000, respectively, to the ABC Partnership. Upon dissolution, after paying all creditors, $20,000 remains. The partnership has suffered a $30,000 loss because $50,000 was contributed to capital and only $20,000 remains. The partnership agreement is silent as to how losses are to be divided, but provides that profits are to be allocated 40% to Alex, 25% to Becky, and 35% to Cindy. Because the partnership agreement is silent as to allocation of losses, they will be allocated in the same proportions as profits: 40% to Alex = $12,000 (i.e., 40% of $30,000); 25% to Becky = $7,500; and 35% to Cindy = $10,500. Thus, Alex is entitled to receive $18,000 ($30,000 capital contribution less $12,000 share of loss); Becky is entitled to receive $7,500 ($15,000 capital contribution less $7,500 share of loss), and Cindy owes $5,500 ($5,000 capital contribution less $10,500 share of loss).

Illustration 9 — Partner Refuses to Pay

If there is a loss and some partners refuse to contribute, are not subject to process (i.e., are not within a court's jurisdiction), or are insolvent, the remaining partners must share the extra loss proportionally. Thus, in the illustration above, if Cindy refused to pay anything else, Alex and Becky would have to share the $5,500 loss that Cindy owes on a 4 to 2.5 basis (Alex would have to deduct an extra $3,385 from his capital and Becky would have to deduct an extra $2,115 from her capital). Of course, if Cindy is solvent, Alex and Becky can seek to recover the $5,500 from Cindy in an action for indemnification.

4 Limited Liability Partnership (Similar to General Partnership)

A limited liability partnership (LLP) is similar to a general partnership in most respects, including the sharing of profits and losses, and generally all of the advantages and disadvantages of a general partnership mentioned above apply to a limited liability partnership. Important differences are listed below.

4.1 Difference: Personal Liability

- **Partners Generally Not Liable for Acts of Fellow Partners, Employees, or Agents**

    An LLP differs from a general partnership in that a partner in an LLP is not personally liable for the obligations or liabilities of the partnership arising from errors, omissions, negligence, malpractice, or the wrongful acts committed by another partner or by an employee, agent, or representative of the LLP.

- **Liable for Own Negligence and Negligence of Those Under Direct Control**

    LLP partners are, of course, liable for their own negligence or wrongful acts and for the negligence and wrongful acts of those under their direct supervision or control.

- **Generally Not Personally Liable for Debts and Contractual Obligations**

    Generally, partners in an LLP are *not* personally liable for the debts and contractual obligations of the LLP.

4.2 Difference: Formation

- **LLP Must File With the State**

    Generally, to become an LLP the partnership must file a document with the state (called a registration, statement of qualification, application for registration, or certificate of limited liability partnership). Some states restrict LLPs only to the learned professions, such as accounting or the practice of law.

- **Contents of Certificate of Limited Liability Partnership**

    Generally, registration must provide information such as the LLP's name, the name and location of its registered office, the number of partners, a description of the partnership business, etc.

5 Limited Partnership

5.1 Nature of a Limited Partnership

A limited partnership is a partnership made up of one or more general partners (who have personal liability for all partnership debts) and one or more limited partners (whose liability for partnership debts generally is limited to their investment).

Pass Key

Examiners sometimes ask whether a limited partnership can be formed with limited liability for all partners. The answer, of course, is *no*—you need at least one general partner who has unlimited personal liability for all partnership obligations.

5.1.1 Generally No Perpetual Life

A limited partnership does not have a perpetual life, unless the partnership agreement provides otherwise.

5.1.2 Similar to a Corporation

A limited partnership can be formed only pursuant to a state statute and only by filing with the state. Limited partners are very much like shareholders. They contribute capital in exchange for a partnership interest, but they do not participate in management.

5.2 Formation of a Limited Partnership

A limited partnership can be formed only pursuant to a state statute and only by filing a certificate of limited partnership with the state.

5.3 Operation of a Limited Partnership

In a limited partnership, management is the responsibility of the general partners, just as in a general partnership.

5.3.1 General Partners

A general partner is personally liable for all partnership debts. If there is a loss, only the general partner can be held personally liable.

- A general partner may also be a limited partner at the same time.
- A general partner may be a secured or unsecured creditor of the partnership.

5.3.2 Limited Partners

A limited partner's liability is limited to his investment and unpaid capital commitments. A limited partner has no right to take part in the management of the business. He is not an agent of the business and generally cannot bind the business in contract. Nevertheless, a limited partner has a right to review the financial information and tax returns of the limited partnership.

- However, under the Uniform Limited Partnership Act of 2001, partners cannot be held personally liable for participating in management. In any case, a limited partner may vote on extraordinary matters without incurring liability (e.g., admission or removal of a general partner, dissolution, amending the certificate of limited partnership, sale of substantially all assets, etc.).
- A limited partner may assign his interest in the partnership.
    - The assignment of a limited partner's interest is like an assignment in a general partnership—the assignee has the limited partner's rights to profits.
    - Unless otherwise agreed, the assignor ceases to be a limited partner upon assignment of all of his limited partnership interest.
- A new partner can be added only upon the consent of all partners.
- A limited partner does not owe a fiduciary duty to the partnership.

5.3.3 Allocation of Profits and Losses

If the partners have agreed on how profits are shared, the agreement governs. Unless otherwise agreed, general and limited partners share profits and losses in proportion to the value of the partners' contributions. Remember, though, a limited partner is not liable for any loss beyond his or her capital contribution.

5.4 Termination of a Limited Partnership

5.4.1 Methods of Dissolution

A limited partnership may be dissolved by:

- the occurrence of the time or event stated in the partnership agreement;
- written consent of all partners (i.e., unanimous written consent to dissolve);
- withdrawal or death of a general partner; or
- judicial decree.

5.4.2 Death of a Limited Partner Does Not Cause Dissolution

Note that the death of a limited partner will not dissolve the partnership.

5.4.3 Order of Distribution of Assets

After dissolution, if the limited partnership is terminated, assets are distributed in the following order:

1. To creditors, including partners who are creditors;
2. To former partners in satisfaction of liabilities that were not paid on their withdrawal; and
3. To partners, first to return their contributions, and then to distribute profits.

5.4.4 Loss Situation

If there is a loss, only the general partners are personally liable; limited partners have no personal liability beyond their capital commitments.

6 Limited Liability Company

6.1 Nature of a Limited Liability Company

6.1.1 Basic Characteristics

An LLC is an entity designed to provide its owners, who are called members, with two main features:

- The limited liability that shareholders of a corporation enjoy (i.e., owners are not personally liable for obligations of the business entity).
- The ability to be taxed like a partnership (i.e., profits and losses flow through the LLC and are treated as the owners' personal profits and losses, unlike profits of a corporation, which are taxed at the corporate level and again when distributed to the shareholders). (Note: Under tax laws, LLCs are taxed as a partnership unless they elect to be taxed as a corporation.)

6.1.2 Controlling Law (Statute vs. Operating Agreement)

LLC members may, but need not, adopt operating agreements with provisions different from the LLC statute, and generally the operating agreements will control. The operating agreement is just that: an agreement among members regarding how they will operate or run their business. Its intent is to forestall and resolve disputes among the members. These agreements are not filed with the state. Indeed, under the Uniform Limited Liability Company Act, such operating agreements need not be in writing.

6.2 Formation of a Limited Liability Company

An LLC is formed by filing articles of organization with the secretary of state.

6.2.1 Contents of Articles

Most states require the articles to include the following:

- a statement that the entity is an LLC;
- the name of the LLC, which must include an indication that it is an LLC;
- the street address of the LLC's registered office and name of its registered agent;
- if management is to be vested in managers, a statement to that effect; and
- the names of the persons who will be managing the company.

6.2.2 Number of Members

Most states now allow one person to form an LLC.

6.3 Operation of a Limited Liability Company

6.3.1 Generally All Members May Participate in Management

Unless the articles or an operating agreement provides otherwise, all members have a right to participate in management decisions of the LLC.

- **Member-Managed Limited Liability Company**

    If the members are managing the LLC, each member is an agent of the LLC and has the power to bind the LLC by acts apparently carrying on the business of the LLC.

- **Manager-Managed Limited Liability Company**

    If management is by managers, each manager is an agent of the LLC and has the power to bind the LLC. In this case, the members are not agents of the LLC and do not have the power to bind the LLC.

6.3.2 Voting Strength Proportional to Contributions

Voting strength is proportional to contributions. For example, a member who contributed 5 percent of the LLC's current capital is entitled to 5 percent of the total vote.

6.3.3 Profit and Loss Allocated According to Contributions

Unless the articles or an operating agreement provide otherwise, profits and losses of an LLC are allocated on the basis of the members' contributions in most states. Under the Uniform Limited Liability Company Act (ULLCA), which is followed by only a few states but which is sometimes specifically tested on the exam, profits are shared equally, regardless of capital contributions.

6.3.4 Transferability of Ownership and Rights

Most statutes provide that unless the operating agreement provides otherwise, a member of an LLC may not transfer all of her interest in the LLC without the consent of all other members. A member is free to assign her interest in distributions (e.g., of profits or on dissolution) but is not free to assign any rights to manage the LLC. Thus, transferability of ownership is similar to that of a partnership.

6.3.5 Books and Records

Each member of an LLC is entitled to inspect and copy the books and records of the LLC during regular business hours.

6.4 Termination of a Limited Liability Company

An LLC will dissolve upon:

- expiration of the period of duration stated in the articles;
- the consent of all members;
- the death, retirement, resignation, bankruptcy, incompetence, etc., of a member (unless the remaining members vote to continue the business)—*these events dissociate the member*; or
- a judicial decree or administrative order dissolving the LLC for violation of law.

NOTES

MODULE 5 Business Structures: Part 2

REG 6

1 Corporation

1.1 Nature of a Corporation

1.1.1 Distinct Legal Entity

A corporation is a legal entity (i.e., it exists as an entity distinct from its shareholders). As a distinct legal entity, usually only the corporation is liable for corporate obligations. Generally, shareholders, directors, and officers are not personally liable for contracts made by their corporation. Neither are they liable for corporate torts, except to the extent the shareholder, officer, or director participated in the tort.

1.1.2 Taxation

- **C Corporation**

  Generally, a corporation is taxed as an entity distinct from its owners. It must pay taxes on any profits it makes. Stockholders generally do not have to pay tax on the profits of the corporation until they are distributed (e.g., as dividends under the tax laws). Such a corporation is known as a C corporation.

- **S Corporation**

  The tax laws permit certain corporations to elect to be taxed like partnerships (i.e., profits are not taxed at the corporate level but rather are treated as income of the shareholders). There are a number of restrictions on S corporations, such as:

  - stock can be held by no more than 100 persons;
  - shareholders must be individuals, estates, or certain trusts;
  - the corporation must generally be a domestic corporation;
  - there can be only one class of stock; and
  - foreign shareholders are generally prohibited.

1.1.3 Owned by Shareholders but Managed by Directors

Corporations are owned by their shareholders, but unless the articles of incorporation provide otherwise, the shareholders do not run the corporation. The power to run the corporation is vested in the board of directors, which is elected by the shareholders.

1.1.4 Perpetual Life

A corporation generally has a perpetual life.

1.1.5 Freely Transferable Ownership

One of the key distinguishing characteristics of a corporation is that its owners (shareholders) are free to transfer all of their ownership rights to others, unless otherwise agreed.

1.2 Formation of a Corporation

1.2.1 Created Under Statute

Corporations are created by complying with a state incorporation statute. A majority of states follow the Revised Model Business Corporation Act, or RMBCA. This outline is based on that act.

Pass Key

A number of past corporation questions have simply asked which of four statements is true. As simple as it may seem, the key to a number of these questions has been that corporations are governed by statute.

1.2.2 Promoters Procure Capital Commitments

Promoters enter into contracts before the corporation is formed to obtain financing and things the corporation will need once formed. Promoters are personally bound on the contracts they make. The corporation is not bound unless and until the corporation adopts the contracts after the corporation is formed, either expressly or by accepting the benefits of the contracts. However, even if the corporation adopts a promoter's contract, the promoter remains liable unless there is a *novation* (an agreement that the third party will release the promoter and substitute the corporation).

1.2.3 Articles of Incorporation

Incorporators must file articles of incorporation with the state.

- **Items Included in the Articles of Incorporation**

    The articles may include anything the incorporators consider appropriate but, under the RMBCA, the articles must include:

    - the name of the corporation;
    - the names and address of the corporation's registered agent (i.e., the person on whom process may be served if the corporation is sued);
    - the names and addresses of each of the incorporators; and
    - the number of shares authorized to be issued.

    Note: One or more classes of shares must have unlimited voting rights.

Pass Key

The examiners often ask what must be included in the articles of incorporation. Items not in the above list are not necessary. For example, the articles need not include a statement of the states in which the corporation is to do business or have offices, the names of the initial directors or officers, terms of office, etc. Memorize the list and do not be fooled by such other choices.

- **Purpose Clause (Ultra Vires Act)**

    A corporation may include a clause in its articles stating the business purpose for which the corporation was formed. If a corporation has a narrow purpose clause and undertakes business outside the clause (or outside the business permitted by statute), it is said to be acting "ultra vires." A director or officer who authorizes an ultra vires act may be liable to the corporation for damages caused by the act.

Illustration 1   Ultra Vires Act

If a corporation was formed to accomplish the single purpose of operating a restaurant, any action to achieve some other purpose (e.g., buying an oil and lube business) would be ultra vires.

1.2.4 Bylaws (Rules)

In addition to the articles of incorporation, a corporation generally will have bylaws containing rules for running the corporation (e.g., they may set out the authority of the corporation's officers). Bylaws are adopted by the incorporators or the board of directors and may be repealed or modified by the board of directors. They are not part of the articles of incorporation and are not required to be filed with the state.

1.2.5 Disregard of Corporate Entity (Piercing the Corporate Veil)

Courts will sometimes hold the shareholders, officers, or directors of a corporation liable because the privilege of conducting business in corporate form is being abused. This disregard of the corporate entity frequently is called "piercing the corporate veil."

Courts generally will pierce the corporate veil for any of three reasons:

1. Shareholders commingle personal funds with corporate funds or use corporate assets for personal use.

2. The corporation was inadequately (or "thinly") capitalized at the time of formation (shareholders must start the corporation with sufficient capital to reasonably meet the corporation's prospective liabilities).

3. The corporation was formed to commit fraud on existing creditors (e.g., a sole proprietor transfers all assets to a newly formed corporation so that the assets are not available to pay the sole proprietor's existing creditors).

Pass Key

Piercing the corporate veil is one of the examiners' favorite corporations issues. Be sure to memorize the three reasons for piercing: commingling personal with corporate funds, inadequate capitalization, and committing fraud on existing creditors. Be mindful of what is *not* on the list. The following do not justify piercing: incorporating as an S corporation, incorporating a partnership, and bankruptcy of a corporation that was adequately capitalized at the outset.

1.3 Financing the Corporation

Corporate capital comes from the issuance of many types of securities, including equity obligations (or stock) and debt obligations (or bonds).

1.3.1 Debt Securities (Bonds)

Bonds include secured mortgage bonds and unsecured debentures, and even bonds that may be convertible into stock (i.e., convertible bonds). Bondholders are creditors.

1.3.2 Equity Securities (Stocks)

Equity securities include shares of the corporation, stock warrants (generally, options to purchase shares granted by the corporation), and stock options (generally, options to purchase stock granted by one other than the issuing corporation). Stockholders are owners of the corporation.

- **Characteristics of Equity Securities**

    A corporation may choose to issue only one class of stock, in which case each share of stock will have the same rights. Alternatively, it may choose to issue several classes or series of stock with varying rights.

- **Consideration for Stock**

    Unless the articles provide otherwise (e.g., by setting a par value for stock), the board of directors has discretion to issue stock at any price it thinks is appropriate. Under the RMBCA, stock may be issued in exchange for any benefit to the corporation (e.g., money, property, promises to perform services in the future, promissory notes, etc.).

1.4 Shareholders: Rights, Duties, Obligations, and Authority

1.4.1 Voting Rights

Shareholders have the right to vote to elect (typically annually) or remove directors. They also have the right to vote on whether to approve fundamental changes to the corporation, such as dissolution.

- **General Rule: One Share, One Vote**

    Unless the articles of incorporation provide otherwise, each share of stock is entitled to one vote.

- **Exception: Cumulative Voting for Directors**

    The articles can give shareholders the right to cumulative voting with respect to electing directors. In cumulative voting, each share is entitled to one vote for each director position that is being filled, and the shareholder may cast the votes in any way, including casting all for a single candidate. This *helps minority shareholders gain representation on the board*.

1.4.2 Distributions (Dividends)

Generally, shareholders do not have a right to a distribution (including cash dividends and repurchases of shares) unless and until it is declared by the board of directors. Once the board declares a distribution, the shareholders are treated as unsecured creditors of the corporation to the extent of the dividend. Distributions decrease the corporation's shareholders' equity.

Pass Key

The fact that shareholders have the status of unsecured creditors once a dividend is declared has been a favorite correct answer choice on a number of past exam questions.

- **Preferred Shareholders**

    A corporation need not give each shareholder an equal right to receive distributions. Shares may be divided into classes with varying rights.

    - **Noncumulative Preferred Shares**

        Shares with a preference usually are entitled to a fixed amount of money (e.g., $5 a year if the preference is a dividend preference) before distributions can be made with respect to nonpreferred shares.

    - **Cumulative Preferred Shares: Dividends Carry Over to Future Years**

        With cumulative preferred shares, if a dividend is not declared in a particular year, the right to receive the preference accumulates and must be paid before nonpreferred shares may be paid any dividend.

Pass Key

Cumulative preferred dividends are an exam favorite. The key is to remember that although these dividends accumulate even if not declared, no dividend can be paid to common shareholders until all cumulative dividends are paid (even for years when dividends were not declared). No dividend is due until it is declared by the board of directors.

- **Stock Dividends**

    Stock dividends are issued from a corporation's own "authorized but unissued shares." Because no assets are distributed, the shareholders receiving the stock generally do not owe any taxes on it, the solvency of the corporation remains the same, and there is no damage to creditors and shareholders (unlike cash dividends). Thus, a stock dividend is not a distribution of corporate assets.

1.4.3 Right to Inspect Books and Records

Upon five days' written notice stating a proper purpose (one related to the shareholder's rights in the corporation), a shareholder may inspect and copy the corporation's records. The shareholder may send an attorney, accountant, or other agent to inspect.

Pass Key

The examiners often ask about shareholders' inspection rights. The key is that the shareholders (or their agents, attorneys, accountants, etc.) can inspect for any proper purpose (e.g., to start a derivative suit, to solicit shareholders to vote for certain directors, etc.), but shareholders can be denied inspection for improper purposes (e.g., to get names for a retail mailing list).

1.4.4 Preemptive Rights

When a corporation proposes to issue additional shares of stock, the current shareholders often want to purchase shares in order to maintain their proportional voting strength. The common law granted shareholders such a right, known as the "preemptive right." Under the RMBCA, preemptive rights do not exist unless the articles of incorporation provide for them.

1.4.5 Derivative Actions

When a corporation has a legal cause of action against someone but refuses to bring the action, the shareholders may have a right to bring a shareholder derivative action to enforce the corporation's rights. Such an action may be brought against directors of the corporation or outsiders.

- **Derivative Action vs. Direct Action**

    Derivative actions may be brought only to vindicate wrongs against the corporation. If a shareholder seeks to vindicate the shareholder's own rights against the corporation, a *direct* action by the shareholder against the corporation is appropriate, rather than a derivative action.

1.5 Directors: Rights, Duties, Obligations, and Authority

Among the specific duties of directors are the election, removal, and supervision of officers (directors generally review the conduct of officers and may remove an officer with or without cause); adoption, amendment, and repeal of bylaws; fixing management compensation; and initiating fundamental changes to the corporation's structure.

1.5.1 Declaration of Distributions

The board of directors has sole discretion to declare distributions to shareholders, including dividends, in the form of cash, property, or the corporation's own shares. The shareholders have no power to compel a distribution. Directors who authorize a distribution in violation of law (i.e., when the corporation is insolvent) are personally liable to the extent the distribution exceeds what would have been lawful. However, they can defend under their right to rely. Moreover, the director can recover from a shareholder who received a contribution knowing that it was unlawful.

1.5.2 Fiduciary Duties and the Business Judgment Rule

Directors are fiduciaries of the corporation and must act in the best interests of the corporation. However, directors are not insurers of the corporation's success. A director will not be liable to the corporation for acts performed or decisions made in good faith, in a manner the director believes to be in the best interest of the corporation, and with the care an ordinarily prudent person in a like position would exercise. (This is sometimes called "the business judgment rule.") Thus, directors will be liable to the corporation only for negligent acts or omissions (e.g., failure to obtain fire insurance, hiring a convicted embezzler as treasurer without performing a background check, etc.).

- **Right to Rely**

    A director is entitled to rely on information, opinions, reports, or statements (including financial statements) if prepared by any of the following:

    - corporate officers, employees, or a committee of the board whom the director reasonably believes to be reliable and competent; or
    - legal counsel, accountants, or other persons as to matters the director reasonably believes are within such person's professional competence.

- **Duty of Loyalty**

    Directors owe their corporation a duty of loyalty and must act in the best interests of their corporation.

    - The duty of loyalty prohibits directors from competing with the corporation, but does not necessarily prohibit directors from transacting business with the corporation (e.g., by buying from or selling to the corporation). An action in which a director has a conflict of interest will be upheld only if:

        — after full disclosure the transaction is approved by a disinterested majority of the board of directors or the shareholders; or

        — the transaction was fair and reasonable to the corporation.

    - The board of directors has the power to set director compensation.

- **Indemnification**

    Generally, corporations are allowed to indemnify directors for expenses for any lawsuit brought against them in their corporate capacity. The corporation may also pay any judgment imposed in a lawsuit on the director, except in a shareholder derivative suit.

1.6 Officers: Rights, Duties, Obligations, and Authority

Officers are individual agents (and employees) of the corporation who ordinarily conduct its day-to-day operations and may bind the corporation to contracts made on its behalf. Note that a person may hold more than one office.

1.6.1 Selection and Removal

Officers are selected by the directors and may be removed by the directors with or without cause. They are not elected by the shareholders.

1.6.2 Authority

Officers are corporate agents and agency rules determine their authority and power. A corporate president will generally have apparent authority to enter into contracts and act on behalf of the corporation in the ordinary course of business.

1.6.3 Fiduciary Duties and Indemnification

Corporate officers, like corporate directors, are subject to fiduciary duties and must discharge their duties in good faith and with the same care as an ordinarily prudent person in a like position. Like directors, officers may be indemnified for expenses and judgments from litigation brought against them in their corporate capacity, and they are protected by the business judgment rule.

1.6.4 May Also Serve as Directors

Officers may also serve as directors of the corporation.

1.6.5 Not Required to Be Shareholders

An officer is not required to be, but may be, a shareholder of the corporation.

Pass Key

The key to several past questions has been the power structure of corporations. Remember, the shareholders generally have no direct power to manage the corporation. They elect the board of directors, but generally, the board does not manage the corporation; instead, it appoints officers to manage on a day-to-day basis. Keep in mind that the shareholders do not elect the officers, and neither do the shareholders have the power to remove officers. Officers serve at the discretion of the board.

1.7 Fundamental Changes

Decisions regarding issues that might fundamentally change the nature of the corporation require shareholder approval through a special procedure. Such fundamental corporate changes include some amendments to the articles of incorporation, dissolutions, mergers, consolidations, share exchanges, and sales of all or substantially all of the corporation's assets.

Pass Key

Remember that the examiners often ask about fundamental corporate changes. The fundamental changes that require shareholder approval include:

Mnemonic: "**DAMS**"

Dissolution

Amendments to the articles of incorporation that materially and adversely affect the shareholders' rights

Mergers, consolidations, and compulsory share exchanges

Sale of substantially all the corporation's assets outside the regular course of business

1.7.1 General Procedure

- **Board Resolution**

    A majority of the board of directors must adopt a resolution setting forth the proposed action and submitting it for a vote at a shareholders' meeting.

- **Notice**

    The corporation must notify all shareholders even if they are not entitled to vote.

- **Shareholder Approval**

    The change must be approved by a majority of the shares voted at the meeting.

- **Filing of Articles**

    A document setting forth the action taken (referred to as "articles") must be executed by the corporation and be filed with the state.

Pass Key

The examiners often ask about fundamental corporate changes. The key points to remember are:

- The board must approve a resolution, but there is no requirement of unanimity.
- The shareholders must be given notice and an opportunity to vote on the change. Approval requires a majority of the votes cast.

- **Right to Dissent/Appraisal Rights**

    Shareholders who have a right to vote on a fundamental corporate change typically have a right to dissent/appraisal right (i.e., the right to have the corporation purchase their shares at a fair price) if the shareholder votes against the fundamental change and it is nevertheless approved.

1.7.2 Amendments to the Articles of Incorporation

The corporation may amend its articles of incorporation in any and as many respects as desired, as long as the provisions, as amended, are lawful.

1.7.3 Merger, Consolidation, and Share Exchange

- **Definitions and Distinctions**

    - **Merger**

        A merger involves one or more corporations joining with another corporation. One corporation survives the merger and continues in existence, while the other merging corporations cease to exist following the merger.

Illustration 2   Merger

XYZ Corp. merges with ABC Corp., and following the merger XYZ Corp. ceases to exist. ABC Corp. now survives, with all of the assets and shareholders that formerly belonged to XYZ Corp.

- **Consolidation**

    A consolidation involves one or more corporations joining together to form a new corporation. Each constituent corporation ceases to exist after the consolidation; only the new corporation goes on. The new corporation is liable for the debts of the old corporation.

- **Share Exchange**

    A share exchange is a transaction in which one corporation acquires all of the outstanding shares of one or more classes of stock of another corporation. Both corporations continue to exist as separate entities.

- **Procedure in General**

    Both corporations in a merger and all corporations involved in a consolidation must follow the general procedure for fundamental corporate changes set out above (board resolution, notice, approval by majority of the shares, and filing). The notice must include a summary of the plan of merger, consolidation, share exchange, etc. In a share exchange, only the corporation whose shares are being acquired need follow the fundamental change procedure. The plan of merger or share exchange must include the terms and conditions of the plan and the manner of converting the corporation's securities.

    - **Merger of Subsidiary (Short-Form Merger)**

        A parent corporation owning 90 percent or more of a subsidiary corporation may merge the subsidiary into the parent without the approval of the shareholders of either corporation or the approval of the subsidiary's board. However, the parent must mail a copy of the plan to each shareholder who has not waived this right.

    - **Effect of Mergers Into a Surviving Corporation**

        A corporation merged into a surviving corporation ceases to exist as a separate entity. The surviving corporation has all rights, liabilities, and obligations of the merged corporations. When a share exchange takes place, the shares are exchanged as the plan provides, and the holders are entitled only to the rights of the exchanged shares.

    - **Fending Off Unwanted Takeover Attempts**

        If a corporation is faced with the prospect of being taken over and the board of directors wants to resist the takeover attempt, it may do so in a number of ways, including:

        — persuading shareholders to reject the offer;

        — suing the person or company attempting the takeover for misrepresentation or omission and obtain an injunction against the takeover;

        — merging with a white knight (a company with which the directors want to merge);

        — making a "self-tender" (an offer to acquire stock from its own stockholders and thus retain control in order to prevent a takeover);

        — paying "greenmail" (i.e., pay the person or company attempting the takeover to abandon its takeover attempt);

        — locking up the crown jewels (i.e., give a third party an option to purchase the company's most valuable assets);

        — undertaking a "scorched earth" policy (which is to sell off assets or take out loans that would make the company less financially attractive); or

        — applying "shark repellent," which means amending the articles of incorporation or bylaws to make a takeover more difficult (e.g., require a large number of shareholders to approve the merger).

1.8 Termination of a Corporation

Dissolution is a fundamental change, requiring director and shareholder approval. Dissolution can also be pursuant to a court order.

After dissolution, the corporation continues in existence for purposes of winding up. Liquidation involves the process of collecting the corporate assets, paying the expenses involved, satisfying creditors' claims, and distributing the net assets of the corporation.

1.9 Calendar Year vs. Fiscal Year

Companies typically have the option of choosing a calendar year-end (a year ending on December 31) or a fiscal year-end (one ending on any day other than December 31). For tax purposes, a fiscal year must first be approved by the IRS.

1.10 Foreign Corporation Must Qualify

A foreign corporation must obtain a certificate of authority from each state in which it does intrastate business. A foreign corporation is a corporation created under the laws of another state. Maintaining an office in the foreign state would be an example of doing business in the foreign state. But merely maintaining a bank account, collecting a debt, or hiring employees in a foreign state are not instances of doing business in the foreign state sufficient to trigger the qualification requirement.

NOTES

NOTES

NOTES

NOTES

NOTES

Be happy & make others happy too :)
Being confident & believing in the power of universe is enough!
Everything is gonna be alright
You have a blessed life! Be thankful
Count your blessings & love with all your heart
Don't be sad, it will pass & you will be loved
You are beautiful, kind & witty :D